"Bird and Harrower have brought toget   who represent many of the best and varied ans........ to the perennial question, 'For whom did Jesus die?' The end result is a helpful collection of writings that dig deep into the biblical text and the history of the church, pushing us to consider this question afresh."

—Brandon D. Smith,
Assistant Professor of Theology and New Testament, Cedarville University,
Cofounder of the Center for Baptist Renewal

"Studies in the history of Christian doctrine simultaneously chasten, nourish, and inspire constructive contemporary theological work. This volume on Amyraut and hypothetical universalism opens the door to a trajectory within church history that promises to do precisely that, particularly in regard to the doctrine of the atonement."

—Adam J. Johnson
Biola University

"This volume addresses a pressing theological issue by assembling colleagues with different points of interest and expertise (interpreters, theologians, historians, philosophers, and preachers). In the best ways, this volume feels like an engaging conversation in which the participants strike different tones, some quite irenic making precisely qualified claims and some a bit fierier, challenging established patterns of thought. The result is a well-rounded look at unlimited atonement within the Reformed tradition through philosophical, theological, historical, and pastoral perspectives."

—Joshua E. Williams,
Associate Professor of Old Testament,
Southwestern Baptist Theological Seminary

UNLIMITED ATONEMENT

Amyraldism and Reformed Theology

MICHAEL F. BIRD & SCOTT HARROWER

EDITORS

KREGEL
ACADEMIC

Published by Kregel Academic, an imprint of Kregel Publications, 2450 Oak Industrial Dr. NE, Grand Rapids, MI 49505-6020

ISBN 978-0-8254-4641-2

2023-10

To Peter MacPherson and Michael McNamara,
faithful preachers of the cross
&
To Roland and Elke Werner
(Christus-Treff and Zinzendorf-Institut Marburg)
who showed me the breadth of God's love.

CONTENTS

Part Three: Amyraldism and Tradition

AUTHORS

James M. Arcadi is associate professor of biblical and systematic theology at Trinity Evangelical Divinity School in Deerfield, Illinois, and, as an ordained Anglican minister, serves at All Souls Anglican Church in Wheaton, Illinois. He is the author of *An Incarnational Model of the Eucharist*, coauthor of *The Nature and Promise of Analytic Theology*, and the coeditor of *Love: Divine and Human* and *The T&T Clark Handbook of Analytic Theology*.

David L. Allen is distinguished professor of preaching, George W. Truett Chair of Ministry, and director of the Southwestern Center for Expository Preaching at Southwestern Baptist Theological Seminary in Fort Worth, Texas. He is the author of several books, including *The Extent of the Atonement: An Historical and Critical Review* and *The Atonement: A Biblical, Theological, and Historical Study of the Cross of Christ*.

Michael F. Bird is academic dean and lecturer in New Testament at Ridley College, Melbourne, Australia. He is the author of *The Gospel of the Lord: How the Early Church Wrote the Story of Jesus*; *Romans* in the Story of God Bible Commentary Series; *An Anomalous Jew: Paul among Jews, Greeks, and Romans*; *The Cambridge Companion to the Apostolic Fathers*, coedited with Scott Harrower; and *The New Testament in Its World*, coauthored with N. T. Wright.

Oliver D. Crisp is professor of analytic theology and director of the Logos Institute in the School of Divinity, University of St. Andrews. He is a founding editor of the *Journal of Analytic Theology* and cochair of the Christian Systematic Theology Unit of the American Academy of Religion. With Fred Sanders he organizes the annual Los Angeles Theology Conference. He is also the chair of the committee for the Society of Christian Philosophers, UK. His recent publications include *Analyzing Doctrine: Toward a Systematic Theology*; *The Nature* *and Promise of Analytic Theology* (coauthored with James Arcadi and Jordan Wessling); *God, Creation, and Salvation: Studies in Reformed Theology*; and *Approaching the Atonement: The Reconciling Work of Christ.*

Joshua R. Farris is professor of theology of science at Missional University and Humboldt Experienced Researcher Fellow at Ruhr Universität Bochum. He recently completed *The Creation of Self: A Case for the Soul* (forthcoming). He is a freelance writer for several academic and news outlets on topics of the soul, science and faith, and public theology. He has edited and authored several volumes, such as *Being Saved; Idealism and Christian Theology; The Routledge Companion to Theological Anthropology; An Introduction to Theological Anthropology: Humans, Both Creaturely and Divine;* and *The Soul of Theological Anthropology: A Cartesian Exploration.* He is the coeditor of the *Routledge Handbook of Idealism and Immaterialism.* He is the international editor of *Perichoresis: The Theological Journal of Emanuel University*; the associate editor of *Journal of Biblical and Theological Studies*; and an international editor for the *European Journal of Philosophy of Religion.*

Jeff Fisher is professor of theology and the director of spiritual formation at The Foundry, a ministry for training and lifelong learning in Grand Rapids, Michigan. He is the author of *A Christoscopic Reading of Scripture* and several articles and chapters on Reformation and post-Reformation theology. He previously taught at Kuyper College and pastored a Christian Reformed Church in Minnesota.

S. Mark Hamilton is the senior managing editor at Davenant Press, research associate at JESociety.org, and NTI/NPI project manager at SPM Oil and Gas, a Caterpillar Company. His most recent publications include "Jonathan Edwards on the Person of Christ" in *The Oxford Handbook of Jonathan Edwards* and "Confessionalism and Causation in Jonathan Edwards (1703–58)," coauthored with C. Layne Hancock, in the *Routledge Handbook on Idealism and Immaterialism.* He and Josh Farris are currently cowriting a two-volume work titled *Reflections on Substitutionary Atonement.*

Scott Harrower is assistant professor of systematic, historical, and moral theology at Ridley College in Melbourne, Australia. He has written on Cranmer's theology of the atonement in addition to works on the Trinity, including *God of All Comfort: A Trinitarian Response to the Horrors of the World*, and edited works in early Christianity including *The Cambridge Companion to the Apostolic Fathers.*

Michael P. Jensen teaches theology at the Sydney College of Divinity and at the Australian College of Theology, and he previously taught at Moore Theological College. His publications include *Martyrdom and Identity: The Self on*

Trial and *Theological Anthropology and the Great Literary Genres*. He is the rector of St. Mark's Anglican Church, Darling Point, in Sydney.

Joshua M. McNall is associate professor of pastoral theology and ambassador of church relations at Oklahoma Wesleyan University. His publications include *The Mosaic of Atonement: An Integrated Approach to Christ's Work* and *A Free Corrector: Colin Gunton and the Legacy of Augustine*.

R. T. Mullins is senior research fellow at the Collegium for Advanced Studies, University of Helsinki. He has published on topics such as God and time, the Trinity, the incarnation, disability theology, and the problem of evil. He is the author of *The End of the Timeless God* and *God and Emotion*. He has previously held research and teaching fellowships at the University of Notre Dame, University of Cambridge, University of St. Andrews, and the University of Edinburgh.

Amy Peeler serves as associate professor of New Testament at Wheaton College, Illinois, and associate rector of St. Mark's Episcopal Church in Geneva, Illinois. Author of *Women and the Gender of God* and *"You Are My Son": The Family of God in the Epistle to the Hebrews*, her primary research interests continue to center on familial themes in the New Testament and Hebrews.

Jonathan Curtis Rutledge is a research fellow in the Center for Philosophy of Religion at the University of Notre Dame. He works at the intersection of value theory, philosophy of religion, and analytic theology and has recently published a monograph titled *Forgiveness and Atonement: Reflections on the Reasons for Christ's Sacrifice*.

Rory Shiner is the senior pastor of Providence City Church in Perth, Western Australia. His PhD was on the thought of Archbishop Donald Robinson.

Christopher Woznicki is an affiliate assistant professor of theology at Fuller Theological Seminary. He was formerly part of the Analytic Theology for Theological Formation Project at Fuller. He received a PhD in Theology from Fuller. His research articles—which focus on atonement, T. F. Torrance, and theological anthropology—have appeared in various journals including *Calvin Theological Journal*, *Journal of Reformed Theology*, *Neue Zeitschrift für Systematisch Theologie und Religionsphilosophie*, and *Philosophia Christi*. His monograph, *T. F. Torrance's Christological Anthropology: Discerning Humanity in Christ*, was published in 2022. He currently serves on staff with Young Life.

PREFACE

L ike many ventures in scholarship, this book has its genesis in a conversation at morning teatime. Mike and I saw the need for a theological volume that would serve our students' development in terms of their theology of God's unlimited love for humanity as it relates to Christ's work on the cross. A number of colleagues at Ridley College have been important for the success of this volume; especially Rebecca Muir for her insightful feedback and editing work, as well as our library staff—Ruth Weatherlake, Alison Foster, and Harriet Sabarez—who have been very helpful and generous with their time and encouragement. We are also grateful to the Australian College of Theology, whose research funding contributed to the progress of this project. Laura Bartlett was a great supporter of this project, and we are grateful to Robert Hand and Shawn Vander Lugt for seeing it through to publication. Our thanks also go to the authors of the works that comprise this volume, as most of these chapters were written during the hardships of COVID-19. We also thank our families for their support throughout the development of this project and dedicate this work to them.

INTRODUCTION

Scott Harrower

There are two points of genesis for this volume: one is the seminary class-room, and the other is historical-theological curiosity. In terms of the classroom, the context is that both Michael and I teach atonement theology as part of the curriculum for the formation of Anglican, Baptist, and non-denominational pastors. Over morning tea one day I mentioned to Mike that I was frustrated by the lack of teaching resources on models of the atonement that make systematic theological sense of biblical verses on Jesus's death for the sins of all people. I was promoting an interpretation of the atonement in which Christ's death is ordained by God as sufficient for the sins and guilt of all people, yet is only efficiently applied to those who have faith. This view known as hypothetical universalism, or as I prefer to call it, unlimited atonement, because it takes the unlimited love of God as its starting point. To my mind, this view was consistent with the thought of medieval and Reformation figures such as Lombard, Amyraut, and Bishop John Davenant. Because there was very little by way of reading and teaching resources for this interpretation of Jesus's death—and the theological framework in which it coherently belongs—we decided to pull this volume together for the good of our students.

Curiosity is the second motivating factor for drawing together this volume. This reaches back to when I was a student myself. Studying French at university required interaction with historic documents from the French Protestant Reformation and their successors. In these documents I read about Moïse Amyraut:[1] his sharp theological mind, virtues, and friendships. However, his life and work were shot through with danger and mystery. I was gripped by the question

---

1. Amyraut's name has been spelled in different ways over the centuries due to the influence of different languages. In this volume, we have chosen to use Amyraut consistently, but have allowed different authors freedom in how they spell his first name.

of why his work on the atonement was rejected by many of Calvin's successors. Yet, why was it so valuable that it was taken up by a number of influential Anglicans in the centuries to come? Who was this man, what was his theology of the atonement, and how was it taken up by his successors? My curiosity also extends to today: Who are the fellow theologians—explicitly Reformed or otherwise—who articulate views consistent with hypothetical universalism or unlimited atonement? I also wonder whether drawing the works of the scholars together in this volume may be a first step toward collectively promoting a more decidedly theological account of the atonement—one in which the majesty and immensity of God's holy love powerfully and coherently energizes how we interpret the reconciling death of Jesus on the cross.

We have divided the volume into sections on (1) the position itself, (2) its historic systematic pedigree, and (3) its expression in various church traditions and their outlooks. Before proceeding to describe these, a note on language is necessary. Readers will note that at various points authors refer to unlimited atonement and/or hypothetical universalism as these relate to the intentions as well as consequences of Jesus's death on the cross. These models of the atonement are slightly different, though they overlap significantly. Oliver Crisp's chapter differentiates these in his opening chapter to the volume; however, we encourage readers to follow the logic and flavor of each author's definitions in their chapters.

In chapter 1, Oliver Crisp introduces the section on the position itself, with his essay "Anglican Hypothetical Universalism." In this opening chapter Crisp writes that according to the doctrine of hypothetical universalism, Christ's reconciling work is sufficient in principle for all humankind, but efficient or effectual only for the salvation of the elect. This represents a kind of moderate Calvinist doctrine about the scope of atonement. On one way of construing this claim, the efficacy of Christ's work depends on the gift of faith given by God. This is dubbed the Anglican version of hypothetical universalism. Crisp's essay outlines and defends this version of the doctrine against a number of standard objections. These include worries about whether this counts as a truly Reformed doctrine; whether it implies a "double payment" for sin (in the person of Christ, and in the person of those who die without faith and are punished everlastingly); and whether it offers a better account of atonement than so-called "Five-Point" Calvinism. The chapter ends with a comparison to the Evangelical Calvinism of Thomas Torrance, which is a rather different sort of moderate Calvinism about the atonement. Please note that his illustration of a pandemic and a vaccine was written before the COVID-19 pandemic and does not reflect his stance on vaccinations or government policies for handling the virus.

Chapter 2 deals with the exegetical practices of Moïse Amyraut, the key early post-Reformation exponent of hypothetical universalism. Michael Bird's chapter, "Amyraut as Exegete," tackles the topic of Amyraut as a biblical interpreter and examines how Amyraut roots his particular blend of Calvinism and hypothetical universalism in his exegesis of Scripture. Bird focuses on Amyraut's treatise *On Predestination* and argues that Amyraut's position amounts to what may be called bi-covenantal universalism, whereby the divine covenants are configured in order to support a universal election on the condition of faith and a specific election rooted in sheer grace. He detects in Amyraut a fusion of principally Pauline and secondarily Johannine themes, and a strong emphasis on assurance taken from Romans 8–11, combined with a sharp account of God's goodness drawn from the Psalms. Amyraut, according to Bird, offers a covenantal arrangement that can consistently and cogently sustain the claim that God's grace is sufficient for all but efficient only for the elect. Bird concludes that Amyraut's leitmotif is the free and sovereign mercy of God.

Chapter 3 is Christopher Woznicki's "Amyraldism and Penal Substitution." The burden of his proposal is to refute the claim that atonement made for all without exception undermines penal substitution. He argues that one can consistently hold to a belief in penal substitution and to the belief that Christ's death was not particular in intent while denying universalism. The argument proceeds as follows: first, defining three terms that are crucial for discussion of our topic: limited atonement, unlimited atonement, and penal substitutionary atonement. With these definitions in place, second, he describes an argument that is often levied against Reformed understandings of unlimited atonement. Briefly, this argument claims that the conjunction of penal substitution and unlimited atonement necessarily lead to universalism. Woznicki then explores several options that a believer in penal substitutionary and unlimited atonement could take to avoid the universalism claim. This leads Woznicki to consider two Reformed versions of unlimited atonement—Ussherian hypothetical universalism and Amyraldism. Of these two positions, he contends that Amyraldism, despite the threat of the "Double Payment Objection," is the preferable way for a penal substitutionary atonement theorist to affirm unlimited atonement.

Chapter 4 deals with unlimited atonement and the doctrine of God. R. T. Mullins's chapter, "The Doctrine of God and Unlimited Atonement," outlines the basics for a Christian doctrine of God, particularly one that coheres with the notion of unlimited atonement, or hypothetical universalism. By basics, he means the sorts of things that most models of God ought to be able to agree upon about the divine nature and divine action. In this way, readers can build in more to their own doctrine of God if they feel inclined to do so as they theologically reflect on the book of nature and the book of Scripture. After articulating the basics of the doctrine of God, Mullins discusses how Calvinists, Molinists, and open theists can develop an understanding of divine providence that is consistent with unlimited atonement.

Chapter 5 illuminates why someone might prefer to adopt a doctrine of unlimited atonement over and above a limited version of the doctrine. In "Unlimited Atonement and the Nature of Forgiveness," Jonathan Curtis Rutledge outlines these reasons. Routledge does this by leveraging a distinction between forgiveness and atonement (i.e., concepts which denote unilateral, one-sided actions) and argues that one's commitments regarding the limits of divine forgiveness can readily be seen to diverge when the context shifts from universal forgiveness to universal atonement. In other words, despite a superficial similarity to the concepts of forgiveness and atonement, their core logics demand that they come apart when considering the scope of their application.

Chapter 6 deals with historical-systematic approaches to a very important theological worry that hovers over unlimited atonement, namely, the problem of double payment. The specter of double payment is approached historically and theologically in "Lombard, Ames, and Polhill: Unlimited Atonement Without Double Payment" by Joshua R. Farris and S. Mark Hamilton. Through a consideration of the "double payment" objection to a version of penal substitution as hypothetical universalism, the authors lay out some of the concerns about coupling penal substitution with hypothetical universalism, with Edward Polhill as a representative. Further, the chapter explores a more viable candidate of hypothetical universalism, namely William Ames's version of Anselmian satisfaction.

Jeff Fisher serves us in chapter 7 with his chapter "Amyraut in Context: A Brief Biographical and Theological Sketch." This chapter locates Moïse Amyraut and his theology on the extent of the atonement in its historical and theological context. It identifies the unique setting of the French Reformed church in the seventeenth century and the Saumur Academy, from which Amyraut's theology developed and spread. The main focus centers on Amyraut's own articulation of "universal grace," which will later be referred to as Amyraldianism (or Amyraldism). It reinforces that this view emerged from within the Reformed tradition, and though it faced strong opposition it was never determined to be heretical or officially outside the bounds of the Reformed confessions. It also isolates the key distinctive features of Amyraldianism from other versions of hypothetical universalism, while recognizing the similarities and overlap of these views. This chapter further demonstrates that there has long been an alternative position to both the Calvinist limited atonement view and the Arminian unlimited atonement view.

Rory Shiner's chapter 8 treats Australian Anglican theologian D. B. Knox. Knox was a key figure in the postwar revival of Reformed theology in Australia and the UK. Rejecting limited atonement, he was a proponent of a hypothetical universalism, perceiving in limited atonement a threat to Reformed theology's renewal. Despite a relatively sparse publishing record, Knox's position had a disproportionate influence in the late twentieth and early twenty-first centuries. Through his influence, the hypothetical universalist account has been an accepted and widely taught position within Sydney Anglican theology in particular. More recently, in wider evangelical discussions of atonement theology Knox's position has, somewhat paradoxically, been itself framed as a threat to Reformed theology's prospects in our era.

In chapter 9 Joshua McNall looks to the twenty-first century to engage with four contemporary versions of unlimited atonement. By highlighting the strengths and weaknesses of each proposal, and by linking them to particular church traditions, McNall draws forth some important lessons to be learned if one wishes to espouse a theologically robust and biblically faithful account of unlimited atonement today.

In chapter 10 James Arcadi argues that the unlimited atonement perspective best characterizes the teaching on the scope of the atonement in the Anglican Thirty-Nine Articles of Religion, which form a basis for theology in the Anglican tradition. Moreover, utilizing the conceptual scheme of dispositional properties, this chapter argues that faith ought to be considered the sole ingredient necessary to make effectual the all-sufficient work of Christ for salvation. Despite some recent work in the Anglican tradition to the contrary, this chapter argues that this dispositional conception of faith best fits ideas found within the Articles and the commentators on them.

"Amyraut and the Baptist Tradition" is David L. Allen's contribution to the volume. In chapter 11 Allen notes that the extent of the atonement has traditionally divided Particular and General Baptists. While it appears that Amyraut did not have a direct influence on Baptists in America, nonetheless the hypothetical universalism of which Amyraldianism is a leading branch has indeed directly influenced Calvinistic Baptist theology, including the Southern Baptist Convention. This influence was predominantly mediated through the impact of Andrew Fuller and his theology.

Social ethics related to unlimited atonement and hypothetical universalism are treated in chapter 12. Here, Michael Jensen attempts to explain how, when held together, both particular and universal aspects of the doctrine of the atonement ought to, and indeed do, provide a resource for clear theological thinking about the church's relationship to the world—a species of what might be called its "social ethics." This is especially so in terms of the inclusive constitution of the community of the cross and the evangelical—and cruciform—practice of loving one's neighbor, even when these are one's enemies. Christians are called upon to live cruciform lives for the sake of the world. Established by the cross of Jesus Christ, the church is not an "us" opposed to "them," but an "us" who exists for the sake of "them."

Amy Peeler rounds out our volume with her sermon on the love of God, "'He Prepareth a Table in the Presence of His Enemies': A Sermon on John 13:1–30 for Maundy Thursday." This chapter is a sermon, demonstrating the pastoral application of this volume within a local church setting. The style of the chapter is therefore distinct from the others in the work in terms of its form, though not in terms of its content. In this chapter, Peeler explores the range of Jesus's love for his enemies. Jesus's love includes his care and affection for his disciples before, during, and after his final supper with them—despite the betrayals that were already in play and would follow the meal.

Taken together, these chapters hope to introduce, describe, and assess God's unlimited atonement for the sins of the world: a hypothetical universalism grounded in God's love. We offer these chapters to the church and the Christian academy in the hope that we may all grow in holy love with God and for one another.

PART ONE

UNDERSTANDING AMYRALDISM

CHAPTER ONE

ANGLICAN HYPOTHETICAL UNIVERSALISM

Oliver D. Crisp

It has long been believed that so-called "four point" Calvinism is an inferior sort of thing—a kind of "Reformed theology lite." The points held in common with the rest of the tradition are, of course, summed up in the acrostic TULIP, which is a modern, not an ancient, summary of the five central dogmatic claims of European Calvinism canonized at the Synod of Dordt.[1] These are Total depravity, Unconditional election, Irresistible grace, and the Perseverance of the saints. The four-point Calvinist, we are told, believes all of the traditional five points of Calvinism, bar one: the claim that the atonement is limited to the elect (the "L" of the TULIP acrostic). According to the "four-pointer" the atonement is, in some sense, *unlimited* or *universal* in scope. Christ dies for the sins of the whole world, not merely for an elect. This, it is said, is a way of watering down traditional Calvinism to make it more palatable to those for whom the notion of a limited atonement is too much to stomach.[2]

Caricatures come and go. Some have greater staying power than others. Yet even those that persist are still nothing more than cartoons that exaggerate certain features at the expense of others. This is certainly true of the

---

1.   The earliest record of the TULIP acrostic is from a periodical in 1913. Kenneth J. Stewart discusses this in *10 Myths About Calvinism: Recovering the Breadth of the Reformed Tradition* (Downers Grove: IVP Academic, 2011), chap. 3. See also Richard Muller, *Calvin and the Reformed Tradition: On the Work of Christ and the Order of Salvation* (Grand Rapids: Baker Academic, 2012), chap. 2.

2.   Chapter originally published in Oliver Crisp, *Freedom, Redemption, and Communion: Studies in Christian Doctrine* (London: T&T Clark, 2021), chap. 5.

persistent popular claim that "four point" Calvinism is an inferior brand of Reformed theology. Recent work in the history of Reformed thought has shown that this is far from the truth, and that, in fact, so-called "four point" Calvinism was part of the fabric of Reformed theology from very early in its development.[3] Far from being a watertight theological "system" that the magisterial Reformers and their progeny developed and then passed on to succeeding generations, Reformed theology is a variegated and broad stream of Christian theology with different tributaries feeding into it, and different and discernible currents and eddies, representing different schools of thought with their own particular doctrinal emphases and distinctive teaching.[4] This includes different views on the nature and the scope of the atonement. That is hardly surprising given that Reformed theology represents a complex theological tradition that is hundreds of years old, and that reaches back to older ways of doing theology in resourcing itself. Nevertheless, the fact that Reformed theology is broader, and more catholic, than is sometimes reported today—including the question of the scope of Christ's reconciling work—is an important claim worth pressing. It seems to me that redressing the balance so as to dispel the notion that "four-point" Calvinism is aberrant is an important contemporary theological task for those who care about the catholicity, as well as the integrity, of the Reformed tradition.

3. The classic modern study is Brian G. Armstrong, *Calvinism and the Amyraut Heresy: Protestant Scholasticism and Humanism in Seventeenth Century France* (Madison: University of Wisconsin Press, 1969). For more recent work, see for example Raymond Blacketer, "Definite Atonement in Historical Perspective," in Charles E. Hill and Frank A. James III, eds., *The Glory of The Atonement: Biblical, Theological and Practical Perspectives* (Downers Grove, IL: IVP Academic, 2004), 304–23; Alan C. Clifford, *Atonement and Justification: English Evangelical Theology 1640–1790: An Evaluation* (Oxford: Oxford University Press, 1990); Lee Gattiss, *For Us and for Our Salvation: Limited Atonement in the Bible, Doctrine, History, and Ministry,* Latimer Studies 78 (London: The Latimer Trust, 2012); W. Robert Godfrey, "Reformed Thought on the Extent of the Atonement to 1618," *Westminster Theological Journal* 37 (1975): 133–71; Michael A. G. Haykin and Mark Jones, eds., *Drawn into Controversie: Reformed Theological Diversity and Debates within Seventeenth-Century British Puritanism,* Reformed Historical Theology 17 (Göttingen: Vandenhoeck and Ruprecht, 2011); Anthony Milton, ed., *The British Delegation and the Synod of Dort (1618–1619),* Church of England Record Society 13 (Woodbridge: Boydell, 2005); Richard A. Muller, *Calvin and the Reformed Tradition*; Stewart, *10 Myths About Calvinism*; G. Michael Thomas, *The Extent of the Atonement: A Dilemma for Reformed Theology from Calvin to the Consensus (1536–1675),* Studies in Christian History and Thought (Milton Keynes: Paternoster, 1997); Jonathan D. Moore, *English Hypothetical Universalism: John Preston and the Softening of Reformed Theology* (Grand Rapids: Eerdmans, 2007); and F. P. van Stam, *The Controversy over the Theology of Saumur, 1635–1650: Disrupting Debates among the Huguenots in Complicated Circumstances* (Amsterdam: APA-Holland University Press, 1988).

4. I have argued this at length in Crisp, *Deviant Calvinism: Broadening Reformed Theology* (Minneapolis: Fortress, 2014), and, more popularly, in Crisp, *Saving Calvinism: Expanding the Reformed Tradition* (Downers Grove, IL: IVP Academic, 2016). Stewart's book, *10 Myths About Calvinism,* is another recent example with a similar theme, as is Muller's *Calvin and the Reformed Tradition.* A recent compendium on Reformed theology that gives a good sense of the breadth of the tradition is Paul T. Nimmo and David A. S. Fergusson, eds., *The Cambridge Companion to Reformed Theology* (Cambridge: Cambridge University Press, 2016).

In previous work, I have given a historical-theological account of how what today is often called "four-point" Calvinism had more than one source and was a widespread early form of Reformed theology that was tolerated within the confessional bounds of Reformed thought.[5] This was even true of some of those who signed the canons of the Synod of Dordt, which is usually thought to be the ultimate source of the "five points" of Calvinism. There are several discernible historic versions of something akin to the modern "four-point" Calvinism in the early period of Reformed theology, including the best known version of Moise Amyraut (1596–1664), whose name is memorialised in the term *Amyraldism*, as well as the distinct version of moderate Calvinism that arose independently of its French cousin in the British Isles under the leadership of Archbishop Ussher of Armagh, John Preston, and Bishop John Davenant, among others.[6] Amyraut's teacher was the Scot John Cameron. So we might say that the two best attested versions of moderate Calvinism in early Reformed thought were, in fact, British in origin: the Anglican and the Scots varieties, the latter of which was made famous once transmitted to Amyraut at the Reformed Academy in Saumur, France.[7]

Be that as it may, the task of this chapter is not to provide further historical-theological argument in support of the pedigree or distribution of versions of moderate Calvinism in early Reformed thought, let alone some historic precedent for the anachronistic "four-point" Calvinism, but rather to give a constructive account of what we might call the moderate Reformed doctrine on the scope of atonement for today. To that end, I will divide the chapter into several parts. In the first, I make some important conceptual distinctions that will furnish the argument that follows. Then, in the second section, I will set out one version of the doctrine that I think is theologically defensible. The third section considers some historic objections to this way of thinking. It also includes a comparison with a modern version of Reformed theology that is a kind of moderate Calvinism, namely, Evangelical Calvinism.[8] Then, in the conclusion, I draw the different threads of the argument together.

5. See *Deviant Calvinism*. The best work on this topic is Moore, *English Hypothetical Universalism*. Richard A. Muller, *Calvin and the Reformed Tradition,* is also very helpful.
6. I am aware of the fact that "four-point" Calvinism and "five-point" Calvinism are anachronisms when applied to early Reformed theology. As I have already intimated, they are modern heuristics that do not map onto the historic discussion. However, the fact is that these are the terms often used today in popular discussion of the topic of the scope of atonement in Reformed thought. So I have chosen to lead with these terms to set the scene, before critiquing the use of them in the next section.
7. The historical background is discussed at length in Moore, *English Hypothetical Universalism*.
8. Evangelical Calvinism takes its cues from the theology of the twentieth-century Scottish theologian Thomas F. Torrance. The best single treatment of the scope of his thought can be found in his work *The Mediation of Christ* (Colorado Springs: Helmers and Howard, 1992 [1984]). The development of Evangelical Calvinism was greatly assisted by the work of Myk Habets and Bobby Grow in their edited volume, *Evangelical Calvinism: Essays Resourcing the Continuing Reformation of the Church* (Eugene, OR: Wipf and Stock, 2012), and its sequel, *Evangelical Calvinism, Vol. 2: Dogmatics and Devotion* (Eugene, OR: Wipf and Stock, 2017).

SOME CENTRAL CONCEPTUAL DISTINCTIONS

To begin with, let us put the misnomer "four-point" Calvinism to rest. Although I opened this chapter with the term because it is the way in which many people think of Amyraldism today, it is not a particularly helpful designation. Aside from being anachronistic when applied to historic Reformed theology, it is also question-begging. Naming a particular view "the authentic doctrine" means that any variant on this will be treated as a deviation from a norm: "the inauthentic doctrine," or at least "the revised doctrine" or something of that nature. But what is at issue here is the very idea that there is such a thing as *the* authentic version of Calvinism from which Amyraldism (or some other account of the scope of Christ's saving work other than that of so-called limited atonement) is a deviation. Opening proceedings by claiming that authentic Calvinism just is five-point Calvinism begs the question at issue.

This in turn depends on a number of dubious popular assumptions about the nature of Reformed thought as well as about its development. For instance, it is often mistakenly thought that Reformed theology has one fountainhead, John Calvin. If Calvin held to a particular view, then, it is said, this is the Reformed view. But this is patently false. Reformed theology has never had a single source, and from the outset there were a plurality of leaders, with Calvin being a second-generation Reformer recruited into the fold by another Reformed pastor, William Farel. Not only that, Reformed theology is historically confessional in nature. That is, in making theological judgments Reformed Christians have always appealed to confessional documents as summaries of their faith, alongside the great catholic symbols of early Christianity. There are a number of such documents from the sixteenth century, and in many Reformed traditions confessions continue to be written into the modern era. These are thought of as subordinate norms, with Scripture as the norming norm. They are fallible and revisable but nevertheless represent an important kind of theological standard in Reformed theology, and one that has more weight at least in ecclesiastical theology than the teaching of any particular theologian—Calvin included.[9]

---

9.   As is well known, there is a debate about the dogmatic shape of Calvin's position on this matter. Some, like Paul Helm, have claimed that Calvin's position is consistent with the later doctrine of particular redemption, according to which Christ dies to effectually purchase salvation only for the elect. However, others have pointed out that there is material in Calvin's work that seems much more optimistic than this, and that Calvin himself speaks of the universal scope of Christ's saving work. For a summary of Helm's position, see his essay "Calvin, Indefinite Language, and Definite Atonement," in David Gibson and Jonathan Gibson, eds., *From Heaven He Came and Sought Her: Definite Atonement in Historical, Biblical, Theological, and Pastoral Perspective* (Wheaton, IL: Crossway, 2013), 97–120. For the view that Calvin's doctrine of the atonement is indefinite in scope, see Kevin Dixon Kennedy, *Union with Christ and the Extent of the Atonement in Calvin,* Studies in Biblical Literature (Bern: Peter Lang, 2002). More recently, Matthew S. Harding has argued that Amyraut's account of the universal scope of atonement in fact parallels Calvin's in important respects. See Harding, "Atonement Theory Revisited: Calvin, Beza, and Amyraut on the Extent of the Atonement," *Perichoresis* 11, no. 1 (2013): 49–73.

More fundamentally, language of "four-point" Calvinism fails to carve the issue at the joint. Often in popular reports of the doctrine, the claim is made that "four-point" Calvinists deny that the atonement is limited to the salvation of the elect. But this is at best a half-truth that obscures the real point at issue. The matter that divides these more moderate Reformed thinkers from their more conservative theological cousins is not whether the reconciling work of Christ is effectual for a particular number of fallen human beings, but rather the nature of the mechanism by means of which this is brought about. Naming this helps dispel the conceptual fog surrounding this doctrine and clarifies why language of "four-point" Calvinism should be set to one side.

Let me explain why. The question about the nature of the mechanism by means of which Christ's reconciling work is made effectual in the believer has two aspects. The first has to do with the scope of salvation brought about by the atonement. We might put it in the form of a question, like this: *For whom does Christ's work bring about reconciliation?* The second has to do with the nature of salvation brought about by atonement. In question form, this would be expressed by saying: *By means of what particular act does Christ bring about reconciliation?* If we want to know how Christ reconciles fallen human beings to Godself, then we are probably concerned with the *nature* of that reconciling work. The question of the *scope* of that saving work is distinct from this concern, however. Put crudely, it is the difference between asking *how* those saved from the fire were saved, and asking *how many* were saved from the conflagration. We are concerned with the latter question: How many fallen human beings does Christ's reconciling work save? Those Reformed theologians who favor the "limited" or "definite" atonement option reply that Christ dies to save only the elect.[10] That is, the intention of God in Christ is that his atonement be effectual only for the elect. There is no divine intention to bring about the salvation of those who are passed over by divine grace and are damned as a consequence. However, this is not the only possible answer to the question of the scope of atonement. Some Reformed theologians appeal instead to a different sort of distinction, one that was introduced into theology

---

10. Many modern defenders of this view dislike the moniker "limited" atonement, preferring instead "definite" atonement or "particular redemption." The problem with the latter two terms is that they are ambiguous. Saying the atonement is limited in its scope to the salvation of some fraction of fallen humanity less than the total number of fallen humanity does get at what distinguishes this view from other accounts. Saying that the atonement is "definite" or "particular" does not. The reason is that the atonement could be for a definite or particular number of humanity for any number of fallen human beings. Those who are universalists, like the Reformed theologian Friedrich Schleiermacher, would affirm with enthusiasm the idea that the atonement is definite and particular in its scope, and would be right to do so: universalism entails the salvation of all humanity without exception. Thus, those who take this view of Christ's reconciling work believe it is particular, definite, and universal in scope. Similarly, defenders of hypothetical universalism can agree that the atonement is definite and particular in one important respect. For these reasons, I shall retain the term "limited" atonement in what follows to distinguish this position from alternatives like versions of hypothetical universalism, of which Amyraldism is a species.

by the great medieval theologian and bishop of Paris, Peter Lombard. In his famous work, *The Sentences*, which became the standard medieval textbook of theology in the ancient universities of Europe, Lombard writes that Christ "offered himself on the altar of the cross not to the devil, but to the triune God, and he did so for all with regard to the sufficiency of the price, but only for the elect with regard to its efficacy, because he brought about salvation only for the predestined."[11] For our purposes, the important thing to notice here is the distinction he makes between the *sufficiency* of Christ's work in principle, and its *effectuality*, or actual distribution to the elect. We might put it a little more formally, thus:

> *Sufficiency-efficiency distinction*: Christ's reconciling work is sufficient in principle for all humankind, but efficient or effectual only for the salvation of the elect.

Compare the way in which there might be a vaccine developed to tackle a particularly nasty disease affecting a given population. Suppose there is enough of the medication to treat the entire population in principle. And suppose that it is offered to the whole population by government proclamation. Still, we might think that there is an important difference between offering the medicine to the whole people, and the question of whether or not the whole population avail themselves of this offer, come to receive the medicine they need to recover, and benefit from its reception. It is this point that the Lombard makes here. This distinction is at the heart of moderate Reformed soteriology. In the way in which it is taken up in the Scots-French strain of Amyraldism, it takes on a particular theological shape. As it is refracted through the work of the Anglicans headed up by the likes of Archbishop Ussher of Armagh, John Preston, and Bishop John Davenant, it takes on a slightly different shape. But both share in common this way of thinking about salvation as dependent upon the sufficiency-efficiency distinction of Lombard.

Given that Amyraldism names only one species of this broader doctrine that sprang up in several different European centres of early Reformed thought, it would be a misnomer to label the larger whole by the smaller part. Instead, historians of doctrine like Andrew Moore and Richard Muller have adopted the language of *hypothetical universalism* because this characterizes the core theological claim shared in common between the different strands of this moderate Reformed understanding of soteriology. The hypothetical universalist embraces the sufficiency-efficiency distinction borrowed from the Lombard. This is said to be *hypothetically* universalist because it implies that Christ's saving work is in principle sufficient to save all of humanity. That is, in principle, his work could save all of humanity. So there is one sense in

---

11.   Peter Lombard, *The Sentences, Book 3: On the Incarnation of the Word*, trans. Guilo Silano (Toronto: Pontifical Institute of Medieval Studies, 2008), 3.20.5.

which it is a universal work, in keeping with much of the New Testament witness, which reports that Christ is the savior of the world (e.g., John 3:16). Defenders of the traditional limited or definite atonement doctrine must take the apparently cosmic passages in the New Testament (e.g., Col. 1:15–20) as indicating that God saves examples of people from all nations, not literally that Christ's work saves the whole world if by this is meant *every single member of the human race*. By contrast the hypothetical universalist can simply say that Christ really does come to save the whole world and mean it without caveat. Christ's work is in principle capable of saving every single member of the human race, and is sufficient to that purpose. How it is said to be effectually applied only to the elect is disputed among those who take this more moderate Reformed soteriology.

Consider, for example, our two candidate versions of hypothetical universalism, namely, Amyraldism, and the Anglican strain of hypothetical universalism espoused by Ussher, Preston, Davenant, and their confreres—which I shall simply refer to as *Anglican hypothetical universalism* from here on in. For the Amyraldians, there are two conceptual or logical stages in God's will regarding human salvation. The first stage is his conditional (and ineffectual) decree to save all humanity depending on their faith. In this sense, we might say that Christ's work is sufficient on the condition of the appropriate human response to this gracious divine act. However, knowing that fallen human beings will not turn to God in faith, there is a second, consequent, and effectual divine decree that ensures that only the elect are given the faith necessary for salvation.

By contrast, the Anglican hypothetical universalists argued more simply on the basis of the Lombardian sufficiency-efficiency distinction to the claim that Christ's work is in principle sufficient to save every single fallen human being, but is effectual only for those to whom the gift of faith is given. On this version of hypothetical universalism, the divine will is not divided into an antecedent ineffectual conditional decree, and a consequent effectual unconditional one. Instead the view turns on the claim that Christ's in-principle sufficient work is made effective for those to whom God bequeaths the gift of faith.

All of this raises an immediate question. This is how the two different versions of hypothetical universalism outlined here differ in substance from the majority Reformed position of limited or definite atonement. The difference lies in the way in which God's intention in the scope of salvation via atonement is connected to the efficacy of that atonement. To explain this more clearly, let us return to the example of the vaccine. In the case that is analogous to versions of hypothetical universalism, I distinguished between offering the medicine to the whole population with the proviso that there is a sufficient amount of the vaccine for all who desire it, and the question of whether or not every individual will avail themselves of this offer, and come to receive the medicine they need to recover. But this now needs some finessing, given what we have just seen about the reasoning that motivates the Amyraldian and Anglican versions of hypothetical universalism, respectively. The supposition that informs both of these versions of hypothetical universalism is analogous to the idea that no one will avail themselves of the proffered vaccine because all the members of the given population are (let us say) implacably opposed to the government and its medical intervention in their lives. Perhaps they are deeply distrustful of government-backed social programs, or perhaps they are vaccine skeptics. Whatever the reason may be, the point is that they all refuse to avail themselves of the vaccine. So the vaccination has to be delivered directly to members of the population by medical personnel in order to vaccinate them. Those who are given the treatment are healed. Those who refuse the treatment perish.

Compare this thought experiment with a vaccine case analogous to the doctrine of limited atonement. In this case, the government has the resources to make enough vaccine for the whole population, and, in fact, concocts a vaccine so potent that even one drop mixed into the drinking water of the whole populace would be sufficient to vaccinate them all. However, in point of fact, and for reasons undisclosed, the government actually decides to formulate enough vaccine for a particular number of the populace chosen at random. Given that no one will voluntarily come to receive the vaccine, the medication is delivered directly to those who have been allotted a chance to survive, to whom it is administered. The rest of the population perishes.

There are structural similarities between these two vaccine stories, though there are also important differences as well. Both scenarios involve the effectual delivery of the vaccine for a particular number of the populace. However, an important difference is that in the first case there is in fact enough vaccine made available for the whole populace, in the second scenario although one drop of the potent vaccine could in principle save the whole population, in fact only enough is made up and delivered for a fraction of those who live there. This helps us see where the nodal difference between hypothetical universalist and limited atonement doctrines really lies. It has to do with a subtle but important distinction regarding *the intention of God in salvation*. In the hypothetical universalist case, although there are different stories told about how the will of God in salvation is expressed, they hold in common the idea that there is a sense in which Christ's atonement is actually sufficient for each and every human being. This is not merely a notional sufficiency. It is a real sufficiency. The same is not true of the limited atonement doctrine, which only holds to a notional idea of the sufficiency of Christ's atonement. The difference between a notional sufficiency and a real sufficiency is this. In the case of a notional sufficiency what is in view is what we might call a conceptual distinction. Christ's reconciling work has the potency to save all of humanity because it is an atonement made by the God-man. In much traditional theology, there is an assumption, going back at least to Anselm, that the God-man has an infinite value because a divine person has an infinite value, and Christ is a divine person with a human nature.[12] Thus, any atoning work made by the God-man will be a work that has an infinite value in principle. We might say that it has that infinite value in abstraction, as it were, from the actual work of atonement just because it is the work of a person of infinite worth, whose work generates an infinite merit. In this way, God could have ensured that Christ's work brought about the effectual salvation of each and every fallen human being because any atoning work of the God-man would have a value sufficient to bring about the salvation of each and every fallen human being. But in point of fact, God has not done this. As the apostle Paul points out in Romans 9, the purpose of God in salvation is for an elect. So, Christ's atonement actually saves only the elect, and this is the particular number of fallen humanity for whom, in the purposes of God, it is actually intended. It is not intended for any other persons. Part of the reason for the insistence of those who adopt a doctrine of limited atonement on this point is that they think the purposes of God cannot be impeded or frustrated by creaturely action; they are irrevocable (Rom. 11:29). So whomever God deigns to elect must be elect according to his good purpose. If he deigns to elect a particular number through the atonement of Christ, then that particular number must be reconciled. The worry, from the point of view of the defender of limited atonement, is that hypothetical universalism posits a divine purpose that is frustrated or at least unfulfilled because of foreseen creaturely action. That is why the kind of sufficiency in view in the limited atonement doctrine can only be a notional or conceptual one.

Not so hypothetical universalism. As we have seen, the kind of sufficiency in view there is a real, not merely notional, sufficiency. A real sufficiency is one that is, in fact, sufficient for the purpose. The hypothetical universalist can agree with the advocate of limited atonement that Christ's work has an in-principle sufficiency for the salvation of each and every fallen human being. But that is not enough. In addition, the defender of hypothetical universalism wants to say that God's purpose is to provide an atonement the actual value of which is sufficient to save each and every fallen human being. To return to our vaccination analogy, it is the difference between the government medical officers saying that they have sufficient raw materials in the laboratory to make enough vaccine for each and every member of the population, and the medical officers actually making up enough of the vaccine from the raw materials sufficient to vaccinate each and every member of the population. The limited atonement doctrine is analogous to the first of these claims; the hypothetical universalist doctrine is analogous to the second. So, according to the hypothetical universalist, God intends to provide an atonement that is actually, really sufficient for the salvation of each and every fallen human

---

12.   I have discussed this in "Salvation and Atonement: On the Value and Necessity of the Work of Christ," in Ivor J. Davidson and Murray A. Rae, eds. *The God of Salvation: Soteriology in Theological Perspective* (Aldershot: Ashgate, 2011), chap. 7.

being. Nevertheless, no fallen human being will avail herself or himself of the atonement offered independent of divine action in bringing about faith in the heart of the fallen human being so that she or he is able to receive the gift of salvation.

AN ARGUMENT FOR ANGLICAN HYPOTHETICAL UNIVERSALISM

With these matters clarified, we may turn to the task of offering a constructive account of the doctrine.[13] We begin with the theological assumption culled from the Lombard:

Sufficiency-efficiency distinction: Christ's reconciling work is sufficient for all humankind, but efficient only for the elect.

In common with other accounts of hypothetical universalism, I shall take this distinction as the point of departure for this constructive account of the doctrine. With this in mind, we can consider these two claims about sufficiency and efficacy in turn. In the previous section we saw that there are several ways of construing this distinction in the Amyraldian and Anglican accounts of the doctrine. There are other versions of hypothetical universalism besides these, of course. It is just that these are perhaps the two that are best known, and the two that we are concerned with here. I favor the Anglican version. The reason is that (a) it is a simpler, more direct way of reasoning to substantially the same conclusion, and (b) it does not require the questionable assumption—disputed by the defenders of limited atonement—that in the purposes of God there is at least one decree that is both conditional and ineffectual, namely, the decree to save all humanity who turn to Christ in faith.

Regarding (a): When weighing up different arguments for substantially the same conclusion, or different hypotheses that explain the same evidence and provide the substantially the same conclusion on the basis of different conceptual models, it is common to prefer the simpler explanation over the more complex. This is not a hard-and-fast theological rule, perhaps, but in general and other things being equal, where there are two competing explanations of the same data that reach substantially the same conclusion, it is preferable to have a simpler explanation rather than a more complex one. The Anglican version of hypothetical universalism is, so it seems to me, more elegant and simpler than the Amyraldian. This is not a sufficient condition for preferring one version of the doctrine over the others, but it is not weightless either.

Regarding (b): We have already noted that the second reason for preferring the Anglican view is significant because it seems problematic to think that anything can frustrate the will of God. Indeed, this is common coin in Reformed theology where a strong doctrine of God's absolute sovereignty and

---

13. In *Deviant Calvinism* I offered another attempt at stating this doctrine, relying on the work of Bishop John Davenant to do so.

meticulous providence over creation means that it is difficult to see how any divine decree can be frustrated or impeded by a creaturely action. This problem does not arise on the Anglican version of the doctrine. On that view, the idea is that God's intention is to provide a means of human salvation that is, in fact, sufficient to atone for the sin of each and every fallen human individual, though it will only be effectual for those to whom the gift of faith is given. Christ's work is really sufficient, not merely notionally sufficient. But it is only efficacious for the elect. We could put the argument a little more formally in order to make its structure clearer, beginning with a minor revision to the sufficiency-efficiency distinction in order to disambiguate the notion of sufficiency in view here. Let us call this the *ordained sufficiency-efficiency distinction*:

> *Ordained sufficiency-efficiency distinction*: Christ's reconciling work is *ordained to be really* sufficient for all humankind, but efficient only for the elect.

On the basis of this distinction, the version of Anglican hypothetical universalism I am interested in goes like this:

1. God intends and ordains that Christ's atoning work be really sufficient for the reconciliation of all humanity, by which is meant *actually* sufficient for the salvation of each and every fallen human being (this we can call *the ordained sufficiency of the atonement*).

2. This ordained actual sufficiency normally requires faith as a condition in order to be made effectual (we can call this *the efficacious condition of faith*).

3. Faith is the gift of God (Eph. 2:8).

4. God normally provides the gift of faith to those whom he has predestined according to his good purposes (Deut. 29:29; Prov. 16:33; Rom. 9; Eph. 1:4–5).

5. Those to whom God provides the efficacious condition of the gift of faith will infallibly be saved by means of the application of the saving benefits of the ordained sufficiency of the atonement.

This completes the argument. But it also raises an important question, having to do with limited cases that are counterexamples to the reasoning of the Anglican version of hypothetical universalism just sketched. These counterexamples comprise those individuals incapable of forming faith, such as those who die in utero, or before the age of reason, or who remain in a permanent vegetative state, or who are severely mentally impaired and incapable of decisions for which they can be held morally responsible. On the face of it, such persons seem to be excluded from salvation according to the Anglican hypothetical universalist argument because they are not fit subjects of the efficacious condition of faith. To put the point slightly differently, these kinds of individuals cannot act in the relevant sort of way that would render them appropriate candidates for praise or blame when it comes to failure to form faith, for they do not appear to be moral agents. On the face of it, this seems to pose a serious problem for the Anglican hypothetical universalist argument just given.

However, note the way in which the argument qualifies the scope of the gift of faith. Ordained actual sufficiency *normally* requires faith as a condition in order to be made effectual. It is *normally* the case that God provides the gift of faith to those whom he has predestined according to his good purposes. This qualification is deliberate. It leaves open the possibility that there are certain individuals, perhaps classes of individuals, who do not fall under the purview of these conditions because they are not appropriate candidates for the ascription of moral praise or blame. For all we know, God ordains the salvation of such individuals as a class and independent of any condition of faith. That seems perfectly consistent with the logic of the Anglican hypothetical universalist scheme, and with God's gracious benevolence to his creatures.

OBJECTIONS AND COMPARISONS

This completes the constructive section of the chapter. We are now in a position to consider three of the most important objections to hypothetical universalism, as well as a brief comparison with another modern version of moderate Calvinism in the form of Thomas F. Torrance's soteriology. The objections have to do with how Reformed this doctrine actually is; with the supposed double payment objection it implies; and with whether it is theologically more satisfactory than the "five-point" Calvinist alternative of limited atonement. Having considered these, we will briefly compare the hypothetical universalist view with that of Torrance and his theological heirs, namely, the Evangelical Calvinists. This seems pertinent for two reasons. First, Evangelical Calvinism is another species of Reformed theology that posits a universal atonement. It is therefore in some respects a kind of theological cousin to hypothetical universalism, being another (contemporary) species of moderate Calvinism. Second, it is important to see how this more recent brand of Reformed soteriology, though universal in scope, is quite distinct from that of hypothetical universalism.

HOW "REFORMED" IS THIS DOCTRINE?

We begin with what might be the most pressing concern from the point of view of the majority voice in contemporary Reformed theology, though it is, in point of fact, the easiest concern to dispel. This has to do with whether the hypothetical universalist doctrine is truly a species of Reformed soteriology. As I indicated in the first section of the chapter, there should be no doubt about this. The very idea that hypothetical universalism is an aberrant Reformed doctrine depends on a tendentious reading of the history, and an anachronistic account of the shape of Reformed thought. Hypothetical universalism has been present from early in the development of Reformed thought, and has persisted as a minority report into the present. There are other moderate accounts of Reformed soteriology as well, which are distinct from hypothetical universalism, such as that of Thomas Torrance or Karl Barth. There is no good reason to think that moderate accounts of Reformed soteriology are less secure than more conservative accounts. Reformed theology is sufficiently broad that it includes more than one way of thinking about this important theological matter. So this objection can be met and rebutted.

THE DOUBLE PAYMENT OBJECTION

Next, we consider the double payment objection. This is often thought to be the single most significant conceptual objection to hypothetical universalism. It can be expressed as follows: If Christ dies for all humanity, then he pays for the sin of all humanity by his atonement. Yet some fallen humans die without faith and are damned as a consequence. How can this be? It suggests a kind of double payment for human sin, which is both unjust and immoral. For the sin of the damned is paid for by Christ's atonement and yet is paid a second time over in the suffering of the damned in hell. But we know that God does not act unjustly or immorally (Hab. 1:13; James 1:13; Heb. 6:10). So there must be something amiss with the reasoning of the hypothetical universalist.

This is a well-crafted objection. However, for the objection to have teeth it needs to be able to make good on the claim that (a) Christ's atonement *effectually* pays for the sin of all fallen humanity, and (b) those who die without faith and are damned also *effectually* pay for their sin in their everlasting punishment in hell. In other words, there must be a kind of symmetry between the efficacy of the payment for sin in Christ's atonement and in the punishment of the damned. Both must generate an actual and effectual payment for sin that is atoning. In the case of Christ, this is actual and effectual, and completed in his sacrificial work on the cross. In the case of the damned, it is actual and effectual, and ongoing in their everlasting suffering in hell.

In the Anglican version of hypothetical universalism I have defended in the previous section there is an ordained sufficiency to Christ's work. It really generates a merit sufficient to atone for the sin of each and every fallen human being. But like the vaccine example, the generation of sufficient vaccines and its delivery are two different things. The ordained sufficiency of Christ's work means that Christ's work is truly sufficient for each and every fallen human being, nothing more. There is no question of an *effectual* atonement for all humanity here. It is perfectly possible for Christ to die for all humanity without this being effectual for all humanity just as it is possible to produce enough vaccine to save a whole populace without the vaccine being delivered to each and every member of the populace.

But once this much is clear, the objection begins to dissolve. Without the admission of an effectual atonement for each and every fallen human being the claim that Christ dies for all humanity no longer poses a problem. On the Anglican hypothetical universalist scheme this just amounts to Christ providing an ordained sufficient atonement. The application of the benefits of this saving work are normally made via the gift of faith, and this is only given to the elect. Thus, the damned (if there be any such) are excluded from the benefits of salvation because they lack the faith by means of which they may appropriate the benefits of Christ's sufficient work. They die in their sin without those benefits. There is no *double* payment involved. There is just the consequence of sin without the interposition of divine grace in the gift of faith by means of which Christ's benefits may be accessed. Like the case of the vaccine, only those to whom the medication is delivered and administered may benefit from it.[14]

But we could reformulate the double payment objection to avoid this response. Suppose the objector replies as follows: even if we grant the claim that Christ's work has an ordained sufficiency as per the Anglican hypothetical universalist, this still means that Christ's work is infinitely more meritorious than the work to which it is put. And that seems to be a problem. For it means God massively overdetermines the merit of Christ's work. Indeed, it seems that there is a superabundance of merit that is otiose—never being put to use in atonement, so to speak. To return to the vaccine analogy, it is like having a massive stockpile of the vaccine that is never deployed, and that remains in a warehouse unused. Such a state of affairs would be an enormous waste of resources. Just so in the case of the atonement, given the argument of the Anglican hypothetical universalist.

But this response can only succeed if the doctrine of limited atonement as most of its defenders understand it is, in fact, false. Here is why. We have already seen that the vast majority of those who defend limited atonement suppose that any atoning work performed by God incarnate will have an infinite value because it is performed by a person of infinite worth, namely, the second person of the Trinity. Admittedly, on the limited atonement view God ensures that the atonement has a value commensurate to the number of those who are elect. But there is a kind of equivocation at the heart of this version of the limited atonement view. For on the one hand, most defenders of this understanding of the scope of atonement want to say that any atoning work performed by a divine person will have an infinite value in abstraction, as it were, from the actual work to which it is put. But on the other hand, they want to claim that in fact, the atonement only has the value to which God assigns it, that is, the effectual salvation of a fraction of humanity who are elect. Which is it? If the work of Christ is notionally sufficient for the salva-

---

14. As I noted previously, for all we know, those incapable of exercising the sort of agency consistent with moral praise and blame, God may yet elect as a class and without faith. That seems plausible to me.

tion of all humanity because of the value of the person performing the work, then how is it that the actual work to which it is put has a value less than an infinite value? I suppose the defender of the limited atonement view might claim that God can ordain that an in-principle infinitely valuable thing will, in fact, save only the elect. In a similar manner, it might be that a vaccine potent enough to save a whole populace with one drop could be decanted into vials that are individually sufficient only to save a single individual, to whom they must be effectually administered. But even if that is the case, the defender of limited atonement can hardly use the same language of infinite merit against the hypothetical universalist. For on the limited atonement view it is also the case that Christ's work has an infinite value. It is just that the value in question is only thought to be notionally sufficient for the salvation of all humanity, not an ordained sufficiency. In both cases, though for different reasons, there is a superabundance of merit in the atonement of Christ.

But there is a third way in which the double payment objection could be reformulated. On this iteration, the concern is that Christ's atonement pays for all human sin in ordained sufficiency except for the sin of unbelief. Then, it appears that the hypothetical universalist is committed to the rather implausible theological claim that those who are damned are suffering only for the sin of unbelief, not for other sins because other sins have been atoned for by the work of Christ. But, it could be argued, the damned cannot be held responsible for failing to believe the great things of the gospel because faith is a divine gift. So the hypothetical universalist ends up holding a view according to which the damned suffer only because they lack saving faith, though they cannot be responsible for this lack of faith because faith is a divine gift. It would be like refusing medication to someone who lacks the ability to walk to a pharmacy to pick it up. Such a person can hardly be responsible for not being able to walk to pick up their medicine!

This is a stronger version of the objection. In response to the question of whether it is merely unbelief that damns a person, it is clear that all Christians would agree that such a condition is normally a reason to think a person is outside the bounds of salvation, other things being equal (i.e., excepting limit cases such as those discussed earlier). So that cannot be the problem. Rather, the concern is that it is this alone that damns a person because the rest of her sin has been atoned for in Christ. This the hypothetical universalist need not concede. As we have already seen, the idea of an ordained sufficiency to the atonement is like the idea of a bank of vaccination ready to be mobilized. It has a potency to deal with the disease affecting the populace. But it needs to be applied to them. This is what is meant by the ordained sufficiency of Christ's work. It has a merit sufficient in fact to atone for the sin of each and every human sinner. But it is only made efficacious upon being delivered to those to whom the gift of faith is given. So the real problem boils down to the question of the gift of faith. Now, all Reformed theologians agree that faith is a divine gift. So this cannot be the point in dispute. Rather, the concern is that the hypothetical universalist is withholding salvation from those who lack the gift of faith, for which they cannot be held responsible. For the gift is not something that they can attain; its bestowal is an act of unmerited grace. But once again, this is a problem common to all Reformed (and more broadly, Augustinian) accounts of salvation. Now, a *tu quoque* response is not a decisive way of addressing the problem, and this is a *tu quoque* response. That said, it is a way of pointing out that those who defend a limited atonement doctrine have exactly the same problem to address since on the limited atonement doctrine only those given the gift of faith are able to receive the benefits of Christ's atonement, and faith is an unmerited divine gift. So this is not a difficulty peculiar to the hypothetical universalist, but a problem common to the sort of Reformed, and more broadly, Augustinian scheme of salvation.

IS HYPOTHETICAL UNIVERSALISM THEOLOGICALLY LESS SATISFACTORY THAN "FIVE-POINT" CALVINISM?

The third objection to which we will turn has to do with whether hypothetical universalism is a less satisfactory account of the scope of atonement than the sort of "five-point" Calvinism of the limited redemption doctrine that is more familiar to most people. By "less satisfactory" in this context, I mean having less explanatory power, or having some explanatory deficit or difficulty not shared by the doctrine of limited atonement. It is often said that hypothetical universalism has a superficial appearance of being more kindly or gentle or "softer" than the doctrine of limited atonement, but that closer analysis demonstrates that appearance in this case is indeed deceptive. For, the objector claims, the hypothetical universalist view only *appears* to be more moderate. It is, in fact, as particular in its account of the salvation of the elect as any doctrine of limited atonement. Thus, there is no real theological gain in endorsing hypothetical universalism apart from the appearance of being more generous or more accommodating than limited atonement. And since this is a false appearance (for both doctrines entail the salvation of the elect alone), this is no more satisfactory than limited atonement. In fact, one might even think that the limited atonement doctrine is *more* satisfactory than hypothetical universalism because it is honest about its entailments and makes them plain up front. By contrast, the hypothetical universalist appears to be more all-encompassing in its embrace of the sufficiency of a universal atonement. But, in fact, this does not necessarily yield a more optimistic account of the scope of atonement than the limited redemption alternative.

I have already made it clear that both limited atonement doctrines and hypothetical universalist doctrines are, in fact, particularist in their soteriology. Both sorts of view presume God elects a particular number of fallen humanity and ensures that they are saved. They differ as to how this is brought about. So this much of the objection is on target, but is no threat to the hypothetical universalist because it is merely pointing out structural similarities between these two versions of Reformed soteriology. Similarly, the claim that the defender of hypothetical universalism employs a kind of conceptual sleight of hand in order to appear more moderate than the advocate of limited atonement is specious. The fact is, hypothetical universalism entails a hypothetically universalist claim about the scope of salvation. In the case of the Anglican doctrine I have defended here, potentially each and every fallen human being could be saved through the ordained sufficient atonement of Christ. The point is that no fallen human being will, in fact, be saved by the atonement without the gift of faith. And this is only given to the elect. So there is no underhand attempt to *appear* more moderate than is in fact the case. The sort of Anglican hypothetical universalism I have in mind is, *in fact*, more moderate in its claims about the ordained sufficiency of Christ's atonement than the limited atonement alternative of a notional sufficiency. Finally, there is the claim that hypothetical universalism is less satisfactory than limited atonement. Much here depends on the grounds on which the claim is staked. A debate could be had about the biblical adequacy of each of these views, and there are biblical texts that could be used in support of each. But if the debate is joined on the theological adequacy of each view, it is difficult to see how the Anglican hypothetical universalist view I have outlined is *less* satisfactory than the limited atonement alternative, unless one thinks that there is something axiologically better about a divine intention constrained by a notional sufficiency as opposed to one that is an ordained sufficiency. But I cannot see why one would think that. So, on balance, I think that the defender of limited atonement has not shown that hypothetical universalism is less satisfactory than the limited atonement alternative. And that is all that is needed to rebut this objection.

THE COMPARISON WITH TORRANCE AND EVANGELICAL CALVINISM

Finally, let us compare the logical form of hypothetical universalism to that of another species of Reformed theology that includes the notion of a universal atonement, that is, Torrancean Evangelical Calvinism.

Earlier I mentioned that there is another, more recent strand of Reformed theology that might be thought to be version of "four-point" Calvinism, but which are different from the hypothetical universalism of early Reformed theologians in the British Isles and France. This is Evangelical Calvinism, which is a branch of Reformed theology indebted to the work of the twentieth-century Scottish divine Thomas F. Torrance (another brand of moderate Scots Calvinism!). There is much about Evangelical Calvinism that is attractive, and it has generated a number of interesting and original lines of theological inquiry. But for our purposes, what is salient is the view these theologians have on the scope of Christ's saving work. The idea is this. Christ's atonement is not a single event on the cross, but a vicarious act that involves his assumption of human flesh in the incarnation. His whole life and ministry are aspects of this vicarious action, culminating in his death and resurrection. Christ's atonement is more than his identification with us in our fallen state. It is his adoption of our fallen state in order to redeem it from the inside out, so to speak, as one of us. This, it is claimed, is the burden of the Pauline notion that Christ becomes sin for us (2 Cor. 5:21), and that he came in the likeness of sinful flesh (Rom. 8:3). The idea is not that he is a sinner, strictly speaking, but that he has a fallen humanity, and that by means of assuming that humanity, he heals not just his own individual human nature, but human nature as such—yours and mine included.

This way of thinking is bound up with the theology of Karl Barth, who took a similar view. It is also connected, in Torrance's mind, with the soteriology of some of the early Greek Fathers, especially Irenaeus and Athanasius. One of the consequences of this Torrancean position is the idea that all of humanity are included in the vicarious work of Christ. By his vicarious action he heals human nature as such, not just the human natures belonging to some fraction of the totality of humanity.[15] And by his vicarious action he *effectually* heals human nature as such. The vicarious action of Christ in atonement is not an in-principle saving act, but one that actually brings about the healing of all human natures. Torrance even goes as far as to say that Christ is the one justified on behalf of all humanity in his vicarious act, so that all humanity is vicariously justified by means of Christ's saving work.[16]

In many ways this is a very strong doctrine of the universality of Christ's atonement. It might be characterised as a version of "four-point" Calvinism in that it affirms Christ's saving work is universal not merely in principle or in its sufficiency, as with hypothetical universalism, but in actuality. Christ's vicarious action (somehow) heals and justifies all of humanity.[17] Nevertheless, Torrance and the Evangelical Calvinists who have followed his lead are unwilling to draw the conclusion that this view implies universalism, which is viewed as a kind of abstraction that does violence to the tensions present in Scripture. Although he is sympathetic to hopeful universalism, which is the notion that we may hope to the salvation of all humanity though we cannot affirm it dogmatically, Torrance says that the true "dogmatic procedure at this point" is "to suspend judgment . . . for here that is the most rational thing reason can do. Whether all men will as a matter of fact be saved or not, in the nature of the case, cannot be known."[18]

---

15.   A very helpful account of Torrance's view on this can be found in Christopher Woznicki, "The One and the Many: The Metaphysics of Human Nature in T. F. Torrance's Doctrine of Atonement," *Journal of Reformed Theology* 12 (2018): 103–26.

16.   Torrance, *The Mediation of Christ*, 86. I discuss this further in Oliver D. Crisp, "T. F. Torrance on Theosis and Universal Salvation," *Scottish Journal of Theology* 74 (2021): 12–25. A much more thorough treatment of this is given in Myk Habets's excellent study, *Theosis in the Theology of Thomas Torrance*, Ashgate New Critical Thinking in Religion, Theology and Biblical Studies Series (Aldershot: Ashgate, 2009).

17.   A very readable recent account of the scope of salvation that draws on the Evangelical Calvinist sensibility, written by one of the contributors to the *Evangelical Calvinism* volumes, is Marcus Peter Johnson, *One with Christ: An Evangelical Theology of Salvation* (Wheaton, IL: Crossway, 2013).

18.   Torrance, "Universalism or Election?" *Scottish Journal of Theology* 2 (1949): 310–18; 314.

It would be churlish not to take Torrance at his word on this matter. Still, on the face of it, this does generate a problem with the internal consistency of his position and that of the Evangelical Calvinists who have followed his lead. For it appears inconsistent to claim hold to both of the following:

1. In the purposes of God, Christ's vicarious act of salvation effectually redeems and justifies all of humanity; and

2. possibly, at least one fallen human being is not effectually redeemed and justified by Christ's vicarious act of salvation.

However, Christopher Woznicki has recently pointed out that Torrance emphasizes that the atonement is unanalyzable because it is ineffable. That is, it is literally a mystery that we cannot express in words.[19] Perhaps that is true. Even if it is, it is difficult to escape the conclusion that Torrance's position relies on a logical sleight of hand. It is one thing to say with respect to a particularly thorny and complex issue, "We cannot fathom how these things are parts of one consistent whole." There are analogues to such concern in things like the way light behaves like waves under certain observational conditions, and as particles under other conditions. But this is not the same as affirming *both* "we know that S is both *x* and *y* at one and the same time," *and* "we cannot know whether S is both *x* and *y* at one and the same time." That does seem inconsistent. Yet it appears to be the conclusion to which Torrance comes in the end.

Whatever we make of Torrance and Evangelical Calvinism, it should be clear that the version of hypothetical universalism I have set out in this chapter does not fall foul of such a worry. It may have other problems, of course. But the hypothetical universalist can consistently claim that there is one sense in which the atonement is universal in its sufficiency, and another sense in which the atonement is particular in its efficacy. Not only that, by elucidating the Evangelical Calvinist view of Torrance (and his followers) we can see that although both it and hypothetical universalism might be thought of as species of moderate Calvinism—in that both deny the claim that the atonement is "limited" to the elect in an important sense—and although both are recognizably Reformed varieties of soteriology, they offer quite distinct, indeed incommensurate, accounts of how to understand the universal scope of atonement.

CONCLUSION

In this chapter I have attempted several things. First, to give some context to the complex discussion of Reformed soteriology. Second, to give some account of several strands of Reformed soteriology, particularly the French/Scots and Anglican versions of hypothetical universalism, and the doctrine

---

19. Woznicki, "The One and the Many," 125.

of limited atonement. I have also given some account of a further modern moderate Reformed soteriology in comparison with hypothetical universalism, namely, Torrancean Evangelical Calvinism. Third, I have offered an account of the nodal difference between limited atonement doctrines and hypothetical universalist doctrines of the scope of atonement, which has to do with divine intention in salvation. Fourth, I have provided a constructive version of Anglican hypothetical universalism and defended it against three sorts of objections: that it is not Reformed; that it cannot overcome the double payment objection; and that it is less satisfactory than limited atonement. The version of the doctrine I have presented here seems to me to be defensible. It is thoroughly Reformed. And it is not, in the final analysis, less satisfactory than its cousin, the doctrine of limited atonement.

CHAPTER TWO

AMYRAUT AS EXEGETE

Building the Biblical Case for a Bi-Covenantal Universalism

Michael F. Bird

Moïses Amyraut (1596–1664) was "a dogmatic theologian, exegete, moralist, and renowned preacher" of the Saumer academy, a Huguenot seminary in western France, in the seventeenth century.[1] Amyraut, like his teacher John Cameron (1579–1625), was concerned about the hardening of Calvinism into a scholastic and dogmatic system with little room for a universal grace as arguably took place under Theodore Beza (1519–1605) in Geneva and by the declarations of the Synod of Dort (1618–1619). Amyraut rejected the supralapsarian and infralapsarian ordering of divine decrees in election and reprobation. He advocated instead the logical priority of the appointment of Christ as the Savior of humanity ahead of the divine decree to save the elect, while also rejecting a decree to deliberately reprobate anyone. Christ becomes, then, the Savior of the whole human race, not merely a chosen group from among fallen humanity.[2] Although views of universal atonement and hypothetical universalism precede Amyraut, and not all subsequent hypothetical

---

1. Eugene et Emile Haag, *La France Protestante* (Paris: Librairie Sandoz et Fischbacher, 1877), 190.
2. See the overview in B. A. Demarest, "Amyraldianism," in *Evangelical Dictionary of Theology*, ed. Walter A. Elwell (Grand Rapids: Baker, 1984), 41; Andrew McGowan, "Amyraldianism," in *The Dictionary of Historical Theology*, eds. Trevor Hart and Richard Bauckham (Grand Rapids: Eerdmans, 2000), 12–13. See also the essays in Alan C. Clifford, ed., *Christ for the World: Affirming Amyraldianism* (Norwich: Charenton Reformed Publishing, 2007).

universalism is Amyraldian,[3] the contribution of Amyraut was to construct a system of covenant theology that undergirded his specific species of hypothetical universalism. According to Amyraut, God had two covenants. First, an absolute and unconditional covenant whereby God saves the elect out of sheer grace. Second, a hypothetical covenant whereby God saves anyone upon the condition of faith. These covenants corresponded to God's electing will and God's saving will. For this reason, Amyraut's hypothetical universalism can be described as a specific model of bi-covenantal universalism. Amyraut's view can be summarized like so:

> The external call of the gospel . . . speaks of a sufficiency of salvation for all, a universal will of God to save all, and an objective grace for all which is needful for their coming to Christ. The subjective grace of salvation is dependent and conditioned upon faith. The objective grace is an offer of pardon to all while the subjective grace of salvation is conditional and only for those who come to Christ. These two graces correspond to the double will of God. The universal grace objectively given corresponds to God's universal will to save all, while the subjective grace flows forth from God's particular will to save only the elect. All of this is rooted in the atonement. The atonement is universal in sufficiency, in intention, and in scope and merits the grace which is objectively for all, but is subjectively given only to those who fulfill the condition of faith.[4]

Or else, in the words of Roger Nicole:

> Amyraut held that God, moved by compassion for the plight of fallen mankind, designed to save all men and sent His Son Jesus Christ as a substitutionary offering for the sins of all men and of every man—this is Amyraut's universalism. This sacrifice is not effectual unto salvation, however, unless God's offer of grace is accepted by man in repentance and faith, which acceptance is the fruit of God's special grace, conferred on those only whom He has chosen—this is the hypothetical aspect of Amyraut's view.[5]

Amyraut, somewhat like Jacob Arminius, was attempting to offer a minority report from *within* the Reformed tradition that ensured the evan-

3.   The wrongful equation of all Reformed hypothetical univeralism with Amyraldianism leads James Eglington ("Early Modern French and Dutch Connections," in *The History of Scottish Theology, Volume 1: Celtic Origins to Reformed Orthodoxy*, eds. Mark W. Elliott and David Fergusson [Oxford: Oxford University Press, 2019], 316) to label Amyraldianism as "an ill-defined, eponymous tradition."
4.   H. Hanko, "History of the Free Offer of the Gospel," *Protestant Reformed Theological Journal* 17 (1983): 15.
5.   Roger Nicole, "Moyse Amyraut (1596–1664) and the Controversy on Universal Grace: First Phase (1634–1637)" (PhD diss., Harvard University, 1966), 3–4.

gelical rather than scholastic substructure of theology, placed predestination within soteriology rather than amidst speculation about divine decrees, and returned to an authentic Calvinism as opposed to its ultra-orthodox version championed by Theodore Beza and then Francis Turretin.[6] According to D. G. Hart, Amyraut's work *Traité de la predestination* advocated a "modified understanding of election [which] attempted to soften the apparently arbitrary treatments of divine sovereignty by stressing the possibility of grace for all people."[7] Amyraut's work *Defensio doctrinae J. Calvini de absoluto reprobationis decreto* (1641) also shows that nothing less than Calvin's legacy was at the heart of the debate.[8] While Amyraut was popular in some circles, influencing Quakers such as William Penn,[9] and even some Westminster Divines,[10] yet he was tried for heresy no less than three times by the French Protestant Synod (1637, 1644, and 1659). As a result, Amyraut and the Saumur Academy he represented was treated with suspicion by the Swiss Reformed churches, which explicitly rejected the *Universalismus hypotheticus* of Amyraldianism in articles of the *Formula Consensus Helvetica* (1675):[11]

> Wherefore, we cannot agree with the opinion of those who teach: 1) that God, moved by philanthropy, or a kind of special love for the fallen of the human race, did, in a kind of conditioned willing, first moving of pity, as they call it, or inefficacious desire, determine the salvation of all, conditionally, i.e., if they would believe, 2) that he appointed Christ Mediator for all and each of the fallen; and 3) that, at length, certain ones whom he regarded, not simply as sinners in the first Adam, but as redeemed in the second Adam, he elected, that is, he determined graciously to bestow on these, in time, the saving gift of faith; and in this sole act election properly so called is complete. For these and all other similar teachings are in no way insignificant deviations from the proper teaching concerning divine election; because the Scriptures do not extend unto all and each God's purpose of showing mercy to man, but restrict it to the elect alone, the reprobate being

---

6. Oliver Crisp (*Deviant Calvinism: Broadening Reformed Theology* [Minneapolis: Fortress, 2014], 6) rightly points out that early Reformed theology was not universal on limited atonement because "there were many who espoused this [universal atonement/hypothetical universalism] view besides and before Amyraut, and Amyraut himself learned it from his Scottish teacher John Cameron."

7. D. G. Hart, *Calvinism: A History* (New Haven, CT: Yale University Press, 2013), 83.

8. Amyraut took heart from Calvin's interpretation of Ezekiel 18:23 to support the notion of two mercies or two wills in God. See Richard A. Muller, *Calvin and the Reformed Tradition: On the Work of Christ and the Order of Salvation* (Grand Rapids: Baker, 2012), 107–25.

9. Stephen W. Angell, "William Penn's Debts to John Owen and Moses Amyraut on the Questions of Truth, Grace, and Religious Toleration," *Quaker Studies* 16 (2012): 157–63.

10. A. Craig Troxel, "Amyraut 'at' the Assembly: The *Westminster Confession of Faith* and the Extent of the Atonement," *Presbyterion* 22 (1996): 43–55.

11. Cited from Martin I. Klauber, "The Helvetic Formula Consensus (1675): An Introduction and Translation," *Trinity Journal* 11 (1990): 103–23.

excluded even by name, as Esau, whom God hated with an eternal hatred (canon VI).

Since all these things are entirely so, we can hardly approve the opposite doctrine of those who affirm that of his own intention and counsel and that of the Father who sent him, Christ died for each and every one upon the condition, that they believe. We also cannot affirm the teaching that he obtained for all a salvation, which, nevertheless, is not applied to all, and by his death merited a salvation and faith for no one individually but only removed the obstacle of divine justice, and acquired for the Father the liberty of entering into a new covenant of grace with all men. Finally, they so separate the active and passive righteousness of Christ, as to assert that he claims his active righteousness as his own, but gives and imputes only his passive righteousness to the elect (canon XVI).

Rather than discuss Amyraut in relation to Calvin's legacy, his relationship to Arminianism, or even the internal debates about federal theology and divine decrees in seventeenth-century continental Reformed theology, in this brief study I would like to instead summarize Amyraut's argument for hypothetical universalism and comment on Amyraut's exegesis of key texts to establish his bi-covenantal universalism, with a view to appreciating Amyraut as a Reformed reader of Holy Scripture. The way I shall proceed is by looking at key sections of Amyraut's *On Predestination* (1634) and how it contributes to his exegetical reasoning from within Calvinistic tradition.[12]

AMYRAUT ON PREDESTINATION

The first step in Amyraut's argument is to claim that "predestination" includes a general sense of divine providence (e.g., Ps. 115:3; Eph. 1:10; Acts 4:28) and a specific sense of individual election (e.g., Rom. 8:29–30; Eph. 1: 5, 11). Logically, then, providence precedes preordination unto salvation.

Second, Amyraut underscores how God is driven by his goodness rather than merely the pursuit of his own glory. It is true that "God has created everything for his glory" insofar that God created all things for himself, and humanity praises God for his glory. However, God's self-sufficiency means he does not need human praise like artists or braggarts who are self-pleased with their inventions. God's purpose is not to elicit praise from creatures; rather, it is the exercise of his own virtues, which in turn elicits such praise. Since "The LORD is good to all" (Ps. 145:9), his goodness is "grand and exquisite but also infinite in proportion with his nature."[13] Whereas God's glory is humanity's

12. Translation and references are from Matthew Harding, trans., *Amyraut on Predestination* (Norwich: Charenton Reformed Publishing, 2017).
13. Harding, trans., *Amyraut on Predestination*, 67.

highest end, God himself is moved to act not by his own glory but by "his pure goodness." For, "with regard to the actions of God himself, it seems that it is more fitting for him to be good, and to act out of his own nature of goodness alone because he is good, than merely to seek the glory of being good."[14] God is propelled, then, not for the recognition of his goodness, but for free exercise and display of his goodness.

Third, concerning God's purpose in the creation of humanity, while God endowed human creatures with sufficient understanding to praise him for his glory (Rom. 1:19–20), nonetheless God sought to unite his wisdom and goodness in a creature more elaborate than any animal of creation (as per Ps. 8:3–6). God, then, made humanity to reflect the perfection of his holiness, virtue, and contentment.

Fourth, as to why God permitted the fall and would not permit humanity to remain in eternal ruin, Amyraut answers that God purposed "to make his goodness exceed the bounds of nature and to overwhelm the whole world with his mercy" by the sending of the Son to atone for sins and to repair the image of God and bring them into a "supernatural covenant."[15] It is a covenant with a reconciler and mediator, none other than the second Adam from heaven, who comes to redeem and repair those in the first Adam.

Fifth, Amyraut sets out his idea of total depravity and original sin. The impact of Adam's sin is that humanity has lost its integrity, holiness, and love. Even the servile fear of God and quest for forgiveness is unable to restore it, for such a wretched condition cannot be restored by oneself! Humans are slaves to sin and even rejoice in their slavery to this rapacious master. Sin is a "totally incurable ulcer"[16] and transmitted in the manner that "leprous fathers breed leprous infants like themselves."[17] Amyraut paraphrases Romans 5:12 as: "This death envelops all men not only in the same condemnation, but also in the same cause of their condemnation, that is, their corruption and active choice of sin."[18] Amyraut's view is that condemnation is transmitted from Adam, but also ratified by the conduct of Adam's progeny.

Sixth, the solution to human corruption is divine mercy. God foreknows and foreordains all things, even the human fall into ruin, yet God has "seen all mankind perishing equally without distinction or difference in the same shipwreck and bottomless and shoreless sea, he has had compassion in this calamity and sought some means to procure the salvation of the world." Such takes place not at the expense of divine retribution, which Christ satisfies, but God has "permitted himself to be overcome by his own mercy."[19]

---

14. Harding, trans., *Amyraut on Predestination*, 67.
15. Harding, trans., *Amyraut on Predestination*, 80.
16. Harding, trans., *Amyraut on Predestination*, 87.
17. Harding, trans., *Amyraut on Predestination*, 88.
18. Harding, trans., *Amyraut on Predestination*, 89.
19. Harding, trans., *Amyraut on Predestination*, 93.

Seventh, we see the heart of Amyraut's thesis in his statement about the purpose of the incarnation:

> Since the misery of men is equal and universal and since the desire that God has had of delivering mankind by such a great Redeemer proceeds from the compassion which he has for them as his creatures which have fallen into such a great ruin, and since they are equally still his creatures, the grace of redemption which he has offered and procured for them ought also to be equal and universal, provided that they are also found to be equally disposed to receive it. And to this extent there is no difference between them. The Redeemer has been taken from their race and made a participant in the same flesh and the same blood with them all, that is, from a same human nature cojoined with him in the divine nature in a unity of person. That sacrifice he offered for the propitiation of their offenses was equally for all; and the salvation that he received from his Father to communicate to men in the sanctification of the Spirit and in the glorification of the body is ordained equally for all, provided—I say—that the necessary disposition to receive it (in men) is equally in the same way.[20]

Notice the main tenets of the argument: (1) The shared and equal plight of humanity; (2) the universal grace of redemption making salvation equally available for everyone; (3) Christ's participation in the same flesh and blood as the whole of humanity; (4) Christ's death rendering the entire sway of humanity as savable; and (5) salvation on condition of faith, and faith emerging as regenerated by the Holy Spirit. God in his goodness leads people of all nations to repentance, and such goodness is in vain if people do not have the opportunity to truly repent. God does not exclude anyone precisely because the whole world is invited to enter into salvation through a universal grace. Salvation requires faith, whether elicited by the preaching of the gospel or by the benevolence of divine providence. Thus, while the grace of salvation is universal and common to all people, it is in a way conditional upon faith, without which it is ineffectual.

Eighth, the problem, as Amyraut recognizes, is that the nature of sin makes people impotent to respond the gospel, even with the light of providence and the light of Christ shining upon them. This line of thinking is more traditional Calvinism, concerned as it is with human depravity and inability, though it raises the obvious question as to how it relates to Amyraut's claim that grace has an equality principle.

Ninth, Amyraut next proceeds to try and resolve this paradox of universal grace and human inability to respond. For Amyraut, God sends Christ as Redeemer "equally and universally to all,"[21] however, to ensure that the sending

---

20. Harding, trans., *Amyraut on Predestination*, 99–100.
21. Harding, trans., *Amyraut on Predestination*, 113.

was not in vain, God predestines some people to salvation by giving them the "gift of faith."[22] In Amyraut's reading of Romans 9, God indeed elects some to salvation by means of faith, but he does not thereby predestine anyone to reprobation; instead, God abandons them to their own blindness and perversity.

Tenth, returning to his equality principle, Amyraut maintains that God is impartial, to the point that he treats humanity with equality in that they have the same maker, misery, and mediator. While God takes upon himself to be merciful to his elect and to pass over others, to prove that he is not arbitrary, God still offers grace to everyone, only requiring that they do not refuse it and strive to make themselves worthy of it. Sadly, people reject this universal grace, which is precisely why a more efficacious mercy is required. God is then neither the author of sin nor the architect of perdition. That God gives to all their due in merely his justice, that he offers salvation on condition of faith to all, and brings some to faith, is testament to his mercy.

Eleventh, the covenantal architecture of Amyraut's system is then spelled out in some detail. Amyraut sees God's counsels or will with a type of conditionality, whereby a favorable outcome is dependent upon the execution of a certain condition. For instance, Adam could have attained perpetual happiness if he continued to persevere in fidelity. Also, Israel could have attained a happy life in Canaan if they have completely observed the law. Similarly, a conditional divine decree in effect is that God has "ordained to save all men by our Lord Jesus, that is, if they do not show themselves to be unworthy through unbelief."[23] Yet, because God knows human slavery to evil and the corruption of their faculties, God has an absolute counsel whereby he imparts faith to those whom he so chooses. God brings the elect to faith by the preaching of the word and by an internal illumination to help them perceive the truth. In which case, God has "ordained to give faith to his elect, executes this decree in a fashion which in no way makes its outcome doubtful and assures by this means the salvation of those who are part of this eternal election."[24]

In sum,

> And truly, the mercy of God consists in two degrees: one which, as it is said, does not go beyond presenting to us the forgiveness of our sins through the Redeemer and takes sovereign pleasure in our salvation providing that through unbelief we do not reject this grace; the other goes so far as to make us believe and prevents salvation from being rejected by us. The first degree is universally manifested to all through the preaching of the gospel, inviting men to faith with the firm and immovable resolution to save them if they believe. Accordingly, the gospel cries through the entire universe,

---

22. Harding, trans., *Amyraut on Predestination*, 113, 118, 155.
23. Harding, trans., *Amyraut on Predestination*, 127.
24. Harding, trans., *Amyraut on Predestination*, 133–34.

Grace, Grace. The second is not particularly manifested to anyone except by its fulfillment, that is, by the feeling of faith engendered in one's soul.[25]

Amyraut thus differentiates a "predestination to salvation" true of everyone from a "predestination to faith" true of only the elect.[26] On such a scheme it is perfectly comprehensible to find in Scripture the teaching that "Christ died universally for all the world," even if it is applied only deliberately to the elect.[27] The final movements of Amyraut's work attempt to presage his Calvinistic credentials by affirming that predestination does not destroy the reality of free will, neither does it lead to spiritual apathy, but predestination does offer a sense of consolation and assurance to the faithful.

AMYRAUT AS CALVINIST AND BIBLICAL INTERPRETER

Amyraut stands with Arminius among those who wanted to soften the hardness of the developing dogmatic Calvinism. However, unlike Arminius, Amyraut was self-consciously attempting to stand within the Calvinistic camp by appealing to a biblical theology of covenant and grace that would prove to be convincing to the exegetical senses of his Calvinist colleagues.

To this end, Amyraut engages in a number of exegetical moves which constitute his case for a bi-covenantal universalism.

First, Amyraut undertakes a rich Pauline and Johannine fusion to establish the universalism of grace and its particular application to the elect through the gift of faith. Amyraut shares the anthropological pessimism of both Paul and John, and he likewise finds the solution to humanity's captivity to sin in the invasive and efficacious grace of the gospel that Paul and John testify to. While God, in his supernatural covenant, determines to save some, nonetheless God also, driven by his sheer goodness, predestines everyone to saveableness, with Jesus Christ dying for the whole world and holding out to them the offer of forgiveness if he or she should respond in faith.

Second, appeal to Paul's epistles does predominate, and Amyraut makes frequent references to Romans 8–11 to establish his thesis. Amyraut's insistence on grace as applying with some measure of equality and universality is an authentic Pauline motif recognizing Paul's point that there is no distinction between Jew and Greek (Rom. 3:22; 10:12), and salvation is for everyone (Rom. 10:13). It is arguably Paul's description of the reign of grace (Rom. 5:21) that inspires Amyraut to imagine the gospel crying "Grace, Grace" through the universe.[28] In addition, Paul's concluding remark that "God has bound everyone over to disobedience so that he may have mercy on them all" (Rom.

25.   Harding, trans., *Amyraut on Predestination*, 146–47.
26.   Harding, trans., *Amyraut on Predestination*, 143.
27.   Harding, trans., *Amyraut on Predestination*, 145.
28.   Harding, trans., *Amyraut on Predestination*, 147.

11:32) arguably drives Amyraut's inference that God wishes to "overwhelm the world with mercy."[29]

Third, concerning the character of God, Amyraut attempts to blunt the edges of a severe Calvinism in three ways: (1) Amyraut uses the Psalms to correct scholastic readings of Paul. This enables Amyraut to prioritize providence over predestination (by appeal to Ps. 115:3) and prioritize God's goodness over his glory (by appeal to Ps. 145:8; 8:3–6). (2) Amyraut argues for election without reprobation, so that the non-elect are not actively consigned to perdition but instead are passively left to the inevitable results of their unbelief and depravity. (3) Amyraut understands the redemptive covenant in light of God's goodness rather than based on an abstract prelapsarian decree since God's justice is superseded by God's restorative mercy.

Fourth, if one had to summarize Amyraut's theology—or at least his soteriology—it would have to be God's *sovereign and free mercy*. For Amyraut God has "his mercy with complete freedom" and is "sovereignly free in the dispensation of his graces."[30] That freedom is, in a polemical sense, the freedom of God to show his goodness and to extend his mercy to all human creatures he so chooses irrespective of how it infringes upon the theological systems of men in Switzerland or Holland.

CONCLUSION

Amyraut is a good candidate to excite debate about Calvin versus the later Calvinists.[31] As it turned out, Protestant scholasticism, for better or worse, developed Calvin into a dogmatic and rigorous Calvinism that meant that the question of whether subsequent generations were truly following Calvin or distorting Calvin was always going to be in the air. We do not know for sure if Calvin would have sided with Amyraut or Beza on predestination and atonement. Many suspect that Calvin, however, despite some sympathies with Amyraut, would have most likely found favor with Beza, who was his hand-picked successor.

Perhaps so, but whether Amyraut was returning the Reformed churches to an authentic Calvinism or was on a slippery slope to Arminianism is moot. Let us remember that the Reformed tradition is not about the legacy of a single man, but about the recovery of the apostolic gospel and the evangelical renewal of the churches. Amyraut's argument for a species of hypothetical universalism, which combines two predestinarian covenants with universal atonement and the universal offer of the gospel, amounts to what I have called

---

29. Harding, trans., *Amyraut on Predestination*, 80.
30. Harding, trans., *Amyraut on Predestination*, 119–20.
31. Cf. Brian G. Armstrong, *Calvinism and the Amyraut Heresy* (Madison: University of Wisconsin Press, 1969); Alan C. Clifford, *Atonement and Justification: English Evangelical Theology 1640–1790* (Oxford: Clarendon, 1990); Alan C. Clifford, *Calvinus: Authentic Calvinism: A Clarification* (Norwich: Charenton Reformed Publishing, 1996); Alan C. Clifford, "Justification: the Calvin-Saumur Perspective," *Evangelical Quarterly* 79 (2007): 331–48.

a bi-covenantal universalism. Amyraut's double predestination is not election and reprobation, but a foreordination to salvation (if accepted) and faith (when illuminated). He offers a covenantal arrangement that can consistently and cogently sustain the claim that God's grace is sufficient for all but only efficient for the elect.

Amyraut's thesis on predestination was not intended as a theological compromise like the Byzantine emperor Zeno's *henotikon*, a kind of half-baked theological fudge on Christology that by trying to satisfy everybody, ends up satisfying nobody. Rather, Amyraut's predestination thesis was derived from a reading of Scripture that takes with the utmost seriousness the incandescent goodness of God, human slavery to sin, the necessity of faith, the efficacy of divine grace, and the sovereign mercy of God. If Calvinism, in whatever permutation it takes, cannot suffer to hear the melodious sound of "Grace" calling to the sinner, or respect the scandalous mercy of God to the reprobate, then it is Calvinism which is all the worse for it.[32]

---

32. Donald Macleod blames Amyraldianism for the gradual liberalism of global Presbyterianism: "Amyraldianism had proved a powerful catalyst, dissolving the bond between the Presbyterian churches and their historic creed. Loosed from their Confessional moorings they were left to drift on uncharted seas with only the undefined 'substance of the faith' for a compass, each preacher free to choose his own position on the ocean of unlimited theological pluralism. Presbyterianism had lost the one thing that bound it together: common preaching. Two ministers in the one Communion could now be as far apart as Friedrich Nietzsche and John Gill." Donald Macleod, "Amyraldus Redivivus: A Review Article," *Evangelical Quarterly* 81 (2009): 210–29.

CHAPTER THREE

AMYRALDISM AND PENAL SUBSTITUTION

Christopher Woznicki

When it comes to Reformed theology, misconceptions abound. One such misconception is that Reformed theology can accurately be encapsulated by the "five points of Calvinism" or by "TULIP."[1] Richard Muller, however, is among those scholars who have persuasively made the case that to reduce Reformed theology to the five points of Calvinism is misleading. Traditional Reformed teaching, which Muller maintains is defined by Reformed confessions, stands in "substantial agreement with the so-called five points—total inability to attain one's salvation, unconditional grace, limited efficacy of Christ's all sufficient work of satisfaction, irresistible grace, and the perseverance of the saints."[2] Yet Reformed teaching also stands in agreement on "the baptism of infants, the identification of sacraments as means of grace, and the unity of the one covenant of grace from Abraham to the eschaton."[3] In other words, "there are more than five points."[4] To this expanded list of Reformed teachings we might add the account of atonement in which atonement is—at least in part—accomplished by the mechanism of Christ's substitutionary death for the penal consequences sinners have incurred.[5]

---

1. Such a misconception is promulgated in popular literature by proponents and opponents of Reformed theology. See for example R. C. Sproul, *What Is Reformed Theology?* (Grand Rapids: Baker, 1997), 189–206.
2. Richard Muller, "How Many Points?" *Calvin Theological Journal* 28 (1993): 427.
3. Muller, "How Many Points?" 427.
4. Muller, "How Many Points?" 427.
5. Stephen Holmes argues that few Reformed Confessions explicitly state that penal substitution is the only orthodox way of narrating the atonement. The Heidelberg Catechism and Belgic confession

Another misconception—one that involves one of the "five points"—is that Reformed theology speaks with one voice about the extent or intent of atonement. It is often assumed that Reformed teaching has a singular understanding about who Christ died for; such an understanding often goes by the terms "limited atonement," "definite atonement," or "particular redemption." In the minds of many, two of the features mentioned above, namely Christ's penal substitutionary death and limited atonement, go hand in hand. To separate these two doctrines, it is said, leads to untoward—and perhaps even unbiblical—consequences. Therefore, we are told, "What therefore God hath joined together, let not man put asunder."

Lee Gatiss is among the chorus of voices who argues for the inseparability of penal substitution and limited atonement. He asserts that if penal substitution and unlimited atonement are true, then it would be the case that "all people are saved from ever bearing the wrath of God themselves."[6] If this is the case, he says, then penal substitution would lead to universal salvation. Universal salvation is unbiblical; therefore, either penal substitution is false, or Jesus was not a penal substitute for all people. Penal substitution is true; thus, we must say that "Jesus died only for those who were chosen."[7] Likewise, Garry J. Williams asserts the inseparability of these two doctrines. He claims: "Penal substitutionary atonement rightly understood entails definite atonement. Conversely, insistence on an atonement made for all without exception undermines belief in penal substitutionary atonement."[8] The burden of this chapter is to refute the claim that atonement made for all without exception undermines penal substitution. I will argue that one can consistently hold to a belief in penal substitution and to the belief that Christ's death was not particular in intent while denying universalism.

My argument proceeds as follows. I begin by defining three terms that are crucial for discussion of our topic: limited atonement, unlimited atonement, and penal substitution. With these definitions in place, I formulate an argument that is often levied against Reformed understandings of unlimited atonement. Briefly, this argument claims that the conjunction of penal substitutionary atonement (PSA) and unlimited atonement necessarily lead to universalism. I formulate this objection as a *reductio ad absurdum* argument and label it the "universalism *reductio*." I then explore several options that a believer in PSA and

---

make use of substitutionary language but do not seem to require penal substitution. The 1560 Scots Confession and the Helvetic Confession, on the other hand, demand penal substitution as one aspect of atonement. See Stephen Holmes, "Penal Substitution," in *T&T Clark Companion to Atonement*, ed. Adam Johnson (London: Bloomsbury, 2017), 305–6.

6.   Lee Gatiss, *For Us and for Our Salvation: "Limited Atonement" in the Bible, Doctrine, History and Ministry* (London: Latimer Trust, 2012), 3.

7.   Gatiss, *For Us and for Our Salvation*, 3.

8.   Garry J. Williams, "The Definite Intent of Penal Substitutionary Atonement," in *From Heaven He Came and Sought Her: Definite Atonement in Historical, Biblical, Theological, and Pastoral Perspective*, eds. David Gibson and Jonathan Gibson (Wheaton, IL: Crossway, 2013), 461.

unlimited atonement could take to avoid the universalism *reductio*. This leads me to consider two Reformed versions of unlimited atonement—Ussherian hypothetical universalism and Amyraldism.[9] Of these two positions I contend that Amyraldism, despite the threat of the "Double Payment Objection," is the preferable way for a PSA theorist to affirm unlimited atonement.

DEFINITIONS

Before making a case for the commensurate nature of penal substitution and the belief that Christ's death was not particular in intent, it seems fitting to clarify several important terms that come up in discussions of limited/ unlimited atonement.

Limited versus Unlimited Atonement

Although the terms "limited" and "unlimited" atonement have become common parlance in discussions about the extent of atonement, these terms are problematic.[10] Richard Muller argues that the language of "atonement" has "been retrojected onto early modern theological debates concerning the sufficiency, efficiency, intention, and extent of Christ's satisfaction."[11] Thus, contemporary debates about limited versus unlimited "atonement" that draw upon early-modern sources, including Reformation-era sources and Reformed Orthodox sources, are anachronistic. But the problem is more serious than mere anachronism. Muller goes on to argue that the term "atonement" actually occludes the heart of the debate. "Atonement" is an English word that means to set at one after discord or strife. This word, "when associated with its actual Latin equivalents . . . stands in what is at best an oblique relationship to the early modern debates over the limitation of Christ's work."[12] "Atonement," Muller proceeds to explain, is typically not used—even in early modern English theology—to discuss the intent of Christ's paschal work; the term that is typically used is "satisfaction."[13] Satisfaction is a technical term which refers to making amends or reparation. When the term is used to describe Christ's work, that is, the *satisfactio vicaria* (vicarious satisfaction), it refers to "Christ's work of

---

9. I have decided to address Ussher's hypothetical universalism instead of Davenant's because Oliver Crisp has already addressed Davenant's views in his chapter in this book.

10. The most obvious problem with the terms is that they appear to be value-laden. The former term appears to place a limit on the wondrous work of the cross, but the latter term appears to have a more expansive or gracious understanding of Christ's salvific work. These terms are, however, slightly misleading. Roger Nicole, to cite one example, has highlighted the fact that all evangelicals assert some limit upon the extent of Christ's salvific work. See Roger Nicole, "The Case for Definite Atonement," *Bulletin of the Evangelical Theological Society* 10 (1967): 200.

11. Richard Muller, *Calvin and the Reformed Tradition: On the Work of Christ and the Order of Salvation* (Grand Rapids: Baker Academic, 2012), 74.

12. Muller, *Calvin and the Reformed Tradition*, 74–75.

13. Muller, *Calvin and the Reformed Tradition*, 75.

propitiation and expiation considered as payment for sin made for believers in their place."[14] Thus, "satisfaction," while related to "atonement," is not equivalent with the notion of atonement. Satisfaction, in scholastic parlance, is something which "must be made for all sin if there is to be redemption and reconciliation."[15] Satisfaction, therefore, ought to be logically distinguished from the concept of reconciliation, redemption, and even atonement.

With the observation that satisfaction is logically distinct from atonement, it seems preferable to speak of "limited satisfaction," "definite satisfaction," or "particular satisfaction" instead of "limited atonement," "definite atonement" or "particular redemption." Yet again, the latter set of terms are so deeply engrained into debates about the intent of atonement—or should I say satisfaction?—that it seems unreasonable to attempt to exchange "satisfaction" for "atonement" or "redemption." With this unfortunate situation in mind, I propose that we continue to use the terms "limited atonement" and "unlimited atonement" while remembering that we are actually discussing the intent of satisfaction made by Christ. With this qualification in mind I suggest the following working definition for limited atonement (LA):

> LA: The satisfaction rendered by Christ on the cross was of infinite value and worth by virtue of Christ's incarnation and its intended object is constituted by those whom God has elected from eternity. The number of the elect is less than the number of all human beings who have existed, currently exist, or will exist.[16]

I suggest adopting the following working definition for unlimited atonement (UA):

> UA: The satisfaction rendered by Christ on the cross was of infinite value and worth by virtue of Christ's incarnation, and its intended object is constituted by all the human beings who have existed, currently exist, or will exist.

Penal Substitutionary Atonement (PSA)

I have defined LA as the view according to which the satisfaction rendered by Christ on the cross was of infinite value and worth by virtue of Christ's incarnation, but its intended object is constituted by those whom God has elected from eternity. So how is satisfaction made?

---

14.   Richard Muller, "Satisfactio Vicaria," in *Dictionary of Latin and Greek Theological Terms: Drawn Principally from Protestant Scholastic Theology*, 2nd ed. (Grand Rapids: Baker Academic, 2017), 352.

15.   Muller, "Satisfactio Vicaria," 352.

16.   This is an adaptation of a definition provided in Raymond A. Blacketer, "Definite Atonement in Historical Perspective," in *The Glory of the Atonement: Biblical, Theological, and Practical Perspectives*, eds. Charles E. Hill and Frank A. James (Downers Grove, IL: IVP Academic, 2004), 305.

According to Anselm, because of sin humans have failed to render to God the honor that is due to him. Anselm explains that God can respond in one of two ways: "Necessarily then, when God's honor is taken away, either it is paid back or else punishment follows. Otherwise, either God would not be just toward himself, or he would lack the power to enforce either repayment or punishment."[17]

On this view human sin is either punished or God's honor is restored through some act of satisfaction. Anselm argued that God, being just, ensures that satisfaction is made by Christ on behalf of human beings. Christ assumes a human nature, lives a sinless life, performs an act of supererogation, generates merit, and gives this merit to believers. This extra merit satisfies God's honor, and thus satisfaction is made.

Anselmian satisfaction and penal substitution resemble one another and are related, but they are different models of atonement.[18] Anselmian satisfaction and penal substitution share several assumptions, including assumptions about divine justice and the need for sin to be punished. Anselm and the penal substitution theorist agree that God's honor has been stolen by sinners and that in order to be just, God's honor must either be repaid, or sinners must be punished for their sin. However, Anselm and the penal substitution theorist provide different accounts of how God's justice is satisfied. Anselm claims Christ satisfied God's justice by repaying God's honor. The penal substitution theorist claims that Christ satisfied God's retributive justice when he acted as a penal substitute. Both Anselm and the penal substitution theorist have an account of how Christ satisfies God's justice on behalf of sinners, therefore both views can legitimately make claims about belonging to the "satisfaction" family of atonement. But what is penal substitution?

Recent literature about the nature of penal substitution identifies four elements that are necessary for labeling an account of atonement a penal substitutionary model. These elements are:

(P1) Sin deserves to be punished by God.

(P2) On the cross, Christ undergoes some harsh treatment from God on behalf of individual sinners.

(P3) Sinners avoid punishment because of Christ's work on the cross.

(P4) God's retributive justice is satisfied by Christ's work on the cross.[19]

---

17. Anselm, "Cur Deus Homo [CDH]," in Anselm: The Basic Works, trans. Thomas Williams (Indianapolis: Hackett, 2007), 237–326 (CDH 1.13).

18. Oliver Crisp writes that "the magisterial Reformers who developed the doctrine of penal substitution did so against the backdrop of the Anselmian doctrine of satisfaction." See Approaching Atonement: The Reconciling Work of Christ (Downers Grove, IL: IVP Academic, 2020), 69.

19. Christopher Woznicki, "Do We Believe in Consequences?" Neue Zeitschrift für Systematische Theolgie und Religionsphilosophie 60 (2018): 213. This list of four conditions has been updated from my

Despite the fact that there are four elements necessary for a view to be classified as penal substitution, there is some debate about how best to understand P2. Some proponents of PSA argue that P2 should be understood as claiming that the harsh treatment Christ endures on the cross on behalf of sinners is a punishment.[20] In a previous essay I labeled this view PSA-1:

PSA-1: Sinners deserve to be punished for their sin. Christ undertakes the punishment for sin that individual sinners deserved. Because of this, sinners do not have to undertake the punishment themselves because God's justice is satisfied by the death of Christ.[21]

Others argue that Christ experiences the consequences that if sinners had themselves undergone would be classified as a punishment.[22] I have previously labeled this view PSA-2:

PSA-2: Sinners deserve to be punished for their sin. Christ undertakes the consequences for sin, which had it fallen upon sinners, would be the punishment for sin that individual sinners deserve. Because of this, sinners do not have to undergo that punishment themselves, yet God's justice is satisfied by Christ.

Despite differences regarding P2, both PSA-1 and PSA-2 are similar in that they both hold to P1–P4. Both views claim that satisfaction is made when Christ dies a substitutionary death on the cross, enduring the harsh treatment (penal or non-penal consequences) that sinners deserved because of their sin. Because of the similarity between the views, it seems best to speak of a family of views called penal substitution rather than one singular account of penal substitution.[23] In what follows, all references to PSA will refer to the family of views as opposed to one particular account of PSA.

SUMMARY

Let us take stock. I have defined LA, UA, and PSA; these preliminary definitions—which might seem like a mere throat-clearing exercise—are crucial for the task of approaching the extent of atonement in a careful manner. I am now in a position to articulate how PSA relates to LA and UA.

---

previous publication as I have been convinced of the necessity of making reference to "individual sinners" in P3.

20. See, for example Thomas Schreiner, "Penal Substitution View," in *The Nature of Atonement: Four Views*, eds. James Beilby and Paul Eddy (Downers Grove, IL: InterVarsity Press, 2006), 67.
21. Woznicki, "Do We Believe in Consequences?" 211.
22. For example, William Lane Craig and J. P. Moreland, *Philosophical Foundations for a Christian Worldview*, 2nd ed. (Downers Grove, IL: InterVarsity Press, 2017), 613.
23. Woznicki, "Do We Believe in Consequences?" 210.

The definition of LA I have provided claims that Christ makes satisfaction only for those whom God has elected for salvation; a penal substitution theorist who believes in LA would say that Christ acts as a penal substitute—thus making satisfaction—only for those whom God has elected for salvation. A penal substitution theorist who believes in UA would say that Christ acts as a penal substitute—thus making satisfaction—for all human beings who have existed, currently exist, and will exist. In the following section I consider one objection that could be leveled against holding PSA and UA together.

THE UNIVERSALISM *REDUCTIO* ARGUMENT

A *reductio ad absurdum* is a type of logical argument that attempts to disprove a claim by showing that its implications lead to an absurd conclusion, for example, denying the law of noncontradiction. One particular objection against holding to PSA and UA simultaneously is that it seems to lead to universalism.[24] Recall Lee Gatiss's argument described in the introduction. Although Gatiss does not formulate his objection as a *reductio ad absurdum*, we can increase the force of his objection by formulating it in this manner. Let us call this objection the "universalism *reductio* argument." I suggest that the argument goes as follows:

(1) Universalism is false, that is, not all persons are saved.

(2) UA is true, that is, Christ makes satisfaction for all human beings who have existed, exist, or will exist.

(3) PSA is true, that is, Christ undertakes the harsh treatment for sin that individual sinners deserved.

From the conjunction of (2) and (3),

(4) Unlimited PSA is true, that is, Christ undergoes the harsh treatment that sinners deserve on behalf of all sinners that have existed, exist, or will exist.

(5) If Christ undergoes the harsh treatment that sinners deserved on behalf of every sinner that has existed, exists, or will exist then (Q) all persons are saved.

From (4) and (5),

(6) All persons are saved.

---

24.   See, Gatiss, *For Us and for Our Salvation*, 3.

But (6) contradicts the supposition with which we began. So, the conclusion from (1) and (6) entails the following absurd claim:

(7) All persons are not saved and all persons are saved.

This argument purports to show that holding to both PSA and UA leads to a contradiction; the unlimited PSA theorist affirms a contradiction, namely, "not all persons are saved" and "all persons are saved." Thus, they are led to break the law of noncontradiction. But certainly, this is an absurd conclusion that ought to be avoided.[25]

AVOIDING THE ABSURDITY

The unlimited PSA theorist has several options if she does not want to break the law of noncontradiction. First, she could reject premise (1). If she rejects premise (1)—that universalism is false—then she avoids breaking the law of noncontradiction. However, there are plenty of biblical and traditional theological arguments for why one should accept the truth of premise (1).[26] So it seems as though this will not be a live option for many theologians. Second, she could reject premise (2), but premise (2) is the heart of the disagreement between an LA and UA theorist, so to reject premise (2) would mean capitulating to the LA position. Third, she could deny premise (3)—that is, deny the truth of PSA. This is what some theologians have done. Michael Horton writes that "Arminian theologians frequently express unease with the doctrine of substitution because it entails either Calvinism [LA] or universalism."[27] He cites H. Orton Wiley who says, "It is in this attempt to impute our sin to Christ as His own that the weakness of this type of substitution appears."[28] Fred Sanders concurs with Horton's assessment, stating that "Plenty of Arminian theologians have looked elsewhere for a key idea in their atonement theology and have especially tended to invest in a governmental model."[29] A fourth option is to deny premise (5). There are several ways to do this. Let us examine just two.

USSHERIAN HYPOTHETICAL UNIVERSALISM

One historically significant attempt at denying premise (5) is the view put forth by Archbishop James Ussher (1581–1656). According to Ussher, "The

25. Laurence Horn, "Contradiction," in *The Stanford Encyclopedia of Philosophy* (Winter 2018), ed. Edward N. Zalta, https://plato.stanford.edu/archives/win2018/entries/contradiction.

26. See, for example, Michael J. McClymond, *The Devil's Redemption: A New History and Interpretation of Christian Universalism* (Grand Rapids: Baker, 2018), 999–1066.

27. Michael Horton, "Traditional Reformed View," in *The Extent of Atonement*, ed. Adam J. Johnson (Grand Rapids: Zondervan Academic, 2019), 121–22.

28. Horton, "Traditional Reformed View," 121–22.

29. Fred Sanders, "Response to Michael Horton," in *The Extent of Atonement*, ed. Adam J. Johnson (Grand Rapids: Zondervan Academic, 2019), 146. Despite the fact that "plenty of Arminians" have adopted models besides PSA, Sanders believes that PSA is consistent with Arminian theology.

satisfaction of Christ, only makes the sins of mankind fit for pardon."[30] Thus, it does not follow from the fact that Christ undergoes the harsh treatment that sinners deserved on behalf of every sinner that has existed, exists, or will exist that all are in fact pardoned or saved. How does he arrive at this conclusion? First, Ussher distinguishes between various stages of Christ's salvific work. One stage is Christ's act of making satisfaction; a second and subsequent stage is Christ's work of making intercession for sinners. Christ's intercession takes the possibility of salvation, which is gained by satisfaction, and makes it actual. For whom did Christ make satisfaction on the cross? Garry Williams explains that for Ussher, "Christ did not make satisfaction for any individual specifically, but for human nature qua nature."[31] This move allows Ussher to separate the object of Christ's satisfaction from the object of his intercession. Ussher explains, "The one [satisfaction] may well appertain to the common nature, which the son assumed, when the other [intercession] is a special privilege vouchsafed to such particular persons only, as the father hath given him."[32] This distinction allows Ussher to say that Christ made satisfaction as a penal substitute for human nature, thus rendering it capable of being saved, but that only those humans whom Christ has made intercession for are actually saved.

At first glance Ussher's distinction between satisfaction for generic human nature and intercession that leads to salvation as a way to deny premise (5) seems promising. However, it suffers from two significant problems.

Williams argues that natures are not the right kind of object for substitution. In order to be the proper object for substitution, natures would have to be able to sin, bear guilt and bear punishment. Yet, natures cannot sin or bear guilt or punishment qua natures. "Sins" he says, "are committed *in* a nature, but they are not committed *by* a nature. Natures can do nothing on their own accord. It is persons who act in a nature, persons who sin in a nature, and persons who bear the resulting guilt and punishment in that nature."[33] In other words, in order to be the proper object for substitution, natures would have to be moral agents, but they are not.[34] As such, Christ cannot make satisfaction for a common human nature, thus Ussher's two-part understanding of Christ's salvific work breaks down.

---

30. Williams, "The Definite Intent of Penal Substitutionary Atonement," 463.
31. Williams, "The Definite Intent of Penal Substitutionary Atonement," 464.
32. Williams, "The Definite Intent of Penal Substitutionary Atonement," 464.
33. Williams, "The Definite Intent of Penal Substitutionary Atonement," 465.
34. Williams considers the possibility that Christ could have made satisfaction for human nature *in abstracto* but quickly dismisses the possibility that human nature exists apart from persons in whom it is instantiated. Williams, "The Definite Intent of Penal Substitutionary Atonement," 465.
    Williams's dismissal of an abstract human nature, however, is too quick. Several theories of atonement build upon this very concept. See Benjamin Myers, "The Patristic Atonement Model," in *Locating Atonement*, eds. Oliver D. Crisp and Fred Sanders (Grand Rapids: Zondervan, 2015), 73–74; and Christopher Woznicki, "The One and the Many: The Metaphysics of Human Nature in T. F. Torrance's Doctrine of Atonement," *Journal of Reformed Theology* 12 (2018): 103–26.

Let us assume, despite the argument above, that natures could sin or bear punishment *qua* natures. Ussher's position suffers from a second problem: it is not clear that his understanding of satisfaction is actually a version of penal substitution. In order to be an account of penal substitution, Ussher's account would need to comport with P2—that is, the thesis that on the cross, Christ undergoes harsh treatment from God on behalf of individual sinners. Yet Ussher's account is founded on the claim that on the cross Christ acts as a penal substitute for human nature, qua nature, not for individual sinners. Simon Gathercole explains that substitution entails replacement: "X taking the place of Y and thereby ousting Y: the place that Y previously occupied is now filled by X."[35] In order to undergo harsh treatment from God on behalf of *individual* sinners then Christ would need to take the place of individual sinners, thereby occupying the place that sinners once occupied. Yet, on the Ussherian account it is not sinners whom Christ takes the place of, rather, it is some nature which sinners share. Perhaps Ussher's doctrine of atonement should be considered a version of penal representation. In representation, Gathercole explains, "X does not thereby oust Y but rather embodies Y . . . [there is] usually a presupposition of representation that X belongs to group Y, and so the representative is part of the body represented."[36] Even if we could classify Ussher's account as penal representation—showing that Ussher's account is similar to penal substitution—it would stand outside the PSA family.

All in all, Ussher's doctrine of atonement presents an interesting way to challenge (5), but it falls short because natures are not moral agents, and it is not a version of PSA. To undermine (5) we need another account of atonement.

AMYRALDISM

Ussher's hypothetical universalism represents a rather obscure account of UA in the Reformed tradition. The most well-known Reformed account of UA, however, is Amyraldism. This view's unique contribution to Reformed accounts of UA lies in how it understands the divine decrees. Moïse Amyraut (1596–1664) conceived of the order of God's decrees in the following manner:

D1: The creation of human beings with the purpose of having them glorify him.

D2: The permission of the fall.

D3: The ordination of Christ to make satisfaction for sin on the cross.

D4: Predestination of persons unto salvation.

---

35. Simon Gathercole, *Defending Substitution: An Essay on Atonement in Paul* (Grand Rapids: Baker Academic, 2015), 20.
36. Gathercole, *Defending Substitution*, 20.

Amyraut's understanding of D3 shares similarities with typical Reformed accounts of soteriology. Amyraut thinks of satisfaction in terms of penal substitution. In a passage in *Defense de la Doctrine de Calvin* he writes, "If man had not sinned he would not have fallen into condemnation and death [P1]. If you believe, you will not come into judgment, for the Lord Jesus has satisfied God's justice in your place [P2, P3]. If you do not believe, the wrath of God will remain upon you forever [P4]."[37]

This brief excerpt demonstrates that he affirms the four necessary conditions of penal substitution, that is, P1–P4.[38]

Despite holding to PSA like other Reformed accounts of salvation, Amyraut's framework differs from some accounts in several important ways. For example, according to Amyraut, D4 is conditional. God, in his scheme, ordains that the salvation of human beings would come to pass but only under certain conditions. Amyraut explains,

> The misery of men was equal and universal, and the desire God had of delivering them from it by means of such a great Redeemer proceeded from the compassion he had towards them as his creatures fallen into such great ruin, in that they are all equally his creatures. So the grace of redemption offered and procured from them had to be equal and universal, provided that they should find themselves disposed to receive it.[39]

In order to be "disposed to receive it [salvation]," a person needs to have faith. God, however, foresees that because of the corrupting effects of sin some persons would not be able to fulfill the condition of faith, so God elects certain people to be given faith as a gift. Amyraut says, "God deploys his power in such a way that it overcomes all that there is of corruption in his understanding and will. . . . It is in this plan, therefore that which is called election or predestination

37. Moïse Amyraut, *Defense de la Doctrine de Calvin: Sur le Sujet de l'election ed de la Reprobation* (Samur: Isaac Desbordes, 1644), 606–7. Translation in Brian G. Armstrong, *Calvinism and the Amyraut Heresy: Protestant Scholasticism and Humanism in Seventeenth-Century France* (Madison: University of Wisconsin Press, 1969), 212.

38. Armstrong confirms this reading of Amyraut, saying, "He accepted at least in its broad outlines, the orthodox doctrine of penal, substitutionary theory. That is, Amyraut taught that the sufferings of Jesus were vicarious in that Jesus took the place of sinners, that their guilt and punishment were transferred to him." *Calvinism and the Amyraut Heresy*, 174. Similarly, G. Michael Thomas explains, "Amyraut took for granted the concept of satisfaction, viewing punishment of the sinner, or satisfaction on the sinner's behalf, as absolutely necessary in view of divine justice." *The Extent of Atonement: A Dilemma for Reformed Theology from Calvin to the Consensus* (Carlisle: Paternoster, 1997), 200.

39. Moïse Amyraut, *Brief Traité de la Prédestination et de ses Principales Dépendances* (Saumur: Jean Lesnier & Isaac Desbordes, 1634), 77. For an English translation, see R. Lum, "Brief Treatise on Predestination and Its Dependent Principles: A Translation and Introduction" (PhD diss., Dallas Theological Seminary, 1985).

consists.[40] This nuance in D4 leads to dual understanding of election—not to be confused with "double predestination."[41] Amyraut neatly summarizes his view of dual election saying, "It is necessary to distinguish carefully predestination to salvation and predestination to faith, the latter being the means and condition through which we come to salvation."[42] The former—predestination to salvation—is with regard to the whole human race. The latter—predestination to faith—is reserved only for some. Those who possess only the former but not the latter are not saved.[43] With the nuance between predestination to salvation and predestination to faith it becomes clear that D4 needs to be reformulated. Let us reformulate D4 as follows:

> D4*: Predestination of all human beings unto salvation conditional upon faith.[44]

We can also add a decree subsequent to D4*:

> D5: Predestination of some human beings to have faith, thus, meeting the condition for salvation.[45]

The distinction between predestination to salvation (D4*) and predestination to faith (D5) plays directly into Amyraut's understanding of the intent of atonement.

On Amyraut's scheme the intent of Christ's penal substitutionary death is unlimited—God intends that satisfaction be made for all human beings—but it is also conditional. The conditional nature of the intent of satisfaction directly parallels the conditional nature of D4*. He explains that by the will of the Father, in his philanthropy and charity towards the human race, Christ died for all, provided they believe.[46] Moreover he says that Christ "expiates the sin of *all* in the world *provided they are not unbelieving or impenitent.*"[47]

---

40. Amyraut, *Brief Traitté*, 103.

41. That is, predestination unto salvation and reprobation.

42. Amyraut, *Brief Traitté*, 163.

43. Amyraut, *Brief Traitté*, 165.

44. "He wills that all human beings might be saved. This is true: and he wills this fondly: but this according to that mercy which presupposes the condition, and not the other. If he does not find the condition in them, he does not so will." Moïse Amyraut, "*Sermon sur les paroles du Prophete Ezechiel,*" in *Sermons sur divers textes de la sainte ecriture,* 2nd ed. (Saumur: I. Desbordes, 1653), 61. Cited in Muller, *Calvin and the Reformed Tradition,* 111.

45. "He wills that some of the human race might be saved. This is true: but it is according to this second kind of mercy which does not demand the condition, but creates it: which does not presuppose it but creates it in human beings." Amyraut, *Sermon sur les paroles du Prophete Ezechiel,* 61. Cited in Muller, *Calvin and the Reformed Tradition,* 111.

46. Moïse Amyraut, "Animadversionum Generaliorum," in *Specimen Animadversionum in Excertitationes de Gratia Universali* (Samur: I. Lesnerium, 1648), 187.

47. Amyraut, "Animadversionum Generaliorum," 189. Italics added for emphasis.

Finally, he says, "The sacrifice that he offered for the propitiation of their offenses has been equally offered for all, and the salvation that he has received from this Father to communicate to mean in the sanctification of the Spirit and in the glorification of the body is *intended equally for all*, provided, I say, that the disposition necessary to receive it is in the same way equal."[48]

God, however, only gives faith to some [D5] so it can be said, "Christ died for all conditionally, but only the elect fulfil the condition; so Christ died for the elect with respect to result rather than intention."[49]

Because Amyraut distinguishes between what I have labeled D4* and D5, it is appropriate to say that Amyraut's understanding of the intent of satisfaction is unlimited but that only a limited set of humans will in fact be saved. In order to illustrate how this is so, consider the following scenario:

> In eternity God decrees the creation of the world which includes the set of all human beings. God decrees the creation of this set of humans with the purpose of having them glorify him in the context of union with him [D1]. Let us say that the set of all human beings who will exist in creation consists of four people: {Gwen, Miles, Peter, Wilson}. Subsequent to God's decree to create {Gwen, Miles, Peter, Wilson} to enter into God-glorifying union, God makes a decree regarding the permission of the fall [D2]. Next, because God wants all people to experience union with him, he makes a decree regarding how he will rescue {Gwen, Miles, Peter, Wilson} from their fallen state and restore them to a state in which they can be united to him. In this plan the Son will become incarnate and act as a penal substitute for {Gwen, Miles, Peter, Wilson} on the cross, thus making satisfaction for sin [D3]. Having decreed the manner in which satisfaction will be accomplished God then renders a decree concerning the intended object of Christ's satisfaction. God declares that satisfaction which leads to salvation will be made for the set which includes all human beings, {Gwen, Miles, Peter, Wilson}. Because God intends satisfaction to be made for all the human beings who will exist in creation, {Gwen, Miles, Peter, Wilson}, we can say that the intent of satisfaction is unlimited. This satisfaction, however, will only result in union with God if Gwen, Miles, Peter, and Wilson put their faith in Christ [D4*]. Subsequent to the decree about God's universal intent for the satisfaction rendered by Christ, God decrees that out of the set {Gwen, Miles, Peter, Wilson}, only a smaller set, {Gwen, Miles, Peter}, will be given faith [D5]. Thus, God intends to give the faith, which is the necessary condition for salvation, to a limited set of human beings. In history, Christ dies on the cross as a penal substitute for the sins of Gwen, Miles, Peter, and Wilson. Christ's substitutionary death

---

48. Amyraut, *Brief Traitté*, 38. Italics added for emphasis.
49. Thomas, *The Extent of Atonement*, 203.

will result in the salvation of Gwen, Miles, Peter, or Wilson if any of these individuals put their faith in Christ. In history, God—by the work of the Holy Spirit—gives the gift of faith to Gwen, Miles, and Peter, but not Wilson. Because Gwen, Miles, and Peter put their faith in Christ, Christ's substitutionary death counts on their behalf and leads to their salvation.

On this scheme, God intends to make satisfaction that will lead to the salvation of all human beings—{Gwen, Miles, Peter, Wilson}—therefore we can say that God's intent for satisfaction is unlimited. Yet God intends to give faith only to Gwen, Miles, and Peter; so Gwen, Miles, and Peter are saved, but Wilson is not. Salvation is accomplished for a set smaller than the set that includes all human beings.

If we transition from speaking about the intent of atonement to the actual work of atonement in history, then we should likewise say that Christ's death makes satisfaction for all individuals and will lead to the salvation of all individuals only if they put their faith in him. If they do not put their faith in Christ, then his death on their behalf will not lead to salvation and at-one-ment with God. Those to whom God gives the gift of faith put their faith in Christ and are actually saved.

SUMMARY

Let us take stock prior to addressing an objection related to penal substitution that Amyraldism might fall prey to. Recall, we defined UA as the view according to which the satisfaction rendered by Christ on the cross was of infinite value and worth by virtue of Christ's incarnation, and its intended object is constituted by all the human beings who have existed, currently exist, or will exist. According to Amyraldism, Christ makes satisfaction for all human beings who have existed, currently exist, or will exist. Therefore, Amyraldism is a version of UA. Satisfaction, however, is only one part of atonement; satisfaction is only *part* of setting fallen human beings at one with God. On its own, satisfaction, which is made for all human beings, does not save individuals. Something more than satisfaction is needed; there is a need for faith. Faith, however, is an unconditional gift given by the Holy Spirit to the elect alone. It is only when a person puts their faith in Christ, by virtue of the work of the Spirit in them, that Christ's act of satisfaction leads to their salvation. Because Amyraldians distinguish between Christ's satisfaction—by means of the harsh treatment that Christ undergoes on behalf of individual sinners—and the appropriation of that work—by means of the unconditional gift of faith—they deny that all persons are in fact saved. Thus, if we reconsider (5), the Amyraldian affirms that unlimited PSA is true but denies that all persons are saved. It seems, then, that Amyraldism is one way to challenge the soundness of the universalism *reductio* argument. But does Amyraldism hold up against one of the most significant objections that might be leveled against it?

THE DOUBLE PAYMENT OBJECTION

Perhaps the most concerning problem with Amyraldism is that it seems to fall prey to the "double payment objection." According to this objection it is unjust to inflict punishment upon someone for an act that has already been punished once before. Accordingly, if Christ has acted as a penal substitute, taking on the penal consequences for the sins of all human beings, then it would be unjust for God to demand that any sinner be punished for their sins again, this time in hell. God is not unjust, so God could not demand a second payment; yet Scripture affirms that there will be some number of people in hell. One must conclude, this argument claims, that Christ could not have been a penal substitute for all human beings.

There are a couple of ways that an Amyraldian could respond to this objection. She might deny the retributive nature of hell. Hell, she might want to say, is restorative in nature—even though those in hell will never in fact be restored unto salvation. By denying that hell is retributive then she would avoid the accusation that anyone is being punished twice. This revisionist account of hell, by my lights, is too high a price to pay to maintain UA.

A more promising route that an Amyraldian might take is to challenge the *ipso facto* connection between satisfaction and salvation. Oliver Crisp observes that "the double payment objection depends on the idea that the sense in which Christ's work atones for the sins of the world is a complete and finished action.... Only if it is true does it follow that there is a double payment objection to answer."[50] Amyraldians, in fact, do challenge the connection. In Amyraldism, satisfaction on its own does not lead to salvation; satisfaction only leads to salvation on the fulfillment of the condition of faith. Thus, the Amyraldian can defeat the double payment objection by appealing to their understanding of the divine decrees to show that Christ's satisfaction does not *ipso facto* lead to salvation.

Amyraldians do not present a minority report when denying the *ipso facto* nature of satisfaction. Charles Hodge—who affirmed LA—questioned the claim that satisfaction is *ipso facto* effective for salvation by highlighting the difference between pecuniary and judicial satisfaction. If satisfaction were merely pecuniary, Hodge says, then "it cannot be refused. It *ipso facto* liberates."[51] He explains that in pecuniary satisfaction, "the moment the debt is paid the debtor is free; and that without any condition."[52] For example, if Han Solo owes ten thousand credits to Jabba the Hutt and some unknown stranger pays the debt on Han's behalf, the debt is *ipso facto* remitted. But if satisfaction is not merely pecuniary and it is actually judicial, then satisfaction does not automatically release the guilty party from their culpability nor

50. Oliver D. Crisp, *Saving Calvinism: Expanding the Reformed Tradition* (Downers Grove, IL: IVP Academic, 2016), 139.
51. Charles Hodge, *Systematic Theology, Vol. 2* (Peabody, MA: Hendrickson, 2011), 557.
52. Hodge, *Systematic Theology, Vol. 2*, 557.

does it automatically lead to salvation.[53] Again, Hodge explains that in the case of judicial satisfaction, "if a substitute be provided and accepted it is a matter of grace. His [Christ's] satisfaction does not *ipso facto* liberate."[54] How is it determined who is actually saved by the Christ's satisfaction? Hodge says that "the application of its benefits is determined by the covenant between the Father and the Son."[55] In this covenant, the gift of faith is included together with satisfaction. Hodge believes that faith is a gift of grace that God deigns to give to those for whom he has made satisfaction. For Hodge, it is part of the same decree. This of course need not have been the case; they could have been different decrees—as the Amyraldian would want to say.

The Amyraldian could appeal to Hodge's argument against the *ipso facto* nature of satisfaction to bolster defense against the Double Payment Objection. Since Christ's satisfaction is not pecuniary, it does not render salvation *ipso facto*. Because satisfaction is judicial, God can determine for whom Christ's satisfaction is effective. God graciously decides that it is effective for those who have faith. It then follows that it is possible for Christ to make judicial satisfaction for sin for some person, say Wilson, but that salvation does not follow because Wilson does not have faith. Thus, even though satisfaction has been rendered for Wilson, he isn't saved. So far, Hodge would agree, but Hodge would claim that it is contingently the case that God has actually intended satisfaction for the same people he has granted faith to. The Amyraldian would disagree, saying that the number of persons that God has decided to grant faith to is smaller than those for whom he has intended satisfaction. Because judicial satisfaction does not *ipso facto* save, the Amyraldian can avoid the double payment objection.

The distinction between pecuniary and judicial satisfaction provides one way for the Amyraldian to challenge the *ipso facto* nature of satisfaction, thus helping them to avoid the double payment objection. Michael Lynch—while not defending UA—provides a second way to challenge the absolute application of Christ's satisfaction. Drawing upon the work of Robert Lewis Dabney, Lynch presents the following version of the double payment objection.

Major premise: If Christ was punished for any person's sins, then that person cannot be punished for their sin.

Minor premise: Christ was punished for the elect's sins.

Therefore: The elect cannot be punished for their sins.[56]

53.   Oliver Crisp, *Deviant Calvinism: Broadening the Reformed Tradition* (Minneapolis: Fortress, 2014), 225.
54.   Hodge, *Systematic Theology, Vol. 2*, 557.
55.   Hodge, *Systematic Theology, Vol. 2*, 557.
56.   Michael Lynch, "*Quid Pro Quo* Satisfaction? An Analysis and Response to Garry Williams on Penal Substitutionary Atonement and Definite Atonement," *Evangelical Quarterly* 89 (2018): 66.

Dabney, Lynch explains, challenges the major premise asking, "If justice forbids the same sin to be punished once in Christ and then in a sinner, how can God 'justly hold the elect unbelievers subject to wrath until they believe' (Eph. 2:1–3)."[57] This question is meant to highlight the fact that prior to putting their faith in Christ, even the elect are under God's wrath. But if prior to belief the elect are under God's wrath, despite the fact that satisfaction was made for them on the cross more than two thousand years ago, then it seems as though anyone who affirms that satisfaction automatically entails salvation suffers from the double payment objection. Lynch summarizes his argument saying, "Would not the double-payment argument also forbid God to punish the unbelieving elect for their sins on the grounds that their sins have been punished in Christ?"[58] Dabney, like Hodge, challenges the *ipso facto* nature of satisfaction. He would have us say that only upon faith is satisfaction actually applied, and thus salvation requires more than just satisfaction.

Let us take stock. By highlighting the nature of judicial satisfaction, Hodge denied that Christ's satisfaction alone automatically entailed salvation. Likewise, Dabney denied that satisfaction alone entailed salvation by showing that such a view would lead to the denial of God's wrath against the not-yet-believing elect. Although Hodge and Dabney were by no means arguing for Amyraldism, they provide the Amyraldian with a way to avoid the double payment objection. If the double payment objection depends on the idea that Christ's satisfaction is a complete and finished action that *ipso facto* saves, then the Amyraldian can appeal to both Hodge and Dabney's arguments as further evidence that salvation requires something more than satisfaction; it requires faith. Of course, the Amyraldian would have to provide an argument for *why* God has separated his intention regarding satisfaction and his intention to give faith into two decrees. Presenting this kind of argument, however, is beyond the scope of this chapter, which deals exclusively with the relationship between Amyraldism and penal substitution, and it is likely beyond our ken to know the secret counsel of God.

CONCLUSION

In this chapter I have attempted to show that one can consistently hold to a belief in penal substitution and to the belief that Christ's death was not particular in intent while denying universalism. I have argued that Amyraldism adequately avoids the universalism *reductio* argument by introducing a distinction between God's decree regarding satisfaction and God's decree regarding faith. Thus, Amyraldism avoids universalism. On the other hand, some would object that Amyraldism is open to the double payment objection. I have shown that Amyraldism avoids this objection because it denies

---

57. Robert L. Dabney, *Syllabus and Notes of the Course of Systematic and Polemical Theology,* 2nd ed. (St. Louis: Presbyterian Publishing Company, 1878), 521.
58. Lynch, "*Quid Pro Quo* Satisfaction?" 66.

that satisfaction *ipso facto* saves. Contrary to popular opinion, denying the *ipso facto* nature of satisfaction is not a minority position; Reformed theologians like Charles Hodge and R. L. Dabney similarly denied this feature of satisfaction. The universalism *reductio* argument and the double payment objection present two of the strongest challenges to the claim that one can hold to PSA and UA; yet I have shown that they do not ultimately undermine belief in PSA and UA. Contrary to Garry Williams's claim, PSA does not entail definite atonement.[59]

---

59. I would like to thank Andrew Hollingsworth and Jordan Wessling for the helpful feedback they provided on earlier versions of this essay.

CHAPTER FOUR

THE DOCTRINE OF GOD
AND UNLIMITED ATONEMENT

R. T. Mullins

Writing on the doctrine of God today comes with a level of difficulty and corresponding anxiety that is unprecedented in the history of Christian thought. In the contemporary world, one is presented with a plethora of competing models of God and the God-world relationship.[1] No more are the days of the Middle Ages when one could simply assume the classical theistic conception of God as timeless, immutable, impassible, and simple.[2] During the Reformation and post-Reformation era, Protestant theologians overwhelmingly assumed this classical model of God, but dissent was beginning to show. Various thinkers like Samuel Clarke, Isaac Newton, and Pierre Gassendi rejected attributes like timelessness, though it does not seem that they rejected the other classical attributes.[3] This time period also saw the rise of pantheism founded in part on reflections on divine infinity.[4]

1. Cf. Jeanine Diller and Asa Kasher, eds., *Models of God and Alternative Ultimate Realities* (New York: Springer, 2013); Andrei A. Buckareff and Yujin Nagasawa, eds., *Alternative Concepts of God: Essays on the Metaphysics of the Divine* (New York: Oxford University Press, 2016); John C. Peckham, *The Doctrine of God: Introducing the Big Questions* (London: T&T Clark, 2020).
2. For a systematic articulation of classical theism, see R. T. Mullins, "Classical Theism," in *T&T Clark Handbook of Analytic Theology*, eds. James M. Arcadi and James T. Turner (New York: T&T Clark, 2021).
3. Cf. Emily Thomas, *Absolute Time: Rifts in Early Modern British Metaphysics* (Oxford: Oxford University Press, 2018).
4. John W. Cooper, *Panentheism: The Other God of the Philosophers* (Grand Rapids: Baker Academic, 2006), 64–72.

Subsequent generations developed panentheistic conceptions of God emphasizing God's immanence in the created order.[5] As one moves into the nineteenth century and on into the twentieth, a growing interest in reconceiving
the divine nature in light of the incarnation can be spotted, with theologians
emphasizing that we need a Christlike God.[6] A major theme of twentieth-
century theological and biblical studies is a wide-scale rejection of classical
theism, and the search for an adequate model of God.[7] One might wonder
how successful the search has been given the preponderance of rival models
of God today, and the renewed interest in classical theism.

Given this background, how is one to approach a Christian doctrine
of God? In this chapter, I shall attempt to outline the basics for a Christian
doctrine of God, and particularly one that coheres with the notion of unlimited atonement, or hypothetical universalism. By *basics*, I mean the sorts of
things that most models of God ought to be able to agree upon about the
divine nature and divine action. In this way, readers can build in more to their
own doctrine of God if they feel inclined to do so, as they theologically reflect
on the book of nature and the book of Scripture. Hypothetical universalism
raises serious problems related to the doctrine of God and his decrees because
hypothetical universalism seems to suggest that God does not always get what
he wants, whereas a divine decree strongly suggests that God does in fact get
what he wants. How is this seeming tension to be resolved?

I shall proceed in five steps. In section 1, I define the essential attributes
of God. In section 2, I discuss divine action as it relates to the doctrines of
creation, decree, and providence. At this point, readers will have the basics for
a doctrine of God, and some understanding of the different ways that they can
develop their own model of God with fear and trembling. In section 3, I highlight various prolegomena that any Christian doctrine of God must address
related to creation, human freedom, and unlimited atonement. In section 4, I
demonstrate how one can take the basics of the doctrine of God and develop
solutions to these prolegomena, thus resolving any tension between God's
unlimited atonement and the divine decree. Finally, in section 5, I offer some
concluding remarks.

---

5.   Cf. Benedikt Paul Gocke, *The Panentheism of Karl Christian Friedrich Krause* (New York: Peter Lang,
      2018).

6.   Francis J. McConnell, *The Christlike God: A Survey of the Divine Attributes from the Christian Point
      of View* (New York: Abingdon, 1927). For a historical overview, see David Brown, *Divine Humanity:
      Kenosis and the Construction of a Christian Theology* (Waco, TX: Baylor University Press, 2011).

7.   For example, Charles Hartshorne, *Man's Vision of God and the Logic of Theism* (Hamden: Archon,
      1964); Wolfhart Pannenberg, *Basic Questions in Theology, Vol. 2* (Minneapolis: Fortress, 1971);
      Terence E. Fretheim, *The Suffering of God: An Old Testament Perspective* (Philadelphia: Fortress,
      1984); Sallie McFague, *Models of God: Theology for an Ecological, Nuclear Age* (Philadelphia: Fortress,
      1987); Clark H. Pinnock, Richard Rice, John Sanders, William Hasker, and David Basinger, *The
      Openness of God: A Biblical Challenge to the Traditional Understanding of God* (Downers Grove, IL:
      InterVarsity Press, 1994).

1. A PERFECT BEING AND THE ESSENTIAL ATTRIBUTES OF GOD

Though there are many models of God on offer today, Christian models of God are committed to the claim that God is perfect. The disagreement is over which attributes make a being perfect or the greatest possible being.[8] Thankfully, there has been a great deal of reflection on the method of perfect being theology. Perfect being theology is a philosophical method for determining which properties God has essentially. Perfect being theology is only designed to discern God's essential properties. It is not a method designed to inform a person about God's contingent or accidental properties, like being the *creator of the universe*. In order to establish God's contingent properties, one will have to consider arguments from natural and revealed theology.[9] Given the teachings of Scripture, the Christian theologian will have no difficulty in establishing that God has the contingent and accidental properties of *being the Creator* and *being the Savior*. However, my main interest at the moment is perfect being theology and the essential divine attributes.

Perfect being theology starts by defining God as perfect, or the greatest metaphysically possible being. It offers an analysis of what it means to be the greatest possible being, and then provides a few simple steps for discerning which essential properties the greatest possible being has.[10] The first question for a perfect being theologian to ask is: What does it mean for God to be the greatest metaphysically possible being? In order to answer this question, I need to introduce three concepts: great-making properties, extensive superiority, and intensive superiority.

I shall begin with great-making properties, or what in classical language are called perfections. Yujin Nagasawa says that some property p is a great-making property if, all else being equal, it contributes to the intrinsic greatness of its possessor.[11] Oftentimes, philosophers and theologians state this as any property that it is intrinsically better to have than not have. A great-making property is an intrinsic property that would improve the greatness of any being that has it and would not worsen the greatness of any being that possesses it.[12] Perfect being theologians emphasize that great-making properties cannot entail any liabilities or imperfections.

When it comes to discerning which attributes God has essentially, the perfect being theologian will say that God has whatever properties are intrinsically better to have than not have. Part of the method of perfect being theology is to identify these great-making properties, and to predi-

---

8. For example, Katherin Rogers and William Hasker, "Anselm and the Classical Idea of God: A Debate," in *Philosophy of Religion: The Key Thinkers*, ed. Jeffrey J. Jordan (London: Continuum, 2011).

9. Thomas V. Morris, *Our Idea of God: An Introduction to Philosophical Theology* (Downers Grove, IL: InterVarsity Press, 1991), 28–35.

10. Jeff Speaks, *The Greatest Possible Being* (Oxford: Oxford University Press, 2018), 8–18.

11. Yujin Nagasawa, *Maximal God: A New Defense of Perfect Being Theism* (Oxford: Oxford University Press, 2017), 53–55.

12. Nagasawa, *Maximal God*, 65.

cate them of God. However, there is more at play in the method of perfect being theology.

Merely identifying a list of potential great-making properties is not enough to establish that God is the greatest metaphysically possible being. To be the greatest metaphysically possible being is to have extensive superiority and intensive superiority to all other possible beings.[13] God is extensively superior in that God has all the actual great-making properties. His excellence extends to all the attributes included in perfection. In more classical language, it is said that God has all the perfections that one finds in creatures, and that God is the ultimate source of all the perfections.

God is intensively superior in that God has all the degreed great-making properties to the maximal degree of intensity. I say "degreed properties" because some great-making properties do not obviously come in degrees of intensity. For instance, properties like *existence* and *eternality* are traditionally taken to be great-making properties, but they do not obviously have degrees of intensity in which they can be possessed. Whereas, when it comes to great-making properties like *knowledge* and *power,* God is said to have the greatest possible amount of knowledge and power. His knowledge and power far surpass that of anything else that could possibly exist. This much is uncontroversial. Where disagreements arise is over the modal scope of what is included in, or entailed by, attributes like maximal knowledge or maximal power. This is because theologians disagree on the logical limits of reality or what is ultimately possible.

All models of God that I wish to consider in this chapter agree on the previous account of divine perfection. Further, they agree on a particular set of uncontested essential divine attributes: necessary existence, aseity, self-sufficiency, eternality, maximal knowledge, maximal power, maximal rationality, maximal goodness, and freedom.

Before defining these essential attributes, it is worth clarifying what an essential attribute is. Essential attributes are, by definition, not the sort of thing that a being can gain or lose. It is metaphysically impossible for God to lose an essential attribute. Thus, every model of God is able to affirm that God cannot cease to be perfect in power, love, knowledge, and so on. Arguments to the effect that a particular model of God puts God at risk of losing an essential divine property are more often than not deeply mistaken, because they fail to understand the distinction between essential and accidental properties. Essential attributes are distinct from accidental attributes like *creator* and *redeemer.* Those are accidental attributes that God has if and only if he freely exercises his power to create a universe and redeem fallen creatures. If God did not freely create the universe, God would not have the accidental property of *creator,* but God would have all his essential attributes.

---

13.   Nagasawa, *Maximal God,* 56–57.

With that clarification out of the way, I will define God's essential attributes. I start with the attributes of necessary existence, divine aseity, and self-sufficiency. These are distinct attributes, though these distinctions are not always recognized. Necessary existence is when a being must exist and cannot fail to exist. It might be the case that things other than God necessarily exist, like numbers, the laws of logic, and propositions. These might exist independently of God, or they might be the necessary thoughts of God.[14] Thus, necessary existence does not imply independent existence. Aseity is an attribute that describes God's independent existence, whereas self-sufficiency describes God's independent perfect essence. These attributes can be stated as follows.

Necessary existence: A being necessarily exists if and only if it cannot fail to exist.

Aseity: A being exists *a se* if and only if its existence is in no way dependent upon, nor derived from, anything *ad extra*.

Divine self-sufficiency: A being is divinely self-sufficient if and only if that being's perfect essential nature is not dependent upon, nor derived from, anything *ad extra*.

Necessary existence and aseity entail that God is an eternal being. To say that God is eternal is to say that God exists without beginning and without end. This logically follows from the necessary existence of God. A necessary being does not and cannot begin to exist, nor cease to exist. However, traditional theists have wanted to say more than that God is merely eternal. Traditional theists have maintained that God is timeless. God is timeless if and only if God necessarily exists without beginning, without end, without succession, without temporal location, and without temporal extension. Historically, Christian theists have affirmed a presentist ontology of time which says that only the present moment of time exists. Past moments no longer exist, and future moments do not yet exist. When traditional theists claimed that God is timeless, they would often describe God as existing as a whole in an eternal now or a timeless present. This timeless present is said to lack a before and after.[15]

This can be contrasted with more contemporary theists who claim that God is temporal. Divine temporalists affirm that God is an eternal being—God exists without beginning and without end. Yet divine temporalists affirm that God has succession in his life as well as temporal location. However, there is debate among divine temporalists about how to best understand this

---

14. Cf. Einar Duenger Bohn, *God and Abstract Objects* (Cambridge: Cambridge University Press, 2019).

15. R. T. Mullins, *The End of the Timeless God* (Oxford: Oxford University Press, 2016), chaps. 3–5.

claim.[16] Most temporalists affirm presentism, though not all do. Of the divine temporalists who affirm presentism, they will typically say that God exists in the same present moment as we do. This is because on presentism, whatever exists, exists at the present. The present moment exhausts all of reality. When God creates things, God is making things exist at the present. For this chapter, I shall assume presentism.

With these essential divine attributes in place, I will turn my attention to maximal power. As *a se* and self-sufficient, God's power is not dependent upon nor derived from anything outside of himself. God alone has maximal power. Maximal power is the most power-granting set of abilities that is logically possible.[17] Theologians often describe this attribute by saying that God can perform all logically and metaphysically possible actions. For example, I shall argue later that God has the power to offer unlimited atonement, but God does not have the "power" to manipulate creatures into freely accepting his offer of divine friendship. Such a "power" is no power at all because it is incoherent. To understand this, more nuance is needed in the concept of maximal power. The maximal power-granting set does not simply contain all abilities. This is because not all abilities are powers. Some abilities are liabilities, which are not powers.[18] Liabilities, or weaknesses, make a being less than great. For instance, the ability to perform irrational actions is a liability. Thus, this ability will not be included in the maximal power-granting set of abilities. For most Christian theologians, it should seem quite obvious that a perfectly wise and rational God could not perform irrational actions. As such, she should have no problem denying that God lacks the ability/liability to perform irrational actions.

God has maximal knowledge in that God knows the truth-values of all propositions.[19] That God knows all things is a standard claim, but *how* God knows all things is a matter of dispute.[20] The classical view is that all of God's knowledge is in some sense self-knowledge.[21] The claim is that by having a perfect knowledge of his own nature and will, God is able to know all things. Moreover, in some sense, God's knowledge is the cause of all things.[22] This is alleged to maintain a sense of self-sufficiency. Those who reject classical theism, and affirm that God knows the future, will deny that God's knowledge

16. For more details, see R. T. Mullins, "The Divine Timemaker," *Philosophia Christi* 22 (2020): 207–33.
17. T. J. Mawson, *The Divine Attributes* (Cambridge: Cambridge University Press, 2018), 41.
18. Mawson, *The Divine Attributes*, 42.
19. Richard Swinburne, *The Coherence of Theism* (Oxford: Oxford University Press, 2016), 177.
20. For more details, see R. T. Mullins, "Divine Temporality and Providential Bodgery," *TheoLogica* 4 (2020): 1–28.
21. Augustine, *The Trinity*, 15.13.22.
22. Stephen Charnock, *The Complete Works of Stephen Charnock, Vol. 1* (Edinburgh: James Nichol, 1864), 386. Cf. Katherin A. Rogers, "Foreknowledge, Freedom, and Vicious Circles: Anselm vs. Open Theism," in Benjamin H. Arbour, ed., *Philosophical Essays Against Open Theism* (London: Routledge, 2019).

is all self-knowledge. They will maintain that some of God's knowledge, such as his knowledge of other things, is dependent upon the created things that exist. They can maintain God's self-sufficiency by saying that omniscience is the cognitive power to know all things. God's possession of this power is self-sufficient. God's exercise of this power is dependent upon his will, and the structure of the world that he freely creates. More will be said about divine knowledge below as it relates to God's decree.

What is particularly relevant for the discussion of unlimited atonement is God's maximal goodness and perfect rationality. As I shall argue later, a perfectly good and rational God will create a universe with unlimited atonement. God is perfectly rational if and only if God always acts for a reason.[23] God's perfect rationality and moral perfection are mutually entailing because moral considerations are reasons for acting. God is maximally good if and only if God is appropriately responsive to morally relevant values.[24] A perfectly good person always does what he has most objective reason to do. As omniscient, God will always know what he has most objective reason to do. As omnipotent, God will be free to perform the action that he has most objective reason to do.[25] Moreover, a perfectly good God's actions will give rise to the best possible consequences. In performing these good actions, God will necessarily instantiate virtuous character traits such as generosity, wisdom, and so forth.[26]

Perfect rationality and perfect moral goodness are related to God's freedom. God is free if and only if (1) God is the source of his action, and (2) God has the ability to do otherwise.[27] Yet, there is a constraint on God's free actions related to reason. As perfectly rational, God will always act for a reason. If God does not have a reason to take a particular course of action, then God will not be able to freely choose to take that course of action.[28] To do otherwise is to act irrationally and arbitrarily.

God's perfect moral goodness and perfect rationality are connected to God's emotional life because emotions involve perceptions of and responses to values. Emotions are part of the cognitive equipment that give agents the ability to perceive values in the world. An emotion is a felt evaluation of a situation. An emotion is a mental state with two components: cognitive and affective. An emotion has a cognitive component in that an emotion is always about something, or it mentally represents the world as being a certain way

23. Richard Swinburne, *The Christian God* (Oxford: Oxford University Press, 1994), 128.
24. Mark C. Murphy, *God's Own Ethics: Norms of Divine Agency and the Argument from Evil* (Oxford: Oxford University Press, 2017), 25.
25. Mawson, *The Divine Attributes*, 50.
26. Mawson, *The Divine Attributes*, 47.
27. Millard J. Erickson, *Christian Theology* (Grand Rapids: Baker Books, 2004), 378; Alexander R. Pruss, "Divine Creative Freedom," in *Oxford Studies in Philosophy of Religion*, vol. 7, ed. Jonathan L. Kvanvig (Oxford: Oxford University Press, 2017), 213–14.
28. Kevin Timpe, *Free Will in Philosophical Theology* (London: Bloomsbury Academic, 2014), 23.

or as having a certain value. An emotion is affective in that there is something that it is like to have an emotion. An agent's evaluation of the situation feels a particular way. An object has value to an agent if she perceives it to be worthy of her attention, and worthy of her to act on behalf of the object. Because of this, emotions can be rational or irrational depending on how well they track the values in reality. If an emotional response fails to properly track the value of the object, the emotional response is not rational. If an emotional response properly tracks the value of the object, the emotional response is rational. As omniscient and perfectly rational, God's emotions will always properly track the values in reality.[29]

With this discussion of the divine nature before us, I can now turn to discuss divine action.

2. DIVINE ACTION

Now that one knows what God is, one will rightly ask about what God does.[30] If God is the sort of being who would provide unlimited atonement, it is important to understand how God brings this about. This naturally gives rise to questions about the doctrines of creation, decrees, and providence.

The doctrine of creation *ex nihilo* says that God created the universe out of nothing. This doctrine says that there is a state of affairs where God exists without creation, and a state of affairs where God exists with creation.[31] This is because the eternal God lacks a beginning, whereas creation has a beginning.[32] Call this state of affairs in which God exists all alone God's precreation moment. Depending on one's model of God, one might take this precreation moment to be either timeless or temporal.

As I understand it, free will involves the ability to perform an action at the next subsequent moment. What kind of actions can God freely perform at the moment subsequent to his precreation moment? God can perform a creative action. A creative action is when God voluntarily exercises his power to cause a universe to exist. A universe is a collection of contingent beings that are spatiotemporally related to one another. Since God is perfectly rational, God cannot create a universe without having a purpose or plan for that universe. This purpose or plan is referred to as God's decree.

29. For more details, see R. T. Mullins, *God and Emotion* (Cambridge: Cambridge University Press, 2020).

30. Louis Berkhof, *Systematic Theology* (Edinburgh: The Banner of Truth Trust, 1984), 100.

31. Emil Brunner, *The Christian Doctrine of Creation and Redemption,* trans. Olive Wyon (London: Lutterworth, 1952), 14–15; Alexander Broadie, "Scotistic Metaphysics and Creation Ex Nihilo," in *Creation and the God of Abraham,* eds. David B. Burrell, Janet M. Soskice, and William R. Stoeger (Cambridge: Cambridge University Press, 2010), 53; David Fergusson, *Creation* (Grand Rapids: Eerdmans, 2014), 40; Thomas Ward, *The Divine Ideas* (Cambridge: Cambridge University Press, 2020), 5.

32. Augustine, *The City of God,* 12. John of Damascus, *Exposition of the Orthodox Faith,* 1.7. W. G. T. Shedd, *Dogmatic Theology, Vol. 1* (New York: Charles Scribner's Sons, 1888), 470.

Louis Berkhof says that God's decree is his eternal plan for the created order. The decree to create is not the created universe itself. There is a distinction between the decree and the execution of that decree.[33] Berkhof says that the decree is efficacious and immutable because it is grounded in God's wisdom and omnipotence. Whatever God decrees will certainly come to pass. There can be no sense in which God's decree, or plan, could get screwed up, thus forcing God to issue a new decree or make changes to his decree at some later time.[34]

Arthur W. Pink draws the connection between God's precreation moment and the divine decree as follows: "God was alone when He made His decrees, and His determinations were influenced by no external cause. He was free to decree or not to decree, and to decree one thing and not another. This liberty we must ascribe to Him who is supreme, independent, and sovereign in all His doings."[35]

What is included in God's decree? As I understand it, God's decree could be general or meticulous. On either view, God's decree will specify a particular goal for creation, but each view differs over how God will providentially achieve that goal (in later sections, I shall say more about God's goal for creation as it pertains to unlimited atonement). On a general decree, God adopts general policies for governing the world to that goal. God does not have a specific intention for each and every event that takes place in the universe.[36] On a meticulous decree, God adopts specific-benefit policies for governing the world which would state that every divine act at each moment should achieve a very particular benefit that advances the created universe towards its ultimate end.[37]

In order to understand the difference between these kinds of decrees, it is important to think in terms of whether or not God's decree includes a specific timeline. A timeline is a particular ordering of a series of temporal moments. A moment is what accounts for how things can be in incompatible ways. A moment is the way things are but could be subsequently otherwise. A moment is a *when* something happens. For example, the precreation moment is when God exists. Things are a particular way at this moment—that is, God exists by himself. Things can be subsequently otherwise in that God can freely exercise his power to bring a universe into existence at later moments. God's precreation moment is earlier than all possible subsequent moments or potential timelines.[38] Which particular subsequent moments will occur depends upon how God exercises his freedom.

33. Berkhof, *Systematic Theology*, 1:103–4.
34. Berkhof, *Systematic Theology*, 1:104–6.
35. Arthur W. Pink, *The Attributes of God* (Grand Rapids: Baker Books, 1975), 15.
36. John Sanders, *The God Who Risks: A Theology of Divine Providence* (Downers Grove, IL: IVP Academic, 2007), 226.
37. William Hasker, "An Open Theist View," in *God and the Problem of Evil: Five Views,* eds. Chad Meister and James K. Dew (Downers Grove, IL: IVP Academic, 2017), 61.
38. For more details, see Mullins, "The Divine Timemaker."

What is important to understand is that prior to God's decree to create a universe, there is no fact of the matter as to which series of subsequent moments will obtain. For God, the future is completely open. Surprisingly, this is something that Calvinists, Molinists, and open theists all agree upon. Each of these views agrees that there are no true counterfactuals about what God would do prior to God's free choice to issue a particular decree.[39] In other words, there is no fact of the matter about what God will do before he freely decides on a decree. In God's precreation moment, all of these views agree that God possesses something called *natural knowledge*. This is God's knowledge of all necessary truths about what is and what could be.[40] At God's precreation moment, God knows all of the possible ways that moments can be ordered. God knows all of the logically possible timelines that could obtain. Knowing God's own essence only gives God knowledge of what is possible, or what could take place. God does not know which timeline will in fact obtain because God has not issued a general nor meticulous decree yet.

Calvinists say that God issues a meticulous decree. This means that God freely selects a specific ordering of moments, or a specific timeline. The decree that God issues specifies that a particular universe with a particular timeline will come to exist. God's act of creation brings the universe into existence. In this sense, the decree can be referred to as God's act of predestination since God determines the destiny of all things prior to acting to bring the universe into existence.[41] Subsequent to God's selection of a specific timeline, God is said to have *free knowledge*. This is God's knowledge of what will in fact occur in the specific timeline that he has freely selected. God has this foreknowledge because of the decree that he freely issued.[42] Calvinists are quite clear that God cannot foreknow the future unless he determines which timeline will occur.[43] On this view, creatures do not have libertarian freedom because God has causally determined which specific timeline will occur. Calvinists typically deny

---

39.   Thomas P. Flint, *Divine Providence: The Molinist Account* (Ithaca, NY: Cornell University Press, 1998), 46, 55–57; John Feinberg, *No One Like Him: The Doctrine of God* (Wheaton, IL: Crossway, 2001), 313; Terrance L. Tiessen, "A Response to John Laing's Criticisms of Hypothetical-Knowledge Calvinism," in *Calvinism and Middle Knowledge: A Conversation,* eds. John D. Laing, Kirk R. MacGregor, and Greg Welty (Eugene, OR: Pickwick, 2019), 181. For more details, see Alan R. Rhoda, "The Fivefold Openness of the Future," in *God in an Open Universe: Science, Metaphysics, and Open Theism,* eds. William Hasker, Thomas Jay Oord, and Dean Zimmerman (Eugene, OR: Pickwick, 2011).

40.   Luis de Molina, *On Divine Foreknowledge: Part IV of the Concordia,* trans. Alfred J. Freddoso (Ithaca, NY: Cornell University, 1988), 130–44; Harm Goris, "Divine Foreknowledge, Providence, Predestination, and Human Freedom," in *The Theology of Thomas Aquinas,* eds. Rik Van Nieuwenhove and Joseph Wawrykow (Notre Dame, IN: University of Notre Dame Press, 2005), 111.

41.   Moise Amyraut, *Amyraut on Predestination,* trans. Matthew Harding (Norwich: Charenton Reformed Publishing, 2017), 60.

42.   Berkhof, *Systematic Theology,* 102.

43.   Shedd, *Dogmatic Theology,* 394. Derk Pereboom, "Libertarianism and Theological Determinism," in *Free Will and Theism: Connections, Contingencies, and Concerns,* eds. Kevin Timpe and Daniel Speak (Oxford: Oxford University Press, 2016), 114.

that God can foreknow what creatures will do with libertarian free will.[44] God's providence refers to the execution of that decree to ensure that the details of the decree are fulfilled by either directly bringing about certain events, or by ensuring that creatures bring about certain events.[45] God indirectly brings something about by causing creatures to causally bring about a particular state of affairs.[46]

Molinists wish to affirm that creatures have libertarian freedom, so they add a moment between God's natural and free knowledge. They affirm something called God's *middle knowledge*. This is God's knowledge of counterfactuals of creaturely freedom. Via middle knowledge, God knows what creatures with libertarian freedom would do in any possible circumstance that they might be placed in. God knows this before he issues a decree. On this view, God is able to know all of the possible timelines that he might create, but he is also able to know which timelines are feasible because he knows what creatures would do in each timeline. Molinists say that God uses this middle knowledge to select which universe and which timeline to bring about. On the standard version of Molinism, God issues a meticulous decree because he selects a specific timeline. Subsequent to God's decree, God is said to have free knowledge, and to providentially guide creation to its ultimate goal.[47]

Open theists and Calvinists reject middle knowledge because they think that it is incoherent. They agree that it is impossible for God to know what creatures with libertarian freedom would do, or will do.[48] Yet the open theist parts ways with the Calvinist because the open theist wishes to affirm that creatures have libertarian freedom. In order to preserve creaturely freedom, open theists say that God issues a general decree. The open theist says that prior to God's decree, God knows all the possible orderings of subsequent temporal moments. Given God's commitment to creating a universe that contains beings with libertarian freedom, it is impossible to know what those creatures will in fact freely do in the future. Hence, there is no exhaustive timeline that God can decree. Yet, God knows all of the possible actions that his creatures might perform in any possible circumstance within the universe. Prior to the act of creation, God develops an exhaustive contingency plan for every possible future free action in order to guarantee that he achieves his ultimate goal for creation.[49] Subsequently, God's act of creation, or decree

44.   Francis Turretin, *Institutes of Elenctic Theology, Vol. 1* (Phillipsburg, NJ: P&R, 1992), 212–14.
45.   Amyraut, *Predestination*, 59.
46.   John Webster, "On the Theology of Providence," in *The Providence of God*, eds. Francesca Aran Murphy and Philip G. Ziegler (London: T&T Clark, 2009), 164, 167; Paul Kjoss Helseth, "God Causes All Things," in *Four Views on Divine Providence*, ed. Dennis W. Jowers (Grand Rapids: Zondervan, 2011), 31.
47.   Flint, *Divine Providence*, 42–43.
48.   Berkhof, *Systematic Theology*, 107; Dean Zimmerman, "The A-Theory of Time, Presentism, and Open Theism," in *Science and Religion in Dialogue*, ed. Melville Y. Stewart (Malden, MA: Blackwell, 2010), 791.
49.   Gregory A. Boyd, "God Limits His Control," in *Four Views on Divine Providence*, ed. Dennis W. Jowers (Grand Rapids: Zondervan, 2011). For criticism of Boyd's claim that open theism can guarantee

to create, refers to God willing that a particular universe come to exist. It does not refer to God willing that a particular timeline should come about. Instead, God's decree to create contains a stated goal for the future history of the universe that God intends to providentially bring about in cooperation with his free creatures.

Again, I must emphasize that these are merely the basics for constructing a doctrine of God. In the next section, I shall articulate some problems that a model of God must seek to address in order to develop a robust account of the God-world relation that coheres with conceiving of Christ's atonement as unlimited.

3. PROLEGOMENA

Thus far, I have articulated the basics for a doctrine of God and the God-world relation. As I mentioned in the introduction, there is a tension between so-called hypothetical universalism and the divine decrees. This tension is actually part of a network of related issues. In this section, I shall highlight several of these prolegomena that a theologian must consider. Understanding these prolegomena will allow me to provide a sketch for how to resolve the tension in the next section.

Creation Problems

Moses Amyraut states that before one can address the doctrine of predestination, one must answer why God created anything at all, and why God created humans in particular.[50] In contemporary philosophical theology, these are referred to as the general problem of creation and the particular problem of creation.[51]

Salvation Problems

With regard to human freedom and divine grace, theologians typically affirm the following:

A) Human persons possess the freedom of rational self-determination that is consistent with one's character, judgments, and desires.

B) Human freedom involves the ability to do otherwise at some point in time.

God's purposes, see Johanness Grossl and Leigh Vicens, "Closing the Door on Limited-Risk Open Theism," *Faith and Philosophy* 31 (2011). Other open theists say that God cannot guarantee that his purposes be fulfilled, but the likelihood of divine failure is negligible at best. Richard Rice, *The Future of Open Theism: From Antecedents to Opportunities* (Downers Grove, IL: IVP Academic, 2020), 231.

50. Amyraut, *Predestination*, chaps. 1–2.
51. Cf. Norman Kretzmann, "A General Problem of Creation: Why Would God Create Anything at All?" in *Being and Goodness: The Concepts of the Good in Metaphysics and Philosophical Theology*, ed. Scott MacDonald (Ithaca, NY: Cornell University Press, 1991).

C) God provides efficient grace to the elect to such a degree that the elect willingly cooperate with God's plan of salvation.

A Calvinist like Berkhof says that God's decree is compatible with (A) and (B). God's decree renders future events certain, but it does not deprive humans of their agency. Human persons really could have done otherwise, but it is certain that they will not in fact do otherwise.[52] These are common claims among Calvinists, and are representative of compatibilists more broadly.[53] Calvinists often claim that God's will renders things certain, but does not render them necessary. For example, if God wills that I perform action X at a particular moment of time, then it is certain that I will perform action X at that particular moment.[54] To be sure, Molinists and open theists will deny that a Calvinist can consistently maintain (B), but I shall not explore this issue here.

With regard to (C), Berkhof is clear that God's election of the redeemed is irresistible. He says that human persons can oppose the execution of God's decree to some extent, but that the elect will not ultimately prevail. God influences the elect to make her willing to cooperate with God. However, Berkhof explicitly states that God's influence does not overpower the agency and freedom of the elect.[55] This is a deeply Reformed view.[56] Chapter 3 of The Westminster Confession states that though God ordains all that shall come to pass, God does not do violence to the will of humans, nor does God remove the liberty and contingency of secondary causes. One way to understand this claim is that God offers sufficient grace, and not violent or manipulative grace. Again, Molinists and open theists will question if a Calvinist can consistently maintain this, but each ought to be happy to affirm that God's grace is not violent nor manipulative.

God's Unfulfilled Desires

Pertinent to this volume on unlimited atonement is the problem of God's unfulfilled desires.[57] First Timothy 2:4 says that God desires that all human persons be saved. Second Peter 3:9 says that God is patiently waiting on the final judgment so that all might be saved. Yet, many biblical texts seem to say that not all will repent or be saved (e.g., John 3:18; Heb. 10:36; 1 John 2:17; Rev. 2:21). It would seem then that God's desire for all to be saved is going to be unfulfilled.

52. Berkhof, *Systematic Theology*, 107.
53. Jesse Couenhoven, *Predestination: A Guide for the Perplexed* (London: T&T Clark, 2018), 103–6; Oliver D. Crisp, *Deviant Calvinism: Broadening Reformed Theology* (Minneapolis: Fortress, 2014), chap. 3; Leigh Vicens and Simon Kittle, *God and Human Freedom* (Cambridge: Cambridge University Press, 2019), 56–57. Cf. Richard A. Muller, *Divine Will and Human Choice: Freedom, Contingency, and Necessity in Early Modern Reformed Thought* (Grand Rapids: Baker Academic, 2017).
54. Erickson, *Christian Theology*, 383–84.
55. Berkhof, *Systematic Theology*, 115.
56. Couenhoven, *Predestination*, 105–7.
57. Peckham, *The Doctrine of God*, chap. 2.

A Christian theologian will need to articulate a model of God that can account for this unfulfilled desire. This is sometimes referred to as hypothetical universalism. God desires that all be saved, but all are not in fact saved so actual universalism does not obtain. A Christian model of God will need to explain why hypothetical universalism, and not actual universalism, is true. In this regard, it will need to specify why it is either metaphysically impossible or morally impermissible for God to save everyone.[58] Further, a model of God will need to reconcile this with the notion that God's decrees, be they general or specific, cannot fail to obtain.

4. UNLIMITED ATONEMENT AND GOD'S UNFULFILLED DESIRES

In this section, I shall attempt to sketch some different kinds of solutions to the problem of God's unfulfilled desires. To begin, recall the general problem of creation. Why would God create anything at all? In order to offer an answer that is compatible with multiple theological positions, I will stipulate that God decides to create a universe so that creatures can enjoy everlasting friendship with God. This decision to create a universe so that creatures can enjoy everlasting friendship with God is not based on any foreseen creaturely free action or merit. Instead, this decision is grounded fully in God's good pleasure. Calvinists often appeal to God's "good pleasure" to explain divine action, but the content of "good pleasure" tends to be rather mysterious. Often it is said to be in God's secret will. Other models of God need not be so vague and mysterious here. One can fill in some of the content of God's good pleasure by claiming that God has a natural desire to have friendship with any and all creatures that he might possibly create. She can argue that this desire is a necessary entailment of God's perfect goodness or love.[59] Thus, one can say that God's decision to create is grounded in God's perfectly loving nature, and not on something external to God. Call this the universalist desire.

> *Universalist desire*: God desires to have a genuine, everlasting friendship with any creature that he might possibly make.

The universalist desire can help answer the general problem of creation because it identifies a general motivation for God to create a universe. It can also help address the particular problem of creation because it will narrow down the range of universes that God might create. What kind of universe would God need to create in order to offer everlasting friendship to creatures? A perfectly rational God will create the kind of universe that best satisfies the universalist desire. However, as omniscient, God knows that there are constraints on how creatures can enjoy everlasting friendship with God. Genuine friendship

---

58.   John Kronen and Eric Reitan, *God's Final Victory: A Comparative Philosophical Case for Universalism* (New York: Continuum, 2011), 68–71.

59.   Mawson, *The Divine Attributes*, 46.

requires significant freedom on the part of God and creatures. Further, creatures will have to be established in virtue in order to have a deep friendship with God. Nonetheless, God has the desire to have a friendship with any and all creatures that he might make. Only certain particular universes can provide the environment where something like this can take place.

One can say that the universalist desire serves as a policy or constraint on the kinds of possible universes that God considers for creation. Desires can naturally be said to be fundamental to the divine psychology, and thus prior to any decision that God might make. For example, the Christian God naturally desires that truth, beauty, and goodness be upheld for all eternity. Thus, one can say that God's desires guide his selection of a possible universe to create.

A theologian can also emphasize a second desire in God that guides his selection of a possible universe to create. Call it the incarnation anyway desire.[60]

> *Incarnation anyway desire*: God desires an incarnation because it is the best, or most fitting, way to achieve the universalist desire.

One can say that it is natural, or fitting, that God should desire the closest possible friendship or union with his creatures. An incarnation demonstrates a deep solidarity with his creatures no matter what kind of universe God might create. Moreover, an incarnation would demonstrate an offer of friendship that is universal in scope to all of God's creatures.[61] Thus, the incarnation anyway desire can guide God's selection of a possible universe to create.

With these two desires in place, one can give an account of God's hypothetical universalism. Unlike decrees, desires can go unfulfilled without any obvious loss to divine sovereignty.[62] A decree determines that certain outcomes will obtain. Divine decrees are not the sorts of things that can go unfulfilled. A desire, however, is merely wanting the world to be a certain way in the future. A divine desire can go unfulfilled. To be sure, some Calvinist theologians will not like the notion of divine desires going unfulfilled, but the Calvinist cannot consistently offer a complaint here. This is because Calvinists often talk about God's desire that humans not sin, and yet also claim that God permits humans to sin.[63] Calvinists typically distinguish between God's antecedent will and consequent will, or God's moral will and his permissive will.[64] These distinctions are meant to capture the claim that God desires that all be saved and not sin, but for some good reason God allows sin and reprobation.

---

60. Marilyn McCord Adams, *Christ and Horrors: The Coherence of Christology* (Cambridge: Cambridge University Press, 2006), 174–81. Cf. Edwin Chr. van Driel, *Incarnation Anyway: Arguments for Supralapsarian Christology* (New York: Oxford University Press, 2008).

61. Mawson, *The Divine Attributes*, 46.

62. Vicens and Kittle, *God and Human Freedom*, 52.

63. Feinberg, *No One like Him*, 694–98.

64. Aquinas makes the same distinction between antecedent and consequent will. See Aquinas, *De Veritate* 23.2.

If this is not a problem for divine sovereignty on Calvinism, then it ought not be a problem on other models of God either.

At the precreation moment, God surveys all the possible universes that he might create. God's desire is to create a universe where all creatures freely enter into a deep friendship with him. However, a Christian theologian might stipulate that there are no such possible universes due to something called transworld depravity. According to Alvin Plantinga, a person has transworld depravity if there is no possible universe in which she exists and does not sin. As Plantinga points out, it is possible that every created person suffers from transworld depravity. In which case, it would be metaphysically impossible for God to create a universe with free creatures who do not sin.[65] A model of God can appeal to this in order to explain why God's universalist desire is unfulfilled. It is metaphysically impossible for God's universalist desire to be fulfilled, so it is no strike against God's sovereignty since sovereignty and omnipotence do not involve God having the ability to perform metaphysically impossible actions. Since God's universalist desire cannot help God select which particular universe to create, God will need to turn to other considerations.

A theologian can say that God desires to create a universe where creatures with freedom genuinely accept God's offer of friendship. Yet God knows that the only kinds of universes and timelines where this occurs are ones in which God also offers sufficient grace. Sufficient grace is offered to everyone, but it is only efficient for some. As noted before by Berkhof, efficient grace is irresistible, but it does not overpower the human person. The degree of sufficient grace given to a human person must be such that it does not coerce or manipulate the individual into accepting God's offer of friendship. Otherwise, the sufficient grace does not count as efficient grace. Instead, it becomes manipulative grace, and as stated before, most Christians don't want to affirm manipulative grace. As Paul Helm points out, "Some of God's actions are resistible and are resisted."[66]

Upon taking sufficient grace into consideration, the subset of possible universes and timelines shrinks considerably. God now has a smaller range to select from. Call this subset *sufficient grace universes*. On this view, there are no sufficient grace universes and timelines in which all human persons freely accept the offer of divine friendship. Why is that? Perhaps one can say that some individuals in these universes and timelines would need more grace in order to accept God's offer of friendship. Yet, the kind of grace needed would pass the threshold of efficient grace, and breach into the territory of manipulative grace. These individuals would need to be overpowered in order to accept God's offer of friendship. That kind of overpowering is not some-

65. Alvin Plantinga, *The Nature of Necessity* (Oxford: Clarendon, 1974), 184–89.
66. Paul Helm, "The Augustinian-Calvinist View," in *Divine Foreknowledge: Four Views*, eds. James K. Beilby and Paul R. Eddy (Downers Grove, IL: InterVarsity Press, 2001), 171.

thing that most models of God wish to accept. Most will say that it is morally impermissible for God to engage in manipulative grace, thus further explaining why actual universalism is not possible for God to establish.

These sufficient grace universes have several features. First, they all contain an incarnation because God has the incarnation anyway desire. Second, these sufficient grace universes have fallen creatures because of transworld depravity. Third, these sufficient grace universes contain timelines with a limited number of grace-infused creatures who accept God's offer of friendship, and a limited number of reprobate creatures who do not accept God's offer of friendship. Again, these creatures are reprobate because they would need to be overpowered in order to accept God's offer of friendship, and it is morally impermissible for God to engage in that kind of manipulative grace.

At this point, one might worry that this story looks too much like Molinism or open theism for any self-respecting Calvinist to accept.[67] However, it should be recalled that the redeemed in these possible universes are not elected because of their own merit or good faith. They are not even elected until God decrees that a particular universe and timeline should exist. The redeemed are individuals in possible universes with sufficient grace. It is God's sufficient grace that causally enables the redeemed to cooperate with the Holy Spirit, and accept God's offer of friendship. Their cooperation depends upon God's sufficient grace.

With this in mind, one can say that God has a set of possible sufficient grace universes and timelines from which to create. God's desires are what narrowed down the range of possible universes. If one affirms meticulous providence, God's decree refers to God's selection of one of those possible universes and timelines. God's decree determines with certainty that everything that happens in that universe will in fact come to pass. Thus, God's decree is infallible, and will succeed. If one affirms a general providence, God's decree refers to his general policies that God adopts for the purpose of satisfying the universalist desire to the extent which it is morally permissible and metaphysically possible for God to do so. On open theism, this decree will not specify a particular timeline, but it will include an exhaustive contingency plan to ensure that God gets the result that he wants.

5. CONCLUDING REMARKS

In this chapter, I have attempted to articulate the basics for a Christian doctrine of God that coheres with the doctrine of unlimited atonement. I wish to conclude by briefly mentioning how the doctrine of God connects with theories of salvation.

Careful readers will have noticed that I cast my discussion in terms of God's desire to have everlasting friendship with any possible creature that he might make. As I noted before, this is intentional so as to be compatible with

---

67. Amyraut, *Predestination*, 20.

multiple theological positions. In particular, my hope is to have articulated a framework for thinking about God that is compatible with multiple theories of salvation. There are many theories of salvation in the Christian tradition, and only some of them claim to offer unlimited atonement. If one adopts my account of the universalist desire, then it will be incredibly difficult to affirm a theory of salvation that does not offer unlimited atonement. One would expect that a perfectly good, rational, and omnipotent being with the universalist desire will be incapable of considering a universe in which God does not offer unlimited atonement. A God like this will wish to offer salvation that is unlimited in scope so as to provide all of his creatures with the opportunity to enter into friendship with him.

If what I have said about the doctrine of God is remotely accurate for a Christian to adopt, the remaining task is to fill in the story of the sufficient grace universes by considering competing theories of salvation. For all I know, it might be that there are possible sufficient grace universes that correspond to different theories of salvation. In which case, Christian theologians will need to develop a framework for testing the different theories of salvation. A task like that is one that I shall leave to other contributors of this volume.

CHAPTER FIVE

UNLIMITED ATONEMENT AND THE NATURE OF FORGIVENESS

Jonathan Curtis Rutledge

According to the doctrine of unlimited atonement in the Reformed tradition,[1] Christ's atonement is sufficient for the salvation of all human persons but efficient only for the elect. This claim is brought out in the following words of Moïse Amyraut:

> Since the misery of men is equal and universal . . . and since they are equally still His creatures, the grace of redemption which He has offered and procured for them ought also to be equal and universal, provided that they are also found to be equally disposed to receive it. . . . The sacrifice that He offered for the propitiation of their offenses was equally for all; and the salvation that He received from His Father to communicate to men . . . is ordained equally for all, provided—I say—that the necessary disposition to receive it (in men) is equal in the same way.[2]

---

1. Adherents to some form of this doctrine include the Scottish theologian John Cameron and Moïse Amyraut, who followed in his footsteps. For a helpful discussion of variations on a doctrine of unlimited atonement, see Oliver D. Crisp, *Deviant Calvinism: Broadening Reformed Theology* (Minneapolis: Fortress, 2014), chap. 7, as well as his contribution to this volume.
2. Moïse Amyraut, *Amyraut on Predestination*, trans. Matthew Harding (Norwich: Charenton Reformed Publishing, 2017), 99–100.

Bishop John Davenant, in his comments on Colossians 1:22, articulates this same claim with more directness:

> We gather from this place that a twofold reconciliation is to be seen in the Scriptures: The one general, accomplished by the sacrifice upon the cross. . . . But besides this reconciliation accomplished upon the cross, and generally applicable to all, the Scripture also shews us a particular and applied reconciliation, effected in the heart and conscience of individuals; that is to say, when that sacrifice of Christ, which hath in itself an universal power of reconciling all, is actually applied to reconcile this or that man . . . by the exhibition of faith in the Gospel.[3]

This claim of unlimited atonement is to be understood in strict contrast with the colloquially more familiar Reformed position of limited atonement, which claims that the class of individuals for whom Christ's atonement is sufficient for salvation is *one and the same* as the class of individuals for whom it is efficient—namely, the elect.

It is the goal of this chapter to provide a framework from which one can more easily evaluate or discern the appeal of a doctrine of unlimited atonement. In order to achieve this goal, we begin with a concept bound up with discussions of atonement but that is importantly different from it at the same time. This concept is *forgiveness*, and recent insights on questions about forgiveness—that is, its unilateral nature and sometimes bilateral justification in particular—can help us better understand how to evaluate the claims of the proponents of unlimited atonement.[4]

I proceed as follows: In section 1, I begin by distinguishing between a definition and justification of forgiveness, a distinction which nicely parallels a similar one concerning punishment that is common in discussions of philosophy of law. Then in section 2, I argue that we should understand acts of forgiveness in paradigmatic cases as definitionally unilateral (i.e., as actualizable by the victim alone, whether or not the wrongdoer cooperates with them via some action such as repentance). Some theologians have thought not only that forgiveness is unilateral but moreover that forgiveness is obligatory, such that a wholly perfect agent, such as God, would always forgive.[5] That is, the unilateral nature of forgiveness, they think, entails the universality

---

3.   John Davenant, *An Exposition of the Epistle of St. Paul to the Colossians* (Edinburgh: Banner of Truth Trust, 2009), 254–55; italics are left unchanged from the quoted material.

4.   The account of forgiveness I present is, of course, the one I endorse (see my *Forgiveness and Atonement: Reflections on the Reason for Christ's Sacrifice* [New York: Routledge, forthcoming]). Unsurprisingly, it is a controversial account. However, I think it is the best account available theologically, and I defend this claim briefly in §2 below.

5.   If the language of obligation is worrisome at this point, then put in its place the following claim: forgiveness is something a perfectly good/loving being would always do whether or not they had (or could have) an obligation to do so.

of divine forgiveness for all wrongdoers. This claim is mistaken, and we shall see why in that section. But having completed our foray into the implications of the unilaterality of forgiveness, in section 3 we leverage those insights in a defense of a doctrine of unlimited atonement. The atonement is in many ways a unilateral act as well, insofar as it is wholly the work of one individual, Jesus the Christ.[6] We humans are the benefactors of that atoning work, but we do not ourselves contribute to it (at least not as a condition on, or prior to, participation with Christ).[7] Given the unilateral nature, then, of the atonement, there is a parallel argument to be made that the atonement would be universal in scope. In this last section, I argue that the reasons for resisting the universal implications of divine forgiveness do not translate to the context of atonement, such that a universal atonement, in some sense, is theologically plausible. The result is not a knockdown argument in favor of a doctrine of unlimited atonement, but it does shed light on why such a doctrine might be appealing to many within the Reformed tradition.

1. FORGIVENESS: DEFINITIONS VERSUS JUSTIFICATIONS

In the philosophical literature surrounding punishment, it is common to encounter an emphasis on the distinction between the definition of punishment and its justification.[8] To understand this distinction, it is helpful to have a working definition of punishment with which to proceed, so allow me simply to stipulate one.

Stipulated definition of punishment: Some action counts as punishment if, and only if, it is (i) an infliction of harm upon an alleged wrongdoer for (ii) having violated a norm of some sort, and that harm is implemented (iii) by an appropriate authority.[9]

---

6. Cf. Amyraut, *Amyraut on Predestination*, 96: "in consequence of His suffering to which He so freely and voluntarily submitted in order to . . . procure the salvation of the human race, Christ had the right and the honor Himself of accomplishing the work of their salvation and being the perfect example of it."

7. For discussions of how participation functions in the Gospels and apostolic writings, see Grant Macaskill, *Union with Christ in the New Testament* (Oxford: Oxford University Press, 2013); Erin M. Heim, *Adoption in Galatians and Romans: Contemporary Metaphor Theories and the Pauline Huiothesia Metaphors* (Leiden: Brill, 2017); James B. Torrance, "The Vicarious Humanity of Christ," in *The Incarnation: Ecumenical Studies in the Nicene-Constantinopolitan Creed A.D. 381*, ed. T. F. Torrance (Edinburgh: Handsel, 1981), 127–47.

8. For an early example of this distinction, see Anthony Flew, "The Justification of Punishment," *Philosophy* 29 (1954): 297.

9. See Mark C. Murphy, "Not Penal Substitution, but Vicarious Punishment," *Faith and Philosophy* 26, no. 3 (2009): 255, for a similar definition of punishment. For the classic Flew-Benn-Hart definition of punishment, see Flew, "The Justification of Punishment"; S. I. Benn, "An Approach to the Problems of Punishment," *Philosophy* 33 (1958): 325–41; or H. L. A. Hart, "Prolegomenon to the Principles of Punishment," *Proceedings of the Aristotelian Society* 60 (1960): 1–26.

We could clarify aspects of this definition of punishment—for example, what counts as harm or renders some seat of authority the appropriate one to implement the punishment? There is no need to clarify for our purposes, however, for a merely intuitive interpretation of the three criteria of punishment ought to suffice to distinguish when something *counts* as punishment as opposed to counting as *just* (i.e., justified) punishment.

To see this distinction in the case of punishment, then, suppose that there is a law in one's country *against* raising one's natural-born children. The social and legally binding norms of your country require you to surrender your newborns immediately after birth to the state, and the state then places the newborn in the hands of a different set of parents (i.e., not their biological ones). Suppose that you had managed to have a homebirth completely off the grid, but then after a few years, a law enforcement officer found evidence beyond any reasonable doubt that the child she saw you playing catch with in your yard one day was your own biological progeny. Acting on this evidence, she arrests you for violating the law, which in this case carries with it a life sentence in solitary confinement; that is, a sentence that you subsequently undergo.

Now ask yourself, are you being punished in this scenario according to the definition of punishment stipulated above? You are an alleged wrongdoer, clearly, and you are being harmed. Thus, condition (i) applies. You also violated a legal norm, so condition (ii) applies. And we can reasonably stipulate for the case that the state is the appropriate authority for implementing harms on the basis of legal norm violations. Thus, condition (iii) is satisfied as well. Consequently, you are clearly being punished per the stipulative definition above.

But, you might ask, how can this be punishment? The law under question seems morally problematic for biological parents have a claim-right against anyone else to not be prevented from raising their children if they wish to do so, all things being equal. And only in the most exotic and remote of circumstances (if even those) could we even imagine such a law as being moderately intelligible as a matter of universal policy.[10] In the scenario described we do not find punishment but rather oppression at the hands of a corrupt government.

As natural as this response might sound, it is simply mistaken insofar as it tacitly assumes that punishment and oppression are mutually exclusive. If we recognize that this assumption is problematic, then we can see immediately that in the above scenario it is not that we fail to have a case of punishment, but rather it is that the punishment is *unjust*. That is, if we were to ask for a legitimate justification for the punishment described that went beyond the legal norms by appealing to morality, no legitimate justification would be

---

10.   Such scenarios would have to make it such that it was inevitable in every case that the all things being equal clause of the claim-rights of parents here would fail to be satisfied, even in the cases of those enforcing the law and legislating it.

forthcoming. Thus, whether something counts as punishment is a different question than whether that punishment is justified.[11]

Interestingly, in discussions of forgiveness, it is important to keep these issues separate as well (although careful attention to these distinctions is not always present in the forgiveness literature as it is in the punishment literature).[12] One crucial reason to ensure that we keep these things separate—that is, a definition of forgiveness as opposed to its justification—is that how one defines forgiveness should make a difference downstream to the normative evaluations one makes regarding whether or not it would be good, right, or permissible to forgive a wrongdoer in a particular case. And, of course, these normative questions about forgiveness are intimately bound up with what it means to live out one's Christian faith.

So, as in the punishment case, the importance of the distinction between a definition and justification of forgiveness is most easily seen by simply starting with stipulative definitions of forgiveness. Accordingly, let us begin with the following two definitions of forgiveness:

Foreswearing resentment: S forgives T *iff* S foreswears her resentment of T for T's action, or

Foregoing punishment: S forgives T *iff* S forgoes punishing T for T's action.

With these two different definitions of forgiveness in the background, now consider an unfortunately familiar case of wrongdoing; namely, those occasional moments when a parent is wantonly disrespected, and thus wronged, by one of their teenage children. Call one such teenage offender Duncan, and suppose that after a few minutes have passed, Duncan becomes genuinely repentant for his action.

Now consider the question, "Should Duncan's parents forgive him after he has repented?" If we understand forgiveness as equivalent to foreswearing our resentment of an offender for their action, then after Duncan's repentance, we are very likely to think, for instance, that his parents *should* forgive him for his wrongdoing at least as soon as he repents.[13] And we will think this because the repentance reflects a change in attitude with respect to—in other words, a distancing of oneself from—the wrongdoing under question. And in light of that distancing by Duncan, the resentment seems no longer wholly fitting.

---

11.   Justifications for punishment come in consequentialist, nonconsequentialist, and hybrid varieties. See David Wood, "Punishment: Consequentialism," *Philosophy Compass* 5, no. 6 (2010): 455–69; and David Wood, "Punishment: Nonconsequentialism," *Philosophy Compass* 5, no. 6 (2010): 470–82.

12.   One notable exception is Glen Pettigrove, *Forgiveness and Love* (Oxford: Oxford University Press, 2013).

13.   Indeed, we might think that Jesus's imperative in Luke 17:3 teaches as much when he states, "If another disciple sins, you must rebuke the offender, and if there is repentance, you must forgive" (NRSV). Although, as will become clear, this is not straightforward.

However, suppose we understand forgiveness on the foregoing punishment model instead. Were we to define forgiveness in this way, we might be less inclined to think forgiveness ought to be given to Duncan. And the reason for this is that punishment in such parental moments serves a pedagogical function. But to forego that punishment might preclude Duncan from fully learning and internalizing why disrespecting his parents in this way is a bad thing. Given that this teaching function of punishment, however, is important and good, then forgiveness might reasonably be withheld, on the foregoing punishment definition.

Thus, these two understandings of forgiveness diverge in whether they prescribe forgiveness for Duncan. On the foreswearing resentment definition, forgiveness would be expected, whereas on the foregoing punishment definition, forgiveness would not be expected. How one defines forgiveness, then, clearly can have a reasonable impact on whether one thinks forgiveness would be appropriate in a particular case.

So, one's definition of forgiveness plays an important role in determining the normative claims one might make about when forgiveness is good, appropriate, or justly given. But how is this distinction relevant to understanding a doctrine of unlimited atonement? The main point of connection is this: different features of a definition of forgiveness (e.g., that it is unilateral or bilateral) guide one's determinations of when forgiveness ought, or ought not, be bestowed upon an offender. Similarly, different features of one's definition of atonement (e.g., that it is unilateral or bilateral) guide one's determinations of when the benefits of atonement ought, or ought not, be offered to a sinner. This is the first feature of discussions of forgiveness that should help us to understand the motivations for adopting a doctrine of unlimited atonement. Let us look more closely now at the features of a promising definition of forgiveness inspired from the reading of the psalms and other Scriptures.

2. DOES UNILATERALISM ABOUT FORGIVENESS ENTAIL FORGIVENESS FOR ALL?

In Psalm 32:1–2, the psalmist writes, "Blessed are those whose lawless deeds were forgiven [aphethēsan] and whose sins were covered. Blessed is the man to whom the LORD does not reckon [logisētai] sin."[14] It is rare that Scripture provides a clear and precise definition of a concept, and this passage presents no exception. Nevertheless, there is a common pattern throughout the pages of the psalms of repeating similar, even the same, themes successively in different language,[15] and this particular psalm can, I think, give us an interesting possibility for something like a biblical concept of forgiveness.

---

14. This translation is my own from the LXX text, and I follow Paul, who in Romans 4:7–8 leaves off what we now would think of as the latter half of Psalm 32:2.
15. Cf. John Goldingay, "Repetition and Variation in the Psalms," *The Jewish Quarterly Review,* New Series, 68, no. 3 (1978): 146–51.

That concept of forgiveness can be stated as a translation of the final portion of this passage such that we understand forgiveness to be the action of *not reckoning sin against a sinner*. The translation of this biblical language which I assume in what follows is this:[16]

S forgives T *if* S treats T as if T is excusable for wronging S.[17]

This calls for some elaboration. Someone is excusable for an offense if they indeed caused the offense (i.e., they have *wronged* someone) but there was some sort of mitigating circumstance such that they were not to *blame* for it. Suppose, for instance, that Rosy ordered a latte at a café but did not hear her name called to collect it the first time around. Suppose further that another customer, Roddy, mistook the name called out by the barista (i.e., Rosy) for his own name and mistakenly took and drank Rosy's latte. In such a case, Roddy has wronged Rosy by stealing her latte, but given that Roddy misheard the name, he is not *blameworthy* for wronging Rosy. Thus, when we excuse someone, we neither treat nor believe them to be morally blameworthy for the wrong.[18]

On this definition of forgiveness, however, one does not excuse the wrong done, for one maintains an unwavering belief in the blameworthiness of the wrongdoer. Instead, if one seeks to forgive, then one treats the wrongdoer as one would were the wrongdoer excusable, with the exception that one recognizes that moral blameworthiness remains. In other words, one treats the wrongdoer *as if* they are excusable by no longer counting their wrongdoing as a knock against their moral constitution.[19] I assume this definition of forgiveness in the remainder of this chapter.

Now that the concept of forgiveness as no longer counting one's wrongdoing against them is intuitively clear, let us observe one significant feature of this definition; namely, that so defined the act of forgiveness is a *unilateral* act. That is, in order for forgiveness of another to take place, all that is required is that the person who has been wronged (i.e., the victim) resolve to treat the wrongdoer as if they were excusable for the wrong. And importantly,

---

16. I have restricted my attention to contexts of moral wrongdoing. Scripture, arguably, includes the possibility of nonmoral transgressions as well.

17. There is much more that needs to go into such a definition (e.g., a context of forgiveness that includes the assumption that T has wronged S, S believes this, T is blameworthy for the wrong). See Nicholas Wolterstorff, *Justice in Love* (Grand Rapids: Eerdmans, 2013), 161–77 for elaboration on such a context and the stipulated definition of forgiveness here. For a theological defense of a modified version of this definition, see my *Forgiveness and Atonement*.

18. For a more thorough discussion of excuse, see Erin I. Kelly, "What Is an Excuse?" in *Blame: Its Nature and Norms*, eds. D. Justin Coates and Neal A. Tognazzini (Oxford: Oxford University Press, 2013), 244–62.

19. The underlying notion of blame here is at least a cognitivist one insofar as it requires some sort of mental judgment of *reckoning* or *counting*. It is not merely cognitivist as I understand it, however, and as a result, coming to a place of complete forgiveness requires more than merely cognitive changes but also affective and conative ones.

there is no constraint in the definition itself that is placed upon when it would be appropriate for anyone to bestow forgiveness. As we saw in the previous section, this is because different definitions of forgiveness should make a difference to the normative predictions we make concerning when forgiving someone would be a virtuous or right action. Thus, given that forgiveness is a unilateral action (i.e., does not require cooperation via repentance from a wrongdoer), one might wonder whether such a view of forgiveness entails universal forgiveness. Let us consider an argument toward such a conclusion:

Unilateral forgiveness entails universalism:

1. Forgiveness is unilateral (i.e., only requires the contribution of the offended party).

2. Forgiveness is always good for a sinner (whether or not repentance is present).

3. God loves everyone.

4. Love requires desiring the good for the beloved.

Therefore,

5. God forgives every sinner (from 1–4).

6. Forgiveness of sins entails (eventual) presence in the new creation.

Therefore,

7. All sinners (eventually) reside in the new creation (from 5 and 6).

How, then should we think about this argument? Does it plausibly demonstrate that a unilateral definition of forgiveness entails universal forgiveness of sin? Well, whether or not it does depends on the truth of the following premises: 2, 3, 4, and 6.[20] Let us look at each beginning with those premises we have least reason to reject.

---

20. Premises 5 and 7 are merely the logical consequents of the previous premises, so there is no way to attack those premises of the argument without also attacking the ones I have highlighted in the main body of the text. Premise 1, moreover, could be rejected, but we are assuming its truth for heuristic purposes. I also think that were someone to reject premise 1, they would likely be caught with either an endorsement of semi-Pelagianism (i.e., the view that the beginnings of faith can be attributed solely to the work of a free human agent) or an incoherent view of the definition of forgiveness in the special case of divine forgiveness.

Beginning with premise 3, one might cite such verses as John 3:16 or 1 John 4:8 in support of its truth. Nevertheless, many theologians in the history of Christian thought seem to have rejected it.[21] They might claim, for instance, that God only loves the elect, or rather, that there are two types of divine love corresponding to two different groups of humans, the elect and the reprobate. Accordingly, such a theologian would point out an equivocation between "love" as it appears in premises 3 and 4, which would demonstrate that the argument was actually fallacious. That is, there would be no disambiguation of "love" such that interpreting the entirety of the argument along the lines of that disambiguation would result in a sound argument.

Those theologians inclined to reject premise 3, however, do not seem to fall within the category of proponents of a doctrine of unlimited atonement, for such a doctrine is often motivated by a desire to preserve the *prima facie* readings of such passages as those listed in support of 3's truth.[22] Thus, given our context, allow us to set aside the possibility of rejecting premise 3.

When one considers premise 4 on its own, it seems fairly innocuous. It is merely a necessary condition on when someone counts as loving another, and very plausibly, if one were to *not* desire the good of another, then one would fail to love them.[23] Indeed, the requirement of premise 4 is so minimal and uncontroversial a condition on love for another that no defense is really necessary.

But now, consider premise 6, which claims that if someone's sins are forgiven, then that guarantees their eventual enjoyment of the goods of the new creation.

Notice first what premise 6 does not say. It does not express the obviously true proposition that all participants in the new creation will have had their sins forgiven. This obviously true claim amounts to saying that if we know that some person is a citizen of the new creation, then we can guarantee that their sins have been forgiven. That is true, but that is not what premise 6 says.

---

21. Notice that premise 4 articulates a necessary condition of love. If someone were to affirm 4, then so long as someone claims that God fails to desire a good for some individuals, it will follow that they deny that God loves everyone. For instance Lucian, at a fifth-century Council of Arles, is reputed to have followed a nonstandard reading of Augustine, where the latter is interpreted as denying that God desires salvation for the nonelect. Lucian changed his mind as a result of the council, but clearly, he would have denied premise 3 before that. Florence of Lyons seems to be another case, as are (probably) such figures as Theodore Beza, Caspar Olevianus, William Perkins, and Williams Ames. See David L. Allen, *The Extent of the Atonement: A Historical and Critical Review* (Nashville: B&H Academic, 2016) for a thorough discussion of the above-named theologians and many others.

22. See, for instance, Davenant, *Colossians,* 235–36: "And in all parts of Scripture, this gratuitous love of God is declared to be the cause why the Father sent his Son into the world to obtain for us, John iii. 16, *God so loved the world that he gave his only begotten Son*"; and Amyraut, *Amyraut on Predestination,* 103–4.

23. Caveat: the desires I have in mind are not *occurrent* desires but rather dispositions that give rise to ways of acting. Thus, if one is not disposed to act in service of the good of another person, then one does not love them. This helps to deal with counterexamples involving, for instance, sleeping or unconscious individuals who, despite not having occurrent desires, retain their dispositions.

What premise 6 does say is this: the forgiveness of sins is logically *sufficient* for entry into the new creation. This might well be false even if all participants in the new creation have had their sins forgiven, for it very well may be that something in addition to forgiveness is needed in order to take part in the new creation. How might this go? Well, suppose that God did forgive all of us for sin (i.e., by treating us *as if* our sins were excusable) but that many persons persisted, despite that forgiveness, to resist the promptings of divine love and refused to repent of and acknowledge their wrongdoings. If such a scenario were possible, then these persons (we might call them the reprobate) would be not unlike the souls imagined in C. S. Lewis's *The Great Divorce*, who despite having heaven within their grasp cannot truly reach it due to their steadfast desire to not be at-one with God. One might say as Alan Torrance has that they are forgiven but unable to "repose in forgiveness."[24] And that inability to repose would prevent any true sense of presence in the new creation. Were this how one understood forgiveness and the new creation, then one could reasonably reject premise 6 despite affirming all the other premises of the above argument.

This is not the only way to undermine the argument, however, for notice that the unilateral definition of forgiveness just offered came with an additional suggestion concerning how forgiveness might be *distributed* by God. One might affirm that forgiveness is unilateral without additionally thinking that it ought to be distributed to everyone unconditionally. Here is one way that could go.

Consider premise 2, which claims that forgiveness is always good for a sinner. Were someone to reject this premise, then they would need to do so because they think that forgiveness can sometimes be *bad* for a sinner.[25] That is, they ought to think about a case in which forgiving a wrongdoer might harm the wrongdoer or in some way impede full reconciliation with them. Indeed, on a commonly accepted understanding of love—that is, as composed of desires for the good of and union with the beloved[26]—what the denier of premise 2 needs to imagine is a case of unloving forgiveness. Is such a thing possible?

Suppose that the way God treats a sinner prior to forgiving them in some cases manifests in an experience of divine absence. That is, suppose that God sometimes removes God's presence from our awareness due to our sin. Were

---

24. Cf. Alan J. Torrance, "The Theological Importance of Advocating Forgiveness and Reconciliation in the Sociopolitical Realm," in *The Politics of Past Evil: Religion, Reconciliation and the Dilemmas of Transitional Justice*, ed. Daniel Philpott (Notre Dame, IN: University of Notre Dame Press, 2006), 45–80.

25. Strictly speaking, someone could simply come up with a case where forgiveness was not good, rather than bad, for a sinner. But presenting cases where forgiveness is bad for the wrongdoer is probably needed to avoid the universal salvation implications.

26. Eleonore Stump, "Love, by All Accounts," *Proceedings and Addresses of the American Philosophical Association* 80, no. 2 (2006): 25–43.

God to forgive in such a case, that is, treat us as if we are excusable for our sin, then among the changes in behavior we might expect due to forgiveness, we would expect God's presence to return. But imagine that someone, a sinner, finds the prospect of a life with God utterly deplorable despite acknowledging that rejecting God amounts to some sort of slight against him. If God were to forgive that person and enter into that person's awareness, then God would be treating that person in a way which precisely undermines their express desire to *not* live life under his rule. Parents, similarly, sometimes push their way into parts of their adult children's lives where they are not wanted, and, as we so often see in the plots of television sitcoms, parental pushiness does not always go over well. Often, resentment of the parents, whether reasonable or not, builds up and undermines a true union between those parents and their beloved children. Such a prospect of increased resentment would threaten were God to push Godself into the life of a sinner who consciously rejected his rule as well. Consider, for instance, God treating someone like Thomas Nagel in such a way when Nagel makes the following sort of claim:

> I speak from experience, being strongly subject to this fear myself: I want atheism to be true and am made uneasy by the fact that some of the most intelligent and well-informed people I know are religious believers. It isn't just that I don't believe in God and, naturally, hope that I'm right in my belief. It's that I hope there is no God! I don't want there to be a God; I don't want the universe to be like that.[27]

It is virtually impossible for us to know with a very high degree of confidence how Nagel would react were God to treat him as if this conscious and emphatic rejection of God were excusable, that is, not ushering forth out of Nagel's own considered moral judgment. Nevertheless, it does not seem like much of a stretch to think that such treatment would simply widen the gulf between God and Nagel due to Nagel's fear that God exists becoming reality. If so, then to be forgiven by God would be *bad for* Nagel, and given that God loves Nagel, God would thereby decline to forgive him (out of God's desire for maintaining the closest union with Nagel possible).

So, why might someone deny premise 2 despite affirming a unilateral understanding of forgiveness? They might do so because they think in some cases (e.g., Nagel's case) to forgive would be to fail to love, and God cannot fail in that regard. Thus, while the act of forgiveness might be unilateral, the virtuous distribution of forgiveness is constrained by the requirement that forgiveness should never be unloving.

From the above, then, it is clear that there is no reason to think that affirming a unilateral understanding of forgiveness entails (i.e., requires or guarantees) that all human persons will eventually reside in the new creation. And

---

27.   Thomas Nagel, *The Last Word* (Oxford: Oxford University Press, 1997), 130.

this is because one might either (i) allow that forgiveness is universal in scope but not something in which those who are forgiven universally repose or (ii) deny that forgiveness is universal in scope because it is sometimes unloving to bestow it.

In the next section, we consider whether shifting our focus from the scope of forgiveness to the scope of atonement in an otherwise identical argument provides reason to prefer a restricted scope for the atonement. As we will see, the reasons given to motivate restricting the scope of forgiveness do not translate precisely into the new context of atonement. Even so, they do provide helpful insight regarding the motivations underlying both of the limited and unlimited atonement views more generally. So, let us now turn to questions of atonement.

3. DOES UNILATERALISM ABOUT ATONEMENT ENTAIL ATONEMENT FOR ALL?

The act of atonement is completed in the death, burial, resurrection, ascension, and exaltation of Jesus Christ. As such, it is accomplished as a result of the unilateral action of the God-man; that is, it is accomplished despite our entrenched and stubborn refusal to cooperate with God in his purposes. Given that atonement is unilateral, then, one might wonder whether an argument that is structurally similar to the one in section 2 might allow for equally similar escape routes for those hoping to avoid commitment to a doctrine of universal salvation.[28] Consider that argument:

Unilateral atonement entails universalism:

1*. Atonement is unilateral (i.e., only requires the contribution of one party).

2*. Atonement is always good for a sinner (whether or not repentance is present).

3. God loves everyone.

4. Love requires desiring the good for the beloved.

Therefore,

5*. God atones for every sin (from 1–4).

6*. Atonement for sins entails (eventual) presence in the new creation.

---

28. You can find the claim that unlimited atonement entails universal salvation in, for instance, Lorraine Boettner, *The Reformed Doctrine of Predestination* (Philadelphia: P&R, 1965), 156.

Therefore,

7. All sinners (eventually) reside in the new creation (from 5 and 6).

In the above argument, I have starred (*) premises that have been changed to accommodate the shift from a focus on forgiveness to a focus on atonement such that premises 3, 4, and 7 remain unchanged. Accordingly, there is no need to revisit them. Likewise, there remains no need to discuss premises 1* or 5* given that they are, respectively, merely definitional or logically follow from the prior premises. That leaves us in the structurally similar position of considering whether there are good reasons for rejecting premises 2* or 6*. Let us begin with 6*.

Given the Reformed tradition context of the present chapter, let us simply assume that some form of penal substitution is the correct model of atonement.[29] As such, we can say that for Christ to atone for sin is for Christ to undergo the penalty which would have been our punishment if applied to us for sin.[30] And now ask whether or not Christ's atoning for someone's sins entails their presence in the new creation. At this point, the difference between unlimited and limited atonement positions in responding to this sort of argument comes into view, for they cannot plausibly reject the same premises.

To see this, let us begin by assuming the limited atonement perspective. That is, let us begin by assuming that the class of individuals for whom the atonement is sufficient for salvation is the same as the class of individuals for whom the atonement is efficient for salvation. In such a case, then it seems very implausible to think that 6* could be resisted, for unlike the case of the forgiveness argument in which we saw that someone might be forgiven without reposing in that forgiveness, there is no parallel for the limited atonement theorist. Why? Because in the forgiveness case, there were two goods—that is, forgiveness and the reconciliation achieved by accepting that forgiveness—that could come apart. But the two goods under question here are (a) having one's sins atoned for in a way that is really sufficient and efficient for salvation and (b) salvation itself. According to the limited atonement theorist, possession of the good of having one's sins atoned for *necessitates* possession of salvation, and thus, the goods under question cannot come apart.

---

29. I do not mean to imply that the only Reformed model of atonement is penal substitution. Variations of it are, however, extremely common within that tradition today. Two examples from the proponents of unlimited atonement discussed here can be found in Davenant, *Colossians*, 241; and Amyraut, *Amyraut on Predestination*, 95–96.

30. For recent discussions of penal substitution informing my statement of the position, see William Lane Craig, *The Atonement* (Cambridge: Cambridge University Press, 2018); Oliver D. Crisp, *Approaching the Atonement: The Reconciling Work of Christ* (Downers Grove, IL: IVP Academic, 2020), chap. 6; Eleonore Stump, *Atonement* (Oxford: Oxford University Press, 2018), chap. 3; and Jeremy R. Treat, *The Crucified King: Atonement and Kingdom in Biblical and Systematic Theology* (Grand Rapids: Zondervan, 2014).

What about those endorsing a doctrine of unlimited atonement; that is, a doctrine that allows for the atonement to be sufficient for all persons without it being efficient for them. In this case, we can coherently conceive of three goods (rather than just two) that are in play: (i) atonement that is sufficient, but not efficient, for salvation; (ii) atonement that is both sufficient and efficient for salvation; and (iii) salvation itself. According to *limited* atonement theorists, the first category (i.e., of a sufficient, but not efficient, atonement) is a merely notional one.[31] But for the advocate of *unlimited* atonement, sufficiency without efficiency is not merely notional but real, and as a result, it can be leveraged into a way of rejecting 6*. For the unlimited atonement theorist can point out that there is a difference between *efficient atonement* and *merely sufficient atonement*, the former of which entails salvation but the latter of which does not. Thus, whereas the adherents of limited atonement cannot coherently deny 6*, attacking that premise is especially plausible for proponents of unlimited atonement.

What of 2*, the claim that atonement is always good for a sinner? A rejection of this premise seems as if it would be particularly unappealing to those of an unlimited atonement mindset. According to the adherents of such a position, it is typically the case that divine love motivates God to make atonement for all humanity; that is, to die for the sins of the whole world. Consider Amyraut on this point: "For these words are eternally and universally true, that "It is He who is the propitiation for our sins, and not only ours but also for the sins of the whole world" (1 John 2:2). And this, moreover, that "God desires that all men might be saved, and come to the knowledge of the truth . . . 1 Timothy 4:5–6. . . . He here invites the whole world as to a grace which He has destined for all humankind."[32]

It is not a large step from this claim to the further claim that Christ's atonement is a "grace" that among God's *reasons* for making atonement for all sinners is this: atoning for sins is good for each particular sinner. Consequently, it seems unlikely, at the very least, that a proponent of unlimited atonement might resist the argument from unilateral atonement to universal salvation by rejecting premise 2*.

So, what are the options, then, for avoiding the implication of universal salvation for proponents of unlimited atonement? If my analysis above is correct, the best option is for them to deny premise 6* since there does not seem to be a viable alternative premise to reject. And this diverges from the analysis we saw above regarding the argument that unilateral forgiveness entails universal salvation. For in that argument, we saw that there were plausible ways of rejecting either premise 2 or premise 6.

Now, the reason for rejecting premise 2 in the forgiveness argument was grounded in the claim that forgiving a sinner might be unloving in some

---

31.   The language of "notional" here is borrowed from Oliver D. Crisp's chapter in this book.

32.   Amyraut, *Amyraut on Predestination,* 103.

instances. And since God is essentially loving, anyone convinced that forgiveness might be bad for a sinner in some circumstances had reason to deny premise 2.

When we turned our attention to the parallel atonement argument, we saw that what was fundamentally different with respect to the revised premise 2* was that there was no real possibility of God's offering of atonement being unloving for an unlimited atonement theorist. What conclusions, then, can we draw from these observations about doctrines of limited and unlimited atonement?

First, notice on the one hand that a limited atonement theorist would (on the assumption that they accept premises 3 and 4) be forced to reject 2* lest their views commit them to a doctrine of universal salvation. Unlike in the forgiveness case, however, denying that atonement is a good for all sinners (i.e., denying 2*) seems very difficult to square theologically. It is perhaps for this reason that limited atonement theorists are more likely to reject premises 3 or 4 of the argument, despite the *prima facie* appeal of such premises.

Unlimited atonement theorists, on the other hand, are committed to denying either that God loves only a proper subset of all human persons or that God loves people in two different and exclusive senses (i.e., one consistent with election and another with reprobation). Or to put it another way, unlimited atonement theorists are committed to embracing premises 3 and 4 as both true and employing a univocal sense of "love." This univocal sense of love, then, is tied up with their understandings of both the scope of atonement and forgiveness. Which combination of responses, then, to these two arguments constitutes the best combination?

The answer to this question is, of course, open to debate, but I suggest that the best combination for an unlimited atonement theorist to adopt is a rejection of premise 2 (in the forgiveness argument) and premise 6* (in the atonement argument). As mentioned already, premise 6* is the only premise which an unlimited atonement theorist can plausibly reject. But not only this; a rejection of premise 6* is built into the very theological foundations of such a view. So, rejecting premise 6* demonstrates clearly how it is that the understanding of atonement underlying a doctrine of unlimited atonement does not entail universal salvation.

Why should one insist that it would be better for unlimited atonement theorists to reject premise 2 rather than premise 6 in the forgiveness argument? Although admittedly rejecting either premise (or both) is consistent with a doctrine of unlimited atonement, there is a worry that someone might reject premise 6 on the basis of an inadvisable conflation of the concepts of atonement and forgiveness. As we saw above, it is unclear precisely what *reposing in forgiveness* is supposed to involve given the unilateral nature of forgiveness argued for in §2. In contrast, it is clear what unloving forgiveness would look like, and I provided examples of such a phenomenon in undercutting the plausibility of premise 2. Thus, although a rejection of premise 6 is possible, there remains more work to be done to avoid the charge that one is rejecting premise 6 as an *ad hoc* attempt to avoid the conclusion of the argument. Thus, a rejection of premise 2 (in the forgiveness argument) alongside a rejection of premise 6* (in the atonement argument) is advisable.

4. CONCLUSION

I began this chapter by setting out a foundation for a scriptural understanding of forgiveness and its status as a unilateral action. Upon this foundation, I built an argument that a unilateral understanding of forgiveness entails universal salvation and suggested two ways in which someone might resist that argument. I then offered a revised version of that argument that focused on the unilateral offering of atonement and suggested that unlimited atonement theorists should not respond to those two arguments in the same fashion (i.e., by rejecting parallel premises). What I hope to have shown, then, is that unlimited atonement theorists need not commit themselves to unlimited forgiveness any more than they commit themselves to universal salvation, for those concepts all possess their own inner logics, that is, logics that when teased out cannot be reduced to the implications of the others.

PART TWO

AMYRALDISM IN HISTORY AND THEOLOGY

CHAPTER SIX

LOMBARD, AMES, AND POLHILL

Unlimited Atonement Without Double Payment

Joshua R. Farris and S. Mark Hamilton

Dogmatic *unity* among a confessional majority does not require theological *uniformity*.[1] Retrieving this once-familiar notion has been the herculean labor of several renowned Reformed historiographers over the last half-century, among whom include Heiko Oberman, David Steinmetz, Steven Ozment, and more recently (and prolifically), Richard Muller.[2] Part of the great harvest of this labor has been the contemporary rediscovery that orthodox Reformed theology—not to be confused with Reformed Orthodox theology, which is (roughly speaking) the scholastic arm of this historic tradition—was once hospitable to the idea of a plurality of defensible, albeit sometimes only minority, theological (and philosophical) opinion.

The return to such theological hospitality among some contemporary Reformed thinkers—a move that is now most often broadly referred to as the

---

1. Nor does it require philosophical uniformity, for that matter. Consider, for example, the philosophical rift in the Reformed tradition over Cartesianism. For more on this rift, see Yoshi Kato and Elco van Burg's essays in Adriaan C. Neele, ed., *Petrus van Mastricht (1630–1706): Text, Context, and Interpretation* (Göttingen: Vandenhoeck & Ruprecht, 2020), 127–42 and 155–70, respectively.
2. See for example Heiko A. Oberman, *The Harvest of Medieval Theology* (Cambridge, MA: Harvard University Press, 1967); David C. Steinmetz, *Calvin in Context* (Oxford: Oxford University Press, 1995); Steven A. Ozment, *The Age of Reform 1250–1550: An Intellectual and Religious History of Late Medieval and Reformation Europe* (New Haven, CT: Yale University Press, 1980); Richard A. Muller, *Post-Reformation Reformed Dogmatics: The Rise and Development of Reformed Orthodoxy, ca. 1520 to ca. 1725*, 4 vols. (Grand Rapids: Baker Academic, 2003).

Muller Thesis—is perhaps no more recently evident than in atonement scholarship.[3] Indeed, the very ripest fruit of this rediscovery has, without doubt,
nourished the minds of many of the contributors to this book.[4] That scholars even broadly committed to (or even merely sympathetic to) the theology
of the Reformed tradition are mounting serious inquiries into the doctrine
of unlimited atonement—what some in the Reformed tradition used to call
universal satisfaction or universal redemption or now more commonly and
technically, hypothetical universalism—is a testament to this.[5]

Although it was a minority opinion among attendants to the Synod of Dort
(1618–1619), much has recently been made of the advantage(s) that hypothetical
universalism purportedly has over the Dortian consensus (i.e., limited or definite
atonement),[6] with Dort having in no small measure steered majority Reformed
opinion about the extent of the atonement for more than four centuries.[7] Chief
among these supposed advantages is the claim that hypothetical universalism
occupies the logical high ground for defending the claim that Christ's death was
truly sufficient for all humanity, namely, that his death actually did something
measurable for and potentially applicable to all persons at all times.[8] Notwith-
standing variants of its Scottish, English, and French expressions, however much
recent scholarship finds itself wooed by this and other supposed advantages of
hypothetical universalism, there yet remains an inherent and rather nettlesome
liability that embattles unlimited accounts of Christ's atonement of this sort.[9]
The liability to which we refer is the infamous *double payment objection.*

---

3.   See, for example, Michael J. Lynch, "Confessional Orthodoxy and Hypothetical Universalism:
     Another Look at the Westminster Confession of Faith," in *Beyond Calvin: Diversity in the Reformed
     Tradition,* eds. Bradford Littlejohn and Jonathan Tomes (Landrum, SC: The Davenant Trust,
     2017), 127–48; "*Quid Pro Quo* Satisfaction? An Analysis and Response to Garry Williams on Penal
     Substitutionary Atonement and Definite Atonement," *Evangelical Quarterly* 89, no. 1 (2018): 57.

4.   Martin I. Klauber, "Continuity and Discontinuity in Post-Reformation Reformed Theology: An
     Evaluation of the Muller Thesis," *Journal of the Evangelical Theological Society* 33, no. 4 (1990): 467–75.

5.   See for example Aaron Clay Denlinger, "Scottish Hypothetical Universalism: Robert Baron (c. 1596–
     1639) on God's Love and Christ's Death for All," in Aaron Clay Denlinger, ed., *Reformed Orthodoxy in
     Scotland: Essays on Scottish Theology 1560–1775* (New York: T&T Clark, 2015), 83–102; Jonathan D.
     Moore, *English Hypothetical Universalism: John Preston and the Softening of Reformed Theology* (Grand
     Rapids: Eerdmans, 2007); Hans Boersma, *A Hot Pepper Corn: Richard Baxter's Doctrine of Justification
     in Its Seventeenth-Century Context of Controversy* (Vancouver: Regent College Publishing, 2003).

6.   It is useful to point out that there is a subtle difference, wrapped up in the language of the divine
     decrees, between Reformed accounts of a *limited* and a *definite* atonement. These distinctions are
     notorious for tripping up even the most well-meaning theological discussion. Some argue for
     a definite atonement and think that God decrees that Christ die as the legal representative for
     particular individuals. Others believe in a limited atonement and think that God decrees that the
     benefits accruing from Christ's representative work be conferred only upon those whom he chooses.

7.   For more on a sympathetic reading of hypothetical universalism's place among the Reformed, see Oliver
     D. Crisp, *Deviant Calvinism: Broadening the Reformed Tradition* (Minneapolis: Fortress, 2014).

8.   See, for example, Michael J. Lynch, *John Davenant's Hypothetical Universalism: A Defense of Catholic
     and Reformed Orthodoxy* (Oxford: Oxford University Press, 2021).

9.   The three forms of hypothetical universalism that we have in mind are, of course, those proposed
     by John Cameron (1579–1625; Scottish), John Davenant (1752–1641; English) and Moïse Amyraut

The double payment objection is often couched in terms of questions like: "How can God require that Christ be punished for sin when making atonement for all people—the first payment—and still require the punishment of those who ultimately reject him—the second (or double) payment?" Or, to put the question in a slightly different way: "if Christ makes atonement by being punished for the sin of everyone, how can God require anyone, much less the damned, be punished for sin thereafter?" Such questions get close to the heart of what should still be regarded as a not inconsiderable problem for unlimited accounts of Christ's atonement. Closer still is the question of the mechanism of atonement (more on mechanism in a moment). This is quite important. For it's one thing to assert that Christ *died* for everyone. It's another altogether to assert that Christ was *punished* for everyone. This is because affirming the former opens the explanatory door quite a bit wider, as it were, to several potential mechanisms of atonement than does affirming the latter. It is when we consider the mechanism of the atonement that the double payment problem for unlimited accounts of it comes to the fore. In what follows, we argue that penal substitution is parasitic upon claims of unlimited atonement and as such will either admit of universal salvation or interminably suffer under the burden of a double payment.

In order to narrow the scope of our examination we shall look at this problem through the lens of the *Lombardian formula* as it issues forth from two historic sources: the English Puritan and so-called learned doctor William Ames's (1576–1633) work, *The Marrow of Sacred Divinity*[10] and the Anglican jurist and lay theologian Edward Polhill's (1622–1694) work, *A View of Some Divine Truths*.[11] We begin our examination by hammering out precisely what we mean by the mechanism of atonement and the Lombardian formula. Next, we lay out some of the specifics of the nature of punishment in Polhill's hypothetical universalism. Next, we turn our attention to the subject of punishment in Ames's satisfaction theory of atonement. This useful comparison reveals, in the end, that their respective theories admit of atonement mechanisms that are worlds apart. For Ames, Christ suffers in order to pay a *debt* owed by all humanity. For Polhill, Christ suffers in order to pay a *debt of punishment* that is owed by all humanity. As such, we argue that those who want an unlimited account of Christ's atonement—one that is truly free from the double payment problem—ought to seriously consider taking up something like Ames's (i.e., Anselmian) satisfaction theory rather than Polhill's hypothetical universalism. And with that, let us define some terms.

(1596–1664; French), all of which are thoughtfully distinguished by Lynch, *John Davenant's Hypothetical Universalism*.

10. William Ames, *The Marrow of Theology*, ed. John Dykstra Eusden (Grand Rapids: Baker, 1968).

11. Edward Polhill, "A View of Some Divine Truths Which Are Either Practically Exemplified in Jesus Christ, Set Forth in the Gospel, or May be Reasonably Deduced from Thence," in *The Works of Edward Polhill* (Morgan, PA: Soli Deo Gloria, 1998 [1677]), 1–109 (hereafter, *A View of Some Divine Truths*).

1. MECHANISM AND THE LOMBARDIAN FORMULA

When we talk about the *mechanism* of the atonement, we are talking specifically about the *efficacy* of Christ's sacrifice. That is, we are talking about what his death actually does. No one debates whether Christ did actually die *for* something. The debate is around what his death actually did (i.e., the mechanism) such that its effect (i.e., its efficacy) brought about the reconciliation of God and humanity. Indeed, "*all* atonement models include a mechanism or account of how this [reconciliation] comes about," says Oliver Crisp.[12] Taking Crisp's assertion one step further, it seems that making sense of this or that mechanism is in part determined by how we make sense of the elements of the Lombardian formula.

Most commonly attributed to the Roman Catholic Archbishop Peter Lombard (around 1096–1160), the Lombardian formula says, *satisfactio Christi sufficienter pro omnibus, sed efficaciter tatum pro electis* ("the satisfaction of Christ is sufficient for all humanity but efficient only for the elect").[13] In other words—adding some specific judicial language to help our explanation—what Lombard means is that while the work of Christ's death is *sufficient* to offset God's just demands for all humanity (whatever those may be), this work is only *efficiently* applied to those just demands that are specifically demanded from the elect.[14] Or to put it in more plain language, sufficiency is like the hope of some potential good, whereas efficiency is like the promise that when the potential good is actualized, it will confer that particular good upon those who partake of it. Efficacy, then, is the enduring effect of the once potential good (i.e., sufficiency), actualized (i.e., efficiency). When abstracted from a concrete story, these concepts can sometimes be a bit confusing. So, for the sake of some additional clarity, beginning with sufficiency, consider the following concrete use of these terms in a piece of historical fiction.

When we talk about Lombardian sufficiency, we are talking about the capacity or the potency that Christ's death has to do the thing for which it was purposed. So, imagine for a moment that a vessel from the American (rather than the Japanese) Pacific surface fleet had discovered Louis Zamperini and Russell Philips after their harrowing and record-setting forty-seven days adrift at sea.[15] And imagine that as they are being carefully hauled aboard, mostly lifeless from exposure and starvation, the ship's "sick bay" is instantly prepared to receive them; all the life-saving provisions—food, water, medicine, and so forth—made ready for administration. The readiness of these

12.   Oliver D. Crisp, *Approaching the Atonement: The Reconciling work of Christ* (Downers Grove, IL: IVP Academic, 2020), 181 (emphasis added).

13.   Peter Lombard, *The Sentences*, vol. 3, *On the Incarnation of the Word*, trans. Guilio Ilano (Toronto: Pontifical Institute of Medieval Studies, 2008), 20.5 (86).

14.   For more on Lombard's soteriological dictum, see Peiter Rouwendal, *Predestination and Preaching in Genevan Theology from Calvin to Picket* (Kampen: Summum Academic, 2017).

15.   Laura Hillenbrand, *Unbroken: A World War II Story of Survival, Resilience and Redemption* (New York: Random House, 2014).

provisions would be an indication of the sufficiency of the food and the water and the medicine. Sufficiency is, again, the potential good. Staged and ready, were they to actually receive these provisions, the two half-dead men would, in time, be undoubtedly restored to full health. But if the two men were simply brought to sick bay and left unattended—put within a mere arm's length of the food and water and medicine—they would have perished. Were they *not* to receive said treatment, the provisions to restore their health—the food, water, and medicine—would be no less sufficient. Now, translating this back into the Lombardian notion of Christ's sacrificial offering, we would say something like Christ's death has the *capacity* to do a thing that, if applied, would bring about the reconciliation of humanity to God. This is sufficiency. And this brings us to efficiency.

To say that the food and medicine aboard the vessel are efficient to provide Zamperini and Philips with life-saving nourishment means that *if they receive it*, it will do the thing that it is supposed to do for them, namely, restore their health. Again, the efficiency of this provision remains only promissory, but for its actual application. Once again, if we apply this notion of the Lombardian formula to one specific theory of atonement—take Ames's satisfaction theory as a prime example—then we would say something more specific, like: Christ's death restores honor to God, thereby satisfying the rectoral demands of divine justice for all humanity (more in a moment).[16] Lombardian *sufficiency*, in this case, would be the capacity of Christ's sacrifice to do that for which it was intended, namely, restore honor to God. This much should be quite clear. Lombardian *efficiency*, by contrast—being the potency of Christ's death *in* application—is the cancellation of the debt of honor owed by those who by faith repent and are united to Christ. Or, returning to our analogy, efficiency is the corpsman's (i.e., a US Navy medic) administration of the life-saving food and medicine to Zamperini and Phillips. So much for sufficiency and efficiency.

Once administered—say, intravenously—when we talk about what the water, food, and medicine actually do to the bodies of the two men is to talk about *efficacy*. Efficacy, then, is the mechanism: the good actualized. In the case of Zamperini and Phillips, we might explain efficacy in terms of the positive biochemical effect that a water-glucose solution has upon internal organ malfunction, or that intravenously fed proteins have upon muscular regeneration, or that shade has upon eyes afflicted with forty-seven days of acute and unrelenting UV light exposure. Turning to the atonement, and borrowing a phrase from sacramental theology, we might say that the good actualized is *ex opere operantis* efficacious for making atonement (i.e., from the works of the one working—that is, God). Translating this once again into Ames's satisfaction theory of atonement, we would say something like: efficacy is the assurance that having fully satisfied the demands of God's rectoral justice, together

---

16.   Anselm, *Why God Became Man*, in *The Major Works*, eds. Brian Davies and G. R. Evans (Oxford: Oxford University Press, 1998), 283, 286, 288, 349 (emphasis added).

with the assurance that having pardoned those who by virtue of one's faithful union, Christ confidently delivers them from future condemnation for their yet remaining (though slowly diminishing) moral corruption. So, tying all these threads together, efficacy (i.e., mechanism) is the positive effect that follows from the administration of some guaranteed good.

Now that we've roughed out some definitional boundaries, consider three issuances of the Lombardian formula that have appeared across the atone-ment-theory landscape of the Christian tradition: (A) *sufficient for all but efficient for none* (i.e., penal non-substitution theories);[17] (B) *sufficient for all and efficient for some* (i.e., penal substitution theories);[18] or (C) *sufficient for all and efficient for all* (i.e., non-penal substitution theories).[19] Perhaps the most notable feature of these three expressions of the Lombardian formula—at least the most notable for our purposes here—is the difference between (B) and (C). This is because, as we shall see in a moment, they each explain the efficacy of Christ's work (i.e., the mechanism) in remarkably different and all too often confused terms.[20] As we transition into this next section, we shall see that Polhill opts for (B), while Ames opts for (C). Enter Polhill.

EDWARD POLHILL: SUBSTITUTION, PUNISHMENT, AND HYPOTHETICAL UNIVERSALISM

If among the first names that come to mind when scholars talk about (English) hypothetical universalism are Baxter, Ussher, Preston, or Davenant, among the last is probably Polhill. Edward Polhill was a British jurist and lay Puritan theologian of a unique Reformed-Anglican variety. Beyond the small cache of his literary remains, little is known about Polhill's theological exploits. And yet, in its time Polhill's works commanded the attention and praise of such famed British and American theologians as John Owen, Cotton Mather, and Jonathan Edwards.[21] Corroborating this testimony is David Thomas's nineteenth-century *The Homilist*, which claimed that Polhill's works

---

17. See, e.g., Nathanael Emmons, *Systematic Theology*, in *The Works of Nathanael Emmons*, ed. Jacob Ide (Boston: Crocker and Brewster, 1842), 5.20.

18. See, for example, Richard A. Muller, *Christ and the Reformed Tradition*, 105.

19. Some readers may stumble at this novel arrangement of the Lombardian formula, perhaps thinking that such an arrangement gives way to a doctrine of universal salvation. Alas, this is only the case if you conceive of the mechanism of Christ's sacrifice in terms of his paying a debt of punishment. Were you to reconceive of this mechanism in terms of Christ paying a debt of honor—thereby putting em-*pha*-sis on a different syl-*la*-ble, so to speak—then the claim that Christ's death was both sufficient for and efficient for all moves into the light of possibility.

20. One example of this sort of confusion is evident in Eleonore Stump's recent work, *Atonement* (New York: Oxford University Press, 2018). For an outline of other, similar (and in some cases, more egregious) problems, see Douglas Farrow, "Anselm and the Art of Theology," *Fellowship of Catholic Scholars Quarterly* 42, no. 4 (2020): 255–73.

21. For some glowing commentary on the value of Polhill's mental labors, see John Owen, "Preface," in Edward Polhill, *The Divine Will Considered in Its Eternal Decrees and Holy Execution of Them* (London, 1673).

"[were] highly valued by good judges," and "bear the impress of sober piety and a deep knowledge of the Scriptures."[22]

As deep as Polhill's knowledge of the Scripture appears to have been, so also was the apparent depth of his knowledge of the doctrinal development of the Christian tradition. Aristotle, Plato, Jerome, Ambrose, Aquinas, Anselm, Bonaventure, Luther, Beza, Baxter, Davenant, Bellarmine, Grotius, Suarez, Volkelius, Calvin, and Latimer are just a few of the names that appear page-to-page, consistently, throughout his various works. Where matters more immediate to the subject of the Divine will (the *ordo decretorum*) and the Lombardian formula are concerned, Polhill appears to have taken many of his theological cues from fellow Anglican and famed hypothetical universalist, Bishop John Davenant.

Polhill explicitly affirms that Christ's death is *sufficient for all and efficient for some*, as does Davenant.[23] So too does he ardently affirm some version of penal substitution and with it, a version of hypothetical universalism, again, like Davenant.[24] Putting these affirmations together, it looks like Polhill believes that Christ's work of atonement is, however much sufficient for all, in the end efficacious for only some (i.e., the elect) upon the condition of faith in Christ's death having paid humanity's debt of punishment. And herein lies a problem. For if we cash out the particulars of the penal substitutionary mechanism that underpin Polhill's hypothetical universalist notion of sufficiency and efficiency, namely that Christ's death swallowed up the whole of humanity's debt of punishment, then it looks like the double payment objection follows. Let us take a closer look at just what Polhill affirms.

Polhill on Atonement: A Synthetic Account

For the sake of brevity and clarity, we have synthesized Polhill's thoughts about atonement into the following eight theses. As a meaningful registration of Polhill's ideas about atonement, when taken together, they bring some shape to his thinking on the matter, beginning with the idea that

1. Christ is a representative of (all) humanity, a mediator in the manner that Adam serves as our mediator.

Polhill flatly states that "[Christ] was the representative of mankind."[25] Later he says, "The debt which he satisfied for was ours, not his; he stood as our representative and satisfied for us; he did not only suffer *nostro bono*, that the profit might be ours, but *nostro loco*, that the satisfaction itself might

22. David Thomas, *The Homilist* (London: Ward and Co., 1863), 3.10 (59).
23. Polhill, *A View of Some Divine Truths*, 67, 77, 80.
24. Polhill, *A View of Some Divine Truths*, 79.
25. Polhill, *A View of Some Divine Truths*, 78.

be ours."[26] Christ, on Polhill's thinking, procured both for others. What this means is if Christ represents all by taking the debt of punishment sufficient for all, then he does so efficiently for all. The logic is something like the following: x is definitive for all, Christ takes x thereby achieving both x and y. Christ assumes a debt sufficient for all, which by the previous logic achieves both sufficiency and efficiency.

>   2. The debt Christ pays in death is "plenary" (i.e., absolute), specifically
>   satisfying those retributive demands of the moral law upon humanity.

What Polhill means by this is that Christ not only endures the consequences of violating the moral law (i.e., death), he is considered righteous by the standards of the moral law on behalf of others. "So plenary was that satisfaction, that *if we receive him by faith* we are debtors no longer, all our debts are blotted out of God's book, no more to be charged upon us; a second payment cannot be demanded of us," Polhill explains.[27] And this brings us to the third assertion, namely, that,

>   3. Christ was made punishable for the sins of others by divine imputation.

As we will take up this up in greater detail in the next section, we shall merely point out here that Polhill is quite bold in his assertion(s) about Christ's being punished by imputation. He says in one place—quoting him at length—that

> God's mere will may inflict sufferings, but nothing but justice can inflict punishment. Justice, unless moved, inflicts it not; neither is there any other mover, but that of sin imputed. Where no sin imputed [to Christ] there it is, as to punishment, all one as if there were no sin, and where this is no sin at all there can be no such thing as punishment. We are therefore under a necessity to say, that sin was in tantum, so far imputed to Christ as to render his sufferings penal, and withal we see an accident passing to another by imputation; only here it will be objected, that sin was only imputed to Christ in its effects [i.e., penal consequences]; but, I take it, this suffices not, for the effect of sin is punishment and punishment cannot be where no sin is imputed is a punishment for nothing, that is, it is no punishment; and where there is no punishment, sin is not so much as imputed in the effect.[28]

---

26.   Polhill, *A View of Some Divine Truths*, 87.
27.   Polhill, *A View of Some Divine Truths*, 78.
28.   Polhill, *A View of Some Divine Truths*, 88.

In other words, the penal consequences view of suffering is insufficient to explain what Christ actually endured. Christ's suffering for sin is for Polhill unabashedly punitive. He says, quite clearly,

> Our sins being laid on him, he suffered the same punishment, for the main, that die to us for them. For how doth the Scripture express the punishment of sin? It is death and he died for us; it is the second death, and he suffered deaths, not the death of the body only, but all the deaths in moriendo morieries, as far as his holy humanity was capable thereof; it is wrath, and he was made a curse, not only a ceremonial, but a real curse, even that which he redeems of from.[29]

4. Christ's atoning work is substitutionary, paying the debt to the moral law on behalf of others.

That Christ satisfies the demands of the moral law *for humanity* entails that his work is not only representative, but substitutionary. "Christ suffered *nostro loco*, in our place and stead," he says. He confirms this repeatedly with such statements as, "There was a divine constitution, that Jesus Christ should be our *sponsor*, and *standing in our room*, should *satisfy for us*, that he should be a head to believers, and his satisfaction should so far become theirs, as to justify them against the law; accordingly that satisfaction is truly imputed to them."[30] From here, we see Polhill quite clearly asserting that

5. Christ's accomplishment in death is imputed to the elect.

This does not mean that humanity has an equal share of Christ's nature and could be as perfect as Christ. Rather, Polhill appears to mean that humanity is simply treated as such. He says, explicitly, that

> [the] active and passive righteousness of Christ are not imputed to us, as they are the idem [i.e., the exact same thing], a perfect conformity to the laws he was under; for we were not under the mediatorial law, nor, being once sinners, are we capable of a perfect conformity to the moral law; but they are imputed to us, as they are the tantundem [i.e., equivalent], a plenary satisfaction to the moral law by us broken, for so they are very apt and proper to justify sinners against the law. Neither is Christ's satisfaction imputed to all actually to justify them against the law, for all are

---

29. Polhill, *A View of Some Divine Truths*, 153.
30. Polhill, *A View of Some Divine Truths*, 87 (emphasis added) and 166 (emphasis added).

not justified against it, but it is imputed to believers, as mystical parts and portions of him.[31]

Notice Polhill's care to distinguish between those for whom imputation is an actual, appreciable benefit and those for whom Christ's work would have otherwise and potentially justified, were it (somehow) effectual for them. This is quite important, as we shall see in a moment when we look at proposition eight. Before that, consider that for Polhill,

> 6. Christ takes on, assumes or absorbs not just the penal consequences of humanity's violation of the moral law (i.e., somatic death), but humanity's actual debt of punishment, thereby absolving humanity from any further requirements to the moral law.

Of course, we saw a glimmer of this sixth proposition in proposition three. When Christ absorbs our individual penal debts, he absorbs a loss to himself that is not meted out in any degreed fashion or in a way that merits a surplus of justice that can be granted when some other condition is met. In numerous places, Polhill describes Christ's atoning work as meriting a compensation that brings about a positive satisfaction, but this is logically confused if Christ's atoning work is first and foremost a work of satisfying penal debts. Penal debts may result in positive redemptive benefits, but the mechanism does not amount to a compensatory payment (i.e., as if someone were to pay additional money into your account so as to bring it out of a negative balance into a positive balance). Christ's absorption of a loss is what is being substituted for our penal debts, which is exacting, and this is precisely what effectuates and procures justification, according to Polhill. It is here that the difference between debtor satisfaction versus creditor satisfaction becomes important. For it admits of the distinction between the sufficiency of atonement for all and the efficiency of the atonement for some. What this means is that, according to Polhill, "if a pardon or immunity from punishment be not our righteousness, then Christ's righteousness (which was penal and obediential to an infinite value, and did compensate the very *culpa*, and free us from it) is, as soon as it is made ours by imputation, our righteousness against the law." And, he goes on, "Christ suffered this punishment in our stead. . . . Our sins being laid on him, he suffered the *same* [idem] punishment, for the main, that was due to us for them." This is, again, one of many places where Polhill explicitly affirms the conjoining of two important concepts: penal and substitutionary atonement, which, when taking together, inform our seventh proposition:[32]

---

31.   Polhill, *A View of Some Divine Truths*, 79 (emphasis added).
32.   Polhill, *A View of Some Divine Truths*, 86 and 154 (emphasis added).

7. Christ's death is penal in two senses (as somatic death and wrath-taking).

According to Polhill, "In his act of somatic death, Christ achieves a full and complete payment *for human sin* to the moral law *and* to God. What this means is that his act of atonement requires no further work to save sinners. It is complete, perfect, and *exacting*."[33] That Polhill distinguishes between two sorts of debt—one owed to the moral law and the other to God—is curious. For, as we have already intimated, it is implied (though overlooked by many contemporary theologians) that a commitment to penal substitution necessarily commits one to a debt to the moral law, and not, strictly speaking, to God. Remember that debts of punishment require that the debtor lose this or that. In Christ's playing the substitute debtor when he makes atonement for humanity, he loses his life by absorbing the debt of punishment owed to the moral law on behalf of others. This, we have pointed out elsewhere, means that the public offense against the moral law has been satisfied because the moral law's inflexible judicial requirement (i.e., the punishment of lawbreakers) is satisfied because Christ loses in the affair just as humanity would have lost were Christ not to stand in for them. That Polhill distinguishes debts of punishment that are owed both to the moral law *and* to God, and what is more, that Christ's somatic (i.e., bodily) death pays both debts of punishment is not so easily resolved.[34] And yet, we find a clue to his thinking about this twofold meaning when he distinguishes between Christ's atoning work as payment of the debt of punishment to the law and another debt of punishment that is owed God in terms of his eternal damnation as a consequence for lawbreaking. For at one point he says,

> We must distinguish between punishment as it stands in the law absolutely [i.e., proposition 2], and punishment as it stands there in relation to a finite creature, which cannot at once admit a punishment commensurate to its offence; and so much ever suffer, because it cannot satisfy to eternity. Punishment as it stand in the law absolutely, is [somatic] death; punishment as it stands there in relation to a finite create, is eternal death: the first was really suffered by Christ and the second could not be justly exacted from him, for he paid down the whole sum of sufferings all at once and so swallowed up death in victory.[35]

The obvious question that emerges here is this: How did he *not really* suffer a penalty of eternal death and somehow still "[pay] down the whole sum of sufferings all at once" for all humanity? The answer is found in the

---

33. Polhill, *A View of Some Divine Truths*, 154–58 (emphasis added).
34. Polhill, *A View of Some Divine Truths*, 142.
35. Polhill, *A View of Some Divine Truths*, 166.

previous section, where he cleverly distinguishes between the "immensity" and the "duration" of sufferings for eternal death.[36] Immensity, he says, refers to the cumulative weight of all human sin that is laid upon Christ, whereas duration obviously refers to the extent of the sufferer's suffering. Immensity, he says, is a necessary condition to Christ having suffered the *idem* of punishment. Duration, he says, is accidental to Christ's atonement—in this way, Christ suffering *tantundem* the penalty for sin. For this reason, and because of "the dignity of his person," Polhill concludes that Christ "more than compensated" for what God required in the punitive condition of what constitutes "eternal death."[37] This assertion, one for which he offers little more than the "dignity of his person" argument, this brings us to our eighth and final proposition in Polhill's thinking about the nature and extent of Christ's atonement, namely:

8. Christ suffered the penalty for sin and died for all humanity.

Underlying this distinction is the idea that while God foreknows that some portion of the "to-be-applied" benefits (conditional upon faith/believing and therefore receiving) that Christ secures for everyone will go unanswerable (i.e., they will go unapplied to the damned), it is apparently still required that he suffer for them to the same degree that he suffers to obtain the benefits that will be applied only to the elect.[38] Polhill explicitly affirms not just the value of Christ's death as a penal substitute—à la the "immensity" of Christ's punitive suffering for sinners—but that Christ actually died for *all people*, appealing repeatedly to such scriptural passages as Hebrews 2:9, 2 Corinthians 5:15, and 1 John 2:2.[39] And it is among such appeals that he takes on, though curiously in his own terms, the "momentous" double payment problem.[40] We say that he tackles the double payment problem "in his own words" because he does not explicitly refer to this problem using the term "double payment." He introduced the problem in the form of an objection, and that in two parts, saying,

> Objection 4. If Christ died for all men, then he was a surety for all, and satisfied for the sins of all, and consequently God hath a double satisfaction; one in Christ the surety, and the other in the persons of the damned, which is against the nature of his justice. . . . Christ intercedes for all men

---

36. Polhill, *A View of Some Divine Truths*, 166.
37. Polhill, *A View of Some Divine Truths*, 154.
38. According to Hans Boersma's reading of Richard Baxter, "Baxter distinguishes the absolute promise of the first grace (universal redemption in terms of securing but yet to-be-applied benefits) for the elect and *the legal moral donation for all*." Boersma, *A Hot Pepper Corn*, 198 (emphasis added). Lynch confirms this is also a distinction in both Ussher and Davenant. The logic of Polhill's argument unfolds similarly (see, e.g., *A View of Some Divine Truths*, 169).
39. Polhill, *A View of Some Divine Truths*, 166.
40. Polhill, *A View of Some Divine Truths*, 169.

in such sort as he died for them; I say in such sort, for there is a vast difference between his general intercession for all, and his special intercession for the elect. For as Christ by his blood shed on the cross, merited for all in general, that they might be saved on gospel terms [i.e., by faith], and merited for the elect in special, that they should believe and be saved on gospel terms, and intercedes for the elect that that they may believe and be saved. If Christ died for all, then he was a surety for all and satisfied for sins of all. If Christ so satisfied for the sins of all, then God hath a double satisfaction which is against justice.[41]

Put in other words, the objection that Polhill attempts to answer is: Can God demand payment for punishment that has already been paid by Christ? In answer to this objection and invoking a bit of creditor-debtor language to do so, upon which hangs our understanding of the nature of this problem, Polhill offers up three rebuttals. Taken together, these three rebuttals frame the bulk of his answer to the double payment objection, and by consequence, answer that all too familiar question: Do we believe in penal substitution?

First, he claims that had the actual debtors (i.e., sinners) themselves repaid God their debt, divine justice would not require the second satisfaction (i.e., the punishment of the damned). Second, assuming these debtors require a surety—a sufficient one they could not find among themselves—Polhill considers that God admits a substitute to make payment. In other words, God permits that substitutes can make payments to divine debts, but such substitutes must be able to actually pay these debts, which means they must be paid by divinity itself. Had the debtors found a substitute amongst themselves, he maintains that a second payment God would not be required; with debtors unable to find a substitute, the creditor supplies his own (i.e., himself). This, Polhill argues, requires a second satisfaction, one that finally discharges the debtor's debt. Here Polhill is careful to distinguish between "absolving" (i.e., requiring nothing more) debtors of their debts versus "acquitting" (i.e., still requiring repentance and faith).[42] "If they do neither," he concludes, "they can have no benefit by Christ's satisfaction, and by consequence a second satisfaction [i.e., punishment] may be justly exacted from them."[43]

Summing Up

A great deal more could be said about Polhill's doctrine of atonement. Propositions 1–8 are a mere skeletal structure. And, of course, this was by design. For, what we have tried to show in the preceding is that Polhill's hypothetical universalism lacks the infrastructure necessary to carry the burden of the double payment objection in light of what he says about the nature

---

41.   Polhill, *A View of Some Divine Truths*, 168 (emphasis added).
42.   Polhill, *A View of Some Divine Truths*, 169.
43.   Polhill, *A View of Some Divine Truths*, 169.

of punishment, and what is more, how and for whom Christ pays debts of punishment. No matter how tightly he carves up the nuances of his view, succumbing to the double payment objection appears to be inevitable consequence, despite his final (and somewhat anticipated) voluntarist appeal to divine wisdom. Curiously, he states,

> It is true that God eternally foresaw these rejecters of Christ, and that Christ in time died for them, nevertheless there is no blot hereby cast on divine wisdom; it is no disparagement to the all-wise God to bestow means of eternal bliss on such as he eternally foresaw would abuse the same to their own destruction. . . . God may be said to will the salvation of men through Christ's death two ways: either because he wills that Christ's death should be a price infallibly procuring their faith and salvation, or else because he wills that there should be in Christ's death an aptness and sufficiency to save them on gospel terms; the former will points only at the elect, and is fulfilled in their grace and glory, the latter extends to all men, and is fulfilled in the aptness and sufficiency of Christ's death to save them on gospel terms. In both God's will hath its effect.[44]

While this is a somewhat unique theological construct, it follows that underlying and well-worn path of those who appeal to a divine command theory, according to which God's incontestable wisdom determines the best setup, so to speak, of the various relationships between his decrees to save whoever and however he wills.[45] But, by our lights, in death Christ absorbs the penalty for all humanity; Christ's death procures faith for all humanity; therefore, Christ's death brings about the salvation of all humanity. Thus, either a double payment is required, or—if we take the double payment objection seriously (and some certainly do not)—we must simply deny the compatibility of penal substitution with hypothetical universalism.[46] If Christ pays the debt of punishment for all, then all are reconciled by his atoning work because the debt of punishment has been paid for all.

---

44.   Polhill, *A View of Some Divine Truths*, 169.

45.   Appeals to voluntarism and divine command theory and the uniqueness of Christ's payment of all debts of punishments in defense against the double payment objection continue to be a go-to move among penal substitution theorists long since Polhill. See, e.g., William Lane Craig, *The Atonement* (Cambridge: Cambridge University Press, 2018) and *Atonement and the Death of Christ: An Exegetical, Historical, and Philosophical Exploration* (Waco, TX: Baylor University Press, 2020).

46.   Why then must Christ's substitutionary work be effectual on penal substitution? Could Christ not have absorbed the penal consequences for all, and all not share in the benefits of his work? Having dealt with the "penal consequences" view elsewhere, we will say only three things. First and foremost, this is not Polhill's view. Second, the penal consequences view belongs categorically to version (A) of Lombardian structure that we saw in the previous section when we defined our terms. Third and finally, the penal consequences view resolves (perhaps) a collective problem, not the problem of individual debts of punishment.

Now, for those who wish to maintain an unlimited account of Christ's atonement as a penal substitute, hypothetical universalism is not the answer, in light of the double payment objection. What then is one to do? Abandon unlimited atonement? Perhaps not. Unlimited atonement is not necessarily the problem. It is the mechanism that is the problem. By changing the mechanism of the atonement, one can effectively avoid the double payment objection parasitic on penal substitution and affirm a mechanism that is both sufficient for all and efficient for all (i.e., option C from the previous section). The central distinction is in how one articulates the mechanism in a way that debts (to be distinguished from debts of punishment) can be satisfied by a positive exchange between Christ's work and those who transgress the law. The defense for an unlimited account of Christ's atonement requires a reenvisioning of the mechanism that supports it. In this way, our appeal is to a satisfaction theory of atonement, like that articulated by William Ames. In the next section, we shall see that for Ames, the mechanism of Christ's has to do with satisfying the debt of honor owed to God rather that satisfying a debt of punishment.

WILLIAM AMES, PUNISHMENT, AND SATISFACTION

Probably not a household name with the popular fame of John Calvin, William Ames is a voice to which most contemporary (particularly American) Reformed theologians owe a significant debt.[47] Ames was tutored by the eminent Cambridge Puritan theologian William Perkins and rose to prominence as a British expatriate among the Dutch, serving most notably as advisor to Johannes Bogerman, the president of the synod of Dort. Though he was not a prolific writer compared to some of his contemporaries, his *Medulla Theologiae* (*Marrow of Theology*)—the work for which he is perhaps now most commonly known—shaped theological education in eighteenth-century New England more than any other.[48] Ames's *Marrow* also became the principal inspiration for Peter van Mastricht (1630–1706)—Ames's chief interpreter and expositor—whose *Theologia Theoretica Practica* is as much a commentary on Ames's *Marrow* as anything else, and which Jonathan Edwards (1703–1758) exalted as "the most important book in the world."[49] But for a handful of recent efforts to introduce Ames into the contemporary atonement literature, the precise impact of his Anselmianism[50] on the

---

47. For more on the significance of Ames to the Reformed tradition, see Jan van Vliet, *The Rise of the Reformed System: The Intellectual Heritage of William Ames* (Milton Keynes, UK: Paternoster, 2013).

48. Richard Warch, *School of the Prophets: Yale College, 1701–1740* (New Haven, CT: Yale University Press, 1973), 36.

49. Jonathan Edwards, "Edwards to the Reverend Joseph Bellamy, January 15, 1747," in *The Works of Jonathan Edwards* (New Haven: Yale University Press, 1980), 6:211.

50. See for example Dániel Deme, *The Christology of Anselm of Canterbury* (Aldershot: Ashgate, 2003).

development of Reformed theology (especially in America) has hitherto been, quite literally, relegated to the footnotes of history.[51]

Far from being able to give Ames's atonement theory a full workup, as it were, we shall instead spend our literary capital expositing his doctrine of punishment, which is at the heart of the difference between the mechanism underpinning penal substitution and anselmian satisfaction.[52] This, therefore, is the most direct route to Ames's thinking about what Christ's work does and does not do. Ames's *Marrow* contains several explicit passages to this effect, each one featuring as a dogmatic subcategory of his doctrines of providence, hamartiology, and his soteriology. Let us briefly take each one in turn, beginning with his doctrine of providence.

Punishment and Providence

Ames' doctrine of providence falls into several important subcategories. The subcategory that concerns us here consists of two parts, (1) "common" and (2) "special" government.[53] A fixture of God's "special" government, Ames says, is his issuance of the moral law for his *rational* creatures. This is important because later Ames will go on to say that punishment belongs exclusively to human agents. Here Ames distinguishes between the law that is "[made]" from threats of punishment that he says are "established."[54] God makes law to point his rational creatures to his own moral perfection and holiness. God establishes law in that he sets forth bespoke consequence(s) for those who slough off his general benevolence and regnant (rectoral) authority. This honor is what theologians of the period once often referred to as *rectitude*[55] or, more specifically, God's *rectoral* justice. This is quite significant. Rectoral justice, as we shall see more clearly in a moment, is the judicial cornerstone, so to speak, upon which rely all other aspects of Ames's account of divine justice, including, most notably for our purposes, retributive justice. The first plank of the argument having now been laid, let us look more specifically at Ames's thinking about the nature of punishment in the context of another systematic heading that he aptly titles "Sin's Consequence."

51.   See John Dykstra Eusden, "Editor's Introduction," *The Marrow of Theology*, 20n44.
52.   Summarily speaking, the satisfaction theory of atonement is worked out in systematic detail in St. Anselm's well-known work *Cur Deus Homo*. Lesser known (especially among Protestants) is Anselm's work *Meditatio Redemptionis Humanae* (St. Anselm, "Concerning the Redemption of Mankind," in *The Devotions of Saint Anselm, Archbishop of Canterbury*, ed. Clement C. J. Webb [London: Methuen & Co., 1903], 105–19). Anselm's *Meditatio* is a kind of prayerful, doxological compliment to his more theologically constructive *Cur Deus Homo*.
53.   Ames, *Marrow*, 1.10.110–11.
54.   Ames, *Marrow*, 1.10.110–11.
55.   For an extended and helpful argument about God, truth, and rectitude, see Thomas Williams, "Saint Anselm," *Stanford Encyclopedia of Philosophy* (2020), https://plato.stanford.edu/entries/anselm.

Punishment and Sin's Consequence

Ames states there are two consequences for sin, (1) guilt and (2) punishment.[56] Of guilt, Ames has some interesting things to say. Of punishment, he has comparatively much more to say. Put in a more digestibly simple form, what Ames means by guilt is a sinner's inherent unworthiness (i.e., *reatus culpae*). "Guilt," he says, "is a situation or consequence," or state, rather than a "*form* of sin."[57] It is "that spiritual pollution whereby a sinner is made *destitute of all dignity and honor* and becomes vile."[58] Of course, there is much more that is interesting about Ames's account of guilt that we must simply pass over in light of the interests of this chapter. Let us therefore pivot toward his account of punishment. As we do, we shall move through this section on sin's consequence selectively, considering and commenting on a few key statements and formulas; again, a full workup on Ames's doctrine of punishment would be a chapter unto itself. To that end, let us consider (1) the definition of punishment, (2) punishment as somatic and spiritual death, and (3) the implications of what Ames calls "the consummation of death."[59] We will look closely at these pieces of the Amesian puzzle, as it were, because together they outline how Ames thinks punishment functions in general, which in turn will aid us in laying the final plank in the next section as we discover how it functions when it comes to the death of Christ. Let's begin with a definition.

AMES ON PUNISHMENT
Punishment, Ames explains, is

[an] evil inflicted on the sinner for sin. It is called an evil inflicted, not simply contracted, because it pertains to retributive and avenging justice. [It] follows upon the offence, because it had been prohibited and upon guilt, because the threat of punishment had been such. Therefore, punishment, properly speaking, has no place but in intelligent creatures in whom there is also sin.[60]

Notice that punishment is not *merely* consequential for Ames, as some (penal substitution) atonement theorists have recently and curiously suggested of somatic death. Rather, punishment has a clear statutory origin, the legislator (i.e., God) having established (via law) death (somatic and spiritual alike) as the consequence for sin *by decree*. That is, God punishes, Ames says, because God's honor has been offended by humanity's corruption of his image in them. He

---

56. For some interesting discussion of the medieval and Reformed scholastic views on original sin, as well as the nature of guilt and punishment, see Oliver D. Crisp, "Scholastic Theology, Augustinian Realism, and Original Guilt," *European Journal of Theology* 13, no. 1 (2004): 17–28.

57. Ames, *Marrow*, 1.7.117 (emphasis added).

58. Ames, *Marrow*, 1.7.117 (emphasis added).

59. Ames, *Marrow*, 1.16.125.

60. Ames, *Marrow*, 1.16.125 (emphasis added).

calls this "the defacement of the image of God."[61] Later in his *Marrow* he argues that punishment, recalling our previous section, is "an act of *corrective justice* by which penalty is inflicted on a violator of justice. The end should be the amendment or restraint of the offender, peace and admonition to others and the *preserving of justice and God's honor*."[62] This is quite important. For again, at the heart of the disparity between the satisfaction theory and the penal substitution theory is a fundamental misunderstanding related to the difference between simple debts and debts of punishment; a misunderstanding that plagues penal substitution theorists (especially evangelical adherents) more than any other. We remember that debts of punishment—those belonging categorically to the penal substitution theory—are debts that require that the debtor suffer loss. And this loss, teeing up our section, comes in two forms: somatic and spiritual death. So much for the definition of punishment; let us now consider the difference between somatic and spiritual punishment.

PUNISHMENT AS SOMATIC AND SPIRITUAL DEATH

Now, before we get too much further into the systematic weeds, we do well to remember the specific problem that is at the heart of this chapter. Put positively, the problem is this: if death is a punishment—somatic and spiritual death alike—that penal substitution theorists like Polhill argue Christ absorbed for *all humanity*, it is perfectly consistent with the conclusion that those who are damned, not being among the elect beneficiaries of this atoning work, are punished *again* because God has decreed that it be so. Or to put it more simply, where there is a divine decree to this or that end, despite an apparent logical inconsistency, God can simply make it so. This is voluntarism on full display. With that, let us turn to Ames's account of the sorts of punishments that threaten humanity.

As he transitions from his definition of death to what he calls "a special consideration of it," Ames argues that "in death—the curse of God that lies upon sinners—there are two degrees: the beginning and the consummation. There are two parts: the punishment which is loss [*damnun*] or the part of deprivation, and the punishment which is a matter of consciousness [*sensus*] or the positive part. And there are two kinds of death, spiritual and bodily."[63] Right away, it is worth mentioning that Ames tackles the subject of *spiritual* death across multiple chapters in his *Marrow* (e.g., "Original Sin," "Actual Sin," and "The Consummation of Death"), whereas he tackles what he titles "Bodily Death" as a chapter unto itself. As we already noted, the beginning of spiritual punishment, he says, is the "defacement of the image of God," or what he calls a "letting go of grace and original justice."[64] The fallout of this,

61. Ames, *Marrow*, 1.7.119.
62. Ames, *Marrow*, 2.16.307 (emphasis added).
63. Ames, *Marrow*, 1.12.119.
64. Ames, *Marrow*, 1.12.119.

Ames goes on, is that human "nature is weakened, put out of order," resulting in the "conscious realization [of] spiritual bondage" to both the devil and his earthly principalities.[65] There is, of course, a lot more that could be said of the "beginning" of spiritual death. He goes on, for example, to enumerate a variety of specific implications that the beginning of spiritual death has upon human faculty psychology, among other implications. Leaving all that aside, let us consider the next most important question, namely: What is the "consummation" of spiritual death?

"The consummation of death," Ames flatly says, "is the highest degree of punishment."[66] This statement, on Ames's account, applies to both bodily and spiritual punishment. Later in the *Marrow* Ames states, "The deprivation of the good of happiness in the sinner who is punished . . . corresponds in fact and kind with what the sin deserves."[67] And what does sin deserve? Simply put: death. And what is death but punishment? "The punishment inflicted on man for sin *is death*," says Ames.[68] Now, of the "consummation" of *spiritual* death, he says that it is "a total and final forsaking by which man is separated completely from the face, presence, and favor of God."[69] It is in this execution of divine sentence—what Ames notably calls "vengeance"—that any vestige of the formerly defaced image of God in man is stripped away. At this, the damned undergo what Ames says is "a great and eternal hardening in evil and despair of good."[70] The result of this, he continues, is "a conscious realization [in] a full sense of the bondage to the power of the devil, to which a man is totally delivered."[71] The damned are thus simultaneously emptied of the little good they enjoyed in life and filled to the point of overflowing with an insatiable evil that will consume them eternally. The inaugural step of this descent into the consummation of spiritual punishment occurs, Ames says, in the separation of soul from the body. This is critical to our understanding of the nature of the sort of punishment that Christ endured. To that end, let us turn now to our final section and look at punishment in the context of Ames's discussion of Christ's work of making atonement by satisfaction.

Punishment and Satisfaction

To this point we've labored to make three ideas clear. We began by clarifying that Polhill's commitment to penal substitution (i.e., that Christ dies to pay a debt of punishment) undermines his commitment to the idea that Christ died for all humanity. Second, we clarified that punishment in Polhill's thinking about what God requires of transgressors takes an elevated and

---

65.   Ames, *Marrow*, 1.12.119.
66.   Ames, *Marrow*, 2.16.125.
67.   Ames, *Marrow*, 2.16.307.
68.   Ames, *Marrow*, 1.7.118 (emphasis added).
69.   Ames, *Marrow*, 2.16.125.
70.   Ames, *Marrow*, 2.16.126.
71.   Ames, *Marrow*, 2.16.126.

therefore worrisome position when it comes to cashing out the demands of divine justice at large and what Christ accomplished by his death to meet this demand. Third, we attempted to clarify that Ames's understanding of punishment, contra Polhill, is actually one, lesser part among many other parts of a highly nuanced and multifaceted account of divine justice. As we turn now to Ames's account of punishment in the context of the nature of Christ's satisfaction, we see that Ames did believe that Christ was, in fact, punished. But *how* was he punished? Was his punishment substitutionary? Was it exemplary? Or was it something else altogether? How we answer *these* questions will tip the interpretive scales in favor of one or another view of Ames's account of satisfaction. A clue as to the answer to these questions, it should perhaps now be obvious, is bound up in how the previous section ended, namely, that punishment for Ames is meted out in the separation of the human body and soul.

According to Ames, "There are two parts to redemption: the humiliation of Christ as our mediator and his exaltation."[72] For our purposes, we will focus attention on Ames's account of Christ's humiliation, which he argues is his doing of that which is necessary to secure redemption for humanity. The first part of his humiliation, he goes on, is Christ's taking on a human nature. The last part of his "humiliation is satisfaction and the achievement of merit."[73] The object of his satisfaction, Ames clearly states, "is for the honor of God as a kind of recompense for the injury done to him by our sin (Rom. 3.25)."[74] *This* is Christ's substitutionary work. "Satisfaction," he clearly states, "*takes away* condemnation," not absorbs it.[75] So far, so good, right? Maybe not. It is at this point that Ames offers up an explanation of how Christ does this.

He says, "Sin could not in any way be imputed to him other than *that he might undergo for us the punishment due to sin*."[76] Curious. At first glance, you may well think that Ames is hereby affirming penal substitution. Why would that be? In short, because Ames uses the words *death, pain, suffering*, and, most importantly, *punishment* to describe Christ's death, you might well assume that, of course, he means penal substitution. This is a common mistake that penal substitution theorists seem to make. Just because these terms are put to use to describe the nature of Christ's work, it does not necessarily follow that the author is talking about what many evangelicals today call penal substitution. The careful reader will notice that when Ames speaks of punishment, in this particular context, he is not describing a punishment that is absorbed (i.e., a debt of punishment) by Christ that brings the redemption of humankind. If we keep reading, and reading carefully, we more accurately discern his meaning when he says, "The same force is found in the words,

72. Ames, *Marrow*, 2.20.134.
73. Ames, *Marrow*, 2.20.135.
74. Ames, *Marrow*, 2.20.135.
75. Ames, *Marrow*, 2.20.135.
76. Ames, *Marrow*, 2.20.135 (emphasis added).

he paid the price of redemption for us, Matt 20.28. No mere deliverance or means of deliverance is set forth in that phrase, because the price itself is named and it is intimated to be like payments of silver or gold for salable merchandise, 1 Pt 1.18."[77]

This is not penal substitution. This is satisfaction à la Anselm. For Ames, Christ takes on punishment in a somewhat loose sense as that which is descriptive of the curse that befalls all human beings; Christ's humanity suffers somatic death. This must be held in relation to Ames's clearer comments about Christ's humiliation for human redemption in explicitly Anselmian ways when he characterizes it as an achievement by merit and satisfaction that eliminates or simply cancels (rather than absorbs) the debt of punishment due to us. Thus, for Ames, there is no indication that he thinks of punishment in substitutionary terms. Rather, "Christ was called to perform this [commercial] work, and this work, being performed, was accepted in our name and for our good" and "by bearing [our iniquities] he took away the sins of the world."[78] Again, this sounds like penal substitution, but it's not. We know this because a few chapters later Ames says quite clearly that "the death of Christ was the same in kind and proportion as the death justly due for the sins of men. It corresponded in degree, parts, and kind."[79] In other words, Christ gave himself up to die *the same sort of death* that all humanity dies. The punishment of Christ was, as he says, equal to "all the misery which the sins of men deserved."[80] This does not mean the collective misery of all the saints befell him, à la the penal consequences view. What it means is that Christ suffered somatic death, and with it, the separation of his human soul from his human body, as all humans eventually do. "[Christ's death] was designed to satisfy through victory and not to ruin through surrender."[81] Punishment is hereby described not as a loss to Christ (in his divinity or humanity), but in the context of victory over death, which is consistent with an Anselmian understanding of Christ as the representative sufferer who merits salvation for humans. Christ, in death, did not absorb humanity's debt of punishment. Ames describes Christ's death as the consummation of his work of humiliation, which procures positive merit demanded by divine justice, thereby offsetting the demerit of debt owed by humanity. In this way, Christ's death is truly sufficient for all, because the moral debt has been paid in the death of Christ's human nature. "The death of Christ is the last act of his humiliation in which he underwent extreme, horrible, and most acute pain for the sins of men. . . . It was design to satisfy

77. Ames, *Marrow*, 2.20.135.
78. Ames, *Marrow*, 2.20.136.
79. Ames, *Marrow*, 2.22.142.
80. Ames, *Marrow*, 2.22.141.
81. Ames, *Marrow*, 2.22.141.

[God] through victory and not ruin through surrender."[82] Summarily speaking, the satisfaction offered up by Christ was *for* God, and the superabundant benefits derived there from redounding to humanity. This is the mechanism that underpins Anselmian satisfaction, worked out in a more systematic fashion by a Reformed theologian. It represents a distinct voice in the broader Reformed theological tradition that is not penal substitution, but an Anselmian satisfaction theory of the atonement. In this way Ames provides contemporary Reformed doctrinal discussions a different option those commonly cited (Calvin, Davenant, Owen, etc.) that paints a coherent picture of Christ's atonement as a version of hypothetical universalism.

CODA

While the doctrine of atonement has never not been a subject of great interest among Christian scholars, in the last decade or two, the number of scholarly works that have appeared on the particular work that Christ accomplished by his death has skyrocketed. This is particularly true among analytic theologians, some of whom have turned their interest in the work of Christ into a veritable cottage industry—better perhaps, chop shop—tearing down, bolting on, and rebuilding the doctrine with all manner of conceptual parts and pieces in an effort to explain away this or that problem. We too have contributed to this effort, proffering a theory of atonement that attempts to account for the honor-based claims of the satisfaction and moral government theories (among others) in a single theory that we referred to at the beginning of the chapter as *reparative substitution*. Grappling, as we have here, with worries such as the double payment objection—a worry for which we have hitherto found no truly compelling reason to disbelieve—puts us one step closer to a more fully articulated theory of the atonement that uniquely depicts Christ's work as both sufficient and efficient.

Polhill's work on atonement represents what we might think of as a standard, albeit thoughtful and nuanced, version of penal substitutionary atonement according to which Christ pays a debt of punishment for humanity by his death. After looking closely at what he says about the nature of punishment, and in light of his commitment to hypothetical universalism, Polhill's theory does not achieve what he thinks it does precisely because the mechanism undermines it: Christ's payment of a debt of punishment that is sufficient for all means that he really did suffer punishment for all. If this is, in fact, the case, then Polhill has only so many options: (1) the damned are not actually punished, (2) double payment follows, or (3) all will be saved. Polhill, we saw earlier, opts for double payment, which he thinks is a problem that is overcome with appeals to voluntarism. This, it appears, is the most defensible option for those committed to hypothetical universalism where penal substi-

---

82. Ames, *Marrow*, 2.22.141.

tution is the underlying mechanism. Not so for Ames's Anselmian-inspired satisfaction theory where the mechanism is altogether different.

For Ames, Christ dies to pay a simple debt of honor, which means that he accrues a merit that is not only sufficient for all, but efficient for all. Yes, efficient for all. How is that precisely? Well, for Ames, Christ's death paid the debt of honor fully. The infinite merit of the sacrifice of his infinite self offsets the infinite demerit of human sin. It does not do so in part. In this, Christ's act is one of (superabundant) equity to a debt. In this way, the burden of both the righteous and the damned is properly hung on the doctrine of faith, union, and their efficacy, which is itself fixed upon divine decree. On Ames's way of thinking, all will still die somatically, but not all will die in a state of perpetual or eternal separation from God because by faith some will appropriate the benefits of Christ's sacrifice to God. For Ames, Christ's sacrifice is truly unlimited without any worry of double payment.

CHAPTER SEVEN

AMYRAUT IN CONTEXT:

A Brief Biographical and Theological Sketch

Jeff Fisher

In the popular "Calvinist versus Arminian" debate, one name that sometimes gets raised is Moïse Amyraut. The theological view of Amyraldianism (or Amyraldism) named after him most commonly refers to a perspective on the extent of the atonement. The views related to Amyraut do not
fit with either the Arminian position or the "limited atonement" position
common among Calvinists, nor does it actually fall "between" Calvinism
and Arminianism.[1] Rather, Amyraldianism and related views emerged from
within the Reformed tradition and lie within the bounds of Reformed orthodoxy.[2] Amyraut himself was not seeking to move away from Calvinism. In

---

1. For popular examples of the language that Amyraldianism is "a mediating position" or "between"
   Calvinism and Arminianism, see Michael Horton, *The Christian Faith: A Systematic Theology for Pilgrims
   on the Way* (Grand Rapids: Zondervan, 2011), 517; Roger R. Nicole, "Amyraldianism," in *New Dictionary
   of Theology*, eds. Sinclair B. Ferguson and David F. Wright (Leicester, UK: Inter-Varsity Press, 1988), 17.
2. See especially Richard A. Muller, "Diversity in the Reformed Tradition: A Historiographical
   Introduction," in *Drawn into Controversie: Reformed Theological Diversity and Debates Within
   Seventeenth-Century British Puritanism*, eds. Mark Jones and Michael A. Haykin (Oakville, CT:
   Vandenhoeck & Ruprecht, 2011), 23–25; *Calvin and the Reformed Tradition: On the Work of Christ and
   the Order of Salvation* (Grand Rapids: Baker, 2012), 107–60; *Post-Reformation Reformed Dogmatics:
   The Rise and Development of Reformed Orthodoxy, ca. 1520 to ca. 1725*, 2nd ed., 4 vols. (Grand
   Rapids: Baker, 2003), 1:76–77; Oliver D. Crisp, *Deviant Calvinism: Broadening Reformed Theology*
   (Minneapolis: Fortress, 2014), 175–234; Michael Lynch, "Richard Hooker and the Development of
   English Hypothetical Universalism," in *Richard Hooker and Reformed Orthodoxy*, eds. W. Bradford
   and Scott N. Kindred-Barnes (Göttingen: Vandenhoeck & Ruprecht, 2017), 273–93.

fact, he maintained and defended that what he taught was not only in line with Scripture but was consistent with Calvin's teaching on the subject. Likewise, Amyraut did not perceive his view as contrary to the Canons of Dort but rather well within the bounds of the confessional language. This chapter focuses on the historical situation of Moïse Amyraut (1596–1664) and his particular teaching on the extent of the atonement in context with similar developing views of the time period.[3]

THE CONTEXT OF AMYRAUT'S LIFE

In September 1596, Moïse (sometimes Moyse) was born in the small town of Bourgueil (Touraine), located in the Loire Valley, about twenty-five kilometers east of Saumur, in the French province of Anjou.[4] His family originally came from Alsace and later Orleans. He would become the famous French Reformed pastor in Saumur and professor of theology at the Saumur Academy, known in Latin as Moyses Amyraldus.[5] Though there are no accounts of his childhood or early education, he would have been educated in the humanities and basic philosophy. As a member of a Protestant family, he would have also had an unstable and vulnerable religious life during the early seventeenth century. Amyraut was very young when King Henry IV issued the Edict of Nantes in April 1598 to bring an official end to the recent Wars of Religion between French Catholics and the Protestants known as the Huguenots. This edict gave some rights and liberties to the Protestants to practice their faith but confirmed Roman Catholicism as the state religion.[6] After Henry IV was assassinated in 1610, King Louis XIII further restored Catholic strength, to the extent that by 1620 the Huguenots were so alarmed that they initiated a movement in opposition to the king that led to a series of three religious wars from 1621 to 1629.

---

3. Richard Muller asserts that there is still "merit in continuing this discussion, particularly when it is directed toward identifying the actual historical situation," noting that "Amyraut's views on the subject . . . have been not so much misunderstood as misplaced—incorrectly located—by much of the scholarship on his thought" ("Beyond Hypothetical Universalism: Moïse Amyraut [1596–1664] on Faith, Reason, and Ethics," in *The Theology of the French Reformed Churches: From Henri IV to the Revocation of the Edict of Nantes*, ed. Martin I. Klauber [Grand Rapids: Reformation Heritage, 2014], 205). See also Muller, *Calvin and the Reformed Tradition*, 279.

4. For fuller biographical details, see Alan C. Clifford, "A Quick Look at Amyraut," in *Amyraut on Predestination* (Norwich: Charenton Reformed, 2017), 15–36; and *Christ for the World: Affirming Amyraldianism* (Norwich: Charenton Reformed, 2007), 7–43; Roger Nicole, *Moyse Amyraut: A Bibliography with Special Reference to the Controversy on Universal Grace* (New York: Garland, 1981), 4–68. The most common sources used for these biographical sketches are Pierre Bayle, "Amyraut (Moise)," in *Dictionnaire historique et critique de Pierre Bayle* (Paris: Desoer, Libraire, 1820 [1679]), 507–19; and John Quick, "The Life of Mons. Amyraut," in *Icones Sacrae Gallicanae*, 2 vols. (MS transcript, Dr. William's Library, London, 1700), 1:958–1028.

5. Amyraut's name is spelled variously as Amyraud, Amyrauld, Amiraut, and Amyrault.

6. On the historical relevance of these events, see especially Albert Gootjes, *Claude Pajon (1626–1685) and the Academy of Saumur: The First Controversy over Grace* (Leiden: Brill, 2013), 22–23.

During this time period was when Amyraut received his training and began his ministry. Like his father (and John Calvin), Amyraut first sought to study law, graduating Licentiate in 1616 after one year at the University of Poitiers. At some point when traveling home he visited Samuel Bouchereau, pastor of a Reformed Church in Saumur and the rector of the Saumur Academy.[7] Bouchereau recognized his extraordinary potential and introduced Moïse to the governor of Saumur, Lord Philippe du Plessis-Mornay (1549–1623), a famous Huguenot statesman and founder of the Saumur Academy. Du Plessis-Mornay and several Huguenot pastors encouraged Amyraut to abandon law and study theology instead. While there are very few sources on Amyraut during this period, we know he was admitted as a student to the Saumur Academy, possibly as early as 1618, but certainly before 1621.[8] It is also likely that Amyraut studied in Leiden where the French theologian, André Rivet (1572–1651), had become professor in 1620.[9] It seems that Amyraut sought a ministerial appointment in 1623 that he did not get, but then served as a pastor in Saint-Aignan and one other location before taking the call to pastor in Saumur in 1626.[10]

By 1631, he was a well-known and well-respected Reformed pastor and theologian in the important city of Saumur, especially following the publication of his *A Treatise Concerning Religions* (1631).[11] He became quite involved in several political and ecclesiastical matters, which necessitated that he possess strong intellectual ability and conviction. The series of religious civil wars in France had ended with the Peace of Alès in 1629, again granting tolerance for Protestant worship, but significantly limiting their political privileges. In 1631, Amyraut was appointed on behalf of the National Synod to present to King Louis XIII the protests against infractions of the Edict of Nantes.[12] Given the religious climate, many of Amyraut's writings were devoted to defending Protestantism in France. Based on his ministry, Amyraut has also been

---

7. Muller, "Beyond Hypothetical Universalism," 199. Muller cites several nineteenth- and early twentieth-century French resources on the background of the Saumur Academy.

8. Amyraut studied under John Cameron (ca. 1579–1625), who was a professor at Saumur from 1618 to 1621–1622. See below on Cameron's influence on Amyraut.

9. See Brian Armstrong, *Calvinism and the Amyraut Heresy: Protestant Scholasticism and Humanism in Seventeenth-Century France* (Eugene, OR: Wipf & Stock, 2004 [1969]), 76.

10. Muller, "Beyond Hypothetical Universalism," 200.

11. Moïse Amyraut, *Traitté des religions contra ceux qui les estiment toutes indifferentes* (Saumur: Girard & Lerpinière, 1631, 1652). An early English translation is *A Treatise Concerning Religions, in Refutation of the Opinion Which Accounts All Indifferent* (London: M. Simons, 1660).

12. Alan C. Clifford, "Amyraldian Soteriology and Reformed-Lutheran Rapprochement," in *From Zwingli to Amyraut: Exploring the Growth of European Reformed Traditions*, eds. Jon Balserak and Jim West (Göttingen: Vandenhoeck & Ruprecht, 2017), 157–58; Mary K. Geiter and W. A. Speck, "Moïse Amyraut and Charles II," *Huguenot Society Journal* 30, no. 2 (2014): 157–80; Clifford, "A Quick Look," 30; Djaballah, "Universal Grace," 170. See also Clifford, "A Quick Look," 18, where Clifford expounds on the significance of Amyraut refusing to present their complaints on his knees and gaining the respect of Cardinal Richelieu.

characterized as ecumenical, tolerant, moderate, and broad-minded.[13] He
engaged in dialogue with Lutherans and Roman Catholics in ways that were
apparently well received, even while writing against aspects of Catholicism
such as transubstantiation and justification.[14]

Perhaps the most significant event in Amyraut's life and ministry was his
appointment as professor and chair of theology at the Saumur Academy in 1633.
He would remain at the academy until his death in 1664. In addition to his
role as professor, he was appointed the academy's principal in 1640. With these
roles, Amyraut and the other two professors of theology at Saumur, collectively
known as the "triumvirate," had a profound influence on the development of
Reformed theology, not only in France but throughout Europe.[15]

THE CONTEXT OF THE SAUMUR ACADEMY
AND "SAUMUR THEOLOGY"

During the seventeenth century as many as seven Reformed academies
existed in France for the training of pastors. The most famous and important was the Geneva Academy, but the Saumur Academy also gained renown
and often drew the most students. Established near the end of the sixteenth
century by Du Plessis-Mornay, the curriculum was infused with Reformed
humanism. The students learned theology, philosophy, philology, history, and
politics.[16] Scholars have noted that the Saumur Academy in particular was
more open to the emerging Cartesian philosophy than other academies.[17] The
French philosopher and mathematician René Descartes was born the same
year as Amyraut, and by the 1630s and 1640s his thought and writings had
become very influential. It may be that some of Amyraut's tendencies were
influenced by this perspective.

During his time as a student at the Saumur Academy, Moïse Amyraut
studied under John Cameron, the influential Scottish theologian often
considered the "father of Saumur theology."[18] Amyraut's disposition

---

13. For common examples, see Clifford, "A Quick Look," 20–22, and Djaballah, "Universal Grace," 170.

14. See Clifford, "Amyraldian Soteriology," 166; Muller, "Beyond Hypothetical Universalism," 204.

15. Moïse Amyraut, Louis Cappel, Josué de La Place, *Syntagma thesium theologicarum in Academia Salmuriensi variis temporibus disputatarum* (Saumur: Joannes Lesner, 1664). See Frans Pieter Van Stam, *The Controversy over the Theology of Saumur, 1635–1650: Disrupting Debates among the Huguenots in Complicated Circumstances* (Amsterdam & Maarsen: APA-Holland University Press, 1988); Stephen Strehle, "Universal Grace and Amyraldianism," *Westminster Theological Journal* 51, no. 2 (1998): 345–57; Clifford, "A Quick Look," 33–36; Muller, "Beyond Hypothetical Universalism," 204.

16. See Gootjes, *Pajon and the Academy of Saumur,* 24–26. Gootjes identifies a practical emphasis for both philosophy and theology at the academy.

17. Muller, "Beyond Hypothetical Universalism," 214–16.

18. Gootjes, *Pajon and the Academy of Saumur,* 6. For background on Cameron's contribution to what would later develop into Amyraldism, see Richard Muller, "Divine Covenants, Absolute and Conditional: John Cameron and the Early Orthodox Development of Reformed Covenant Theology," *Mid-America Journal of Theology* 17 (2006): 11–56. On the life of John Cameron, see G. Michael Thomas, *The Extent of the Atonement: A Dilemma for Reformed Theology from Calvin to the*

toward moderation and reconciliation of opposing theological views likely descends from Cameron. Throughout his career, Cameron pastored and taught philosophy and theology in several important locations. Cameron succeeded the Dutch theologian Francis Gomarus as the chair of theology at Saumur in 1618. While Cameron only taught at the Saumur Academy for three years (1618–1621), his legacy extended far beyond that, both through his continued private teaching and through the teachings of his students. The resurgence of religious conflicts forced him to live in London and Glasgow between 1621 and 1623 before returning to Saumur, though upon his return he could only teach privately due to the restrictions of King Louis XIII's edict.[19]

Most noteworthy for our purposes, Cameron taught one of the earliest forms of what would later be considered Amyraldianism. His articulation of certain elements of predestination and the covenant resulted in *both* Reformed and Arminian theologians questioning whether he truly agreed with the Canons of Dort.[20] The most distinctive elements of Cameron's teaching were his views on universal grace, covenant, and efficacious grace. These distinctives developed from Cameron to Amyraut and on to Claude Pajon (1626–1685) and formed the core of the Saumur doctrine of "universal grace" or "Saumur Theology."[21]

Following the death of Amyraut in 1664, the Saumur Academy faced multiple crises because of the controversies regarding its theology on the extent of the atonement and the shifting landscape of religious tolerance in France.[22] In 1685, the Edict of Nantes that had been allowing limited rights and freedoms for French Protestants was revoked. Among many other issues Protestants faced, this soon contributed to the closing of the Saumur Academy.[23] However, the end of the Academy did not end the influence of Amyraut or his teaching on the extent of the atonement.

Consensus (1536–1675) (Carlisle, UK: Paternoster, 1997), 162–86; and Robert Wodrow, "Collections on the Life of Mr. John Cameron, Minister at Bordeaux, Professor of Divinity at Saumur, Principall of the College of Glasgow, and Professor of Divinity at Montauban," in *Collections upon the Lives of the Reformers and Most Eminent Ministers of the Church of Scotland*, 3 vols. (Glasgow: Maitland, 1834–1848), 2.1:81–223.

19. Gootjes, *Pajon and the Academy of Saumur,* 27–28; Richard Muller, "Divine Covenants," 13–14. Because of the tensions between Catholics and Protestants in seventeenth-century France, Cameron was forced to move many times within and outside of France. One of the military campaigns by Louis XIII included the taking of the city of Saumur in April 1621.

20. See Gootjes, *Pajon and the Academy of Saumur,* 27–28.

21. Albert Gootjes, "Calvin and Saumur: The Case of Claude Pajon (1626–1685)," *Church History and Religious Culture* 91, nos. 1–2 (2011): 203–14. Stepehn Strehle likewise summarizes the connections from Cameron to Amyraut in "Universal Grace," 345–48.

22. See especially Gootjes, *Pajon and the Academy of Saumur,* 15–16.

23. Martin Klauber, *Between Reformed Scholasticism and Pan-Protestantism* (Cranbury, NJ: Associated University Press, 1994), 147.

THE CONTEXT OF AMYRAUT'S TEACHING

Much of the previous scholarship regarding Moïse Amyraut unfortunately got trapped within the "Calvin against the Calvinists" debate, following
the works of Basil Hall and others.[24] Brian Armstrong, in particular, incorporated Amyraut into this line of thinking.[25] This "Calvin against the Calvinist"
thesis has been shown to be highly problematic—not only in its conclusions,
but even in its methods and approach.[26] Notably, Amyraut actually serves as
a good case study to demonstrate that he (like all his contemporaries) had
many similarities with Calvin and many differences. Amyraut himself explicitly claimed faithfulness to Calvin on his views regarding predestination and
the atonement, even contrasting what he taught with that of Theodore Beza,
Calvin's successor in Geneva.[27] Any study of Amyraut's writings reveals the
reasoning, syllogisms, methods, and distinctions characteristic of scholasticism and the appeal to the sources, linguistics, and historical interest characteristic of his training in humanism.[28] Unfortunately, still many of those
who have written on Amyraut position themselves in one or the other of
these camps: some arguing that Amyraut was a biblical humanist just like
John Calvin, while others argue that he was just as scholastic as his orthodox
counterparts but diverged significantly from Calvin's theology.[29] Debating

24. See Basil Hall, "Calvin against the Calvinists," in *John Calvin*, ed. G. E. Duffield (Appleford: Sutton Courtnay, 1966), 19–37.
25. Armstrong, *Calvinism and the Amyraut Heresy*. See John Frame's critique of Armstrong's thesis in "Review of Armstrong's Calvinism and the Amyraut Heresy," *Westminster Theological Journal* 34, no. 2 (May 1972): 186–92.
26. See, as representative examples, Richard A. Muller, *After Calvin: Studies in the Development of a Theological Tradition* (New York: Oxford University Press, 2003); "Calvin and the 'Calvinists': Assessing Continuities and Discontinuities between the Reformation and Orthodoxy," *Calvin Theological Journal* 30 (1995): 345–75 and 31 (1996): 125–160; "John Calvin and Later Calvinism: The Identity of the Reformed Tradition," in *The Cambridge Companion to Reformation Theology*, eds. D. Bagchi and D. C. Steinmetz (New York: Cambridge University Press, 2005), 147; Willem J. Van Asselt and Eef Dekker, eds., *Reformation and Scholasticism: An Ecumenical Enterprise* (Grand Rapids: Baker Academic, 2001), 22–24; Robert Letham, "Theodore Beza: A Reassessment," *Scottish Journal of Theology* 40 (1987): 25–40; Carl R. Trueman and R. Scott Clark, eds., *Protestant Scholasticism: Essays in Reassessment* (Waynesboro, GA: Paternoster, 1999).
27. Amar Djaballah, "Controversy on Universal Grace: An Historical Survey of Moïse Amyraut's Brief *Traitté de la Predestination*," in *From Heaven He Came and Sought Her*, eds. David Gibson and Jonathan Gibson (Wheaton, IL: Crossway, 2013), 170.
28. See Muller, "Beyond Hypothetical Universalism," 197–98, 210, 220. Muller opens his chapter noting, "Virtually all of the recent scholarly literature devoted to him has tended either to argue the significance of his thought as a humanistic, Calvinian protest against a rigid, Bezan Scholastic orthodoxy, or to argue that his thought was a highly problematic deviation from the fundamental message of Calvin as well as from the orthodoxy of his time." See also Muller, *Calvin and the Reformed Tradition*, 107–25, 156–60.
29. For example, see Strehle, "Universal Grace," 345–57, and Alan C. Clifford, *Amyraut Affirmed: Or, "Owenism, a Caricature of Calvinism": A Reply to Ian Hamilton's Amyraldianism—Is It Modified Calvinism?* (Norwich: Charenton Reformed Publishing, 2004). Clifford even labels Amyraut's teachings as "authentic Calvinism" since it was Scholastic followers who shifted away from Calvin's teaching ("Amyraldian Soteriology," 162).

and making cases for whether Amyraut taught "authentic Calvinism" actually presents many problems, including anachronistic readings of Calvin's own views and the fact that many thinkers besides Calvin contributed to the diverse and variegated Reformed tradition.

While he is now most known for his views on the extent of the atonement, Amyraut was a preeminent theologian and prolific writer in his day on many theological subjects. His other major publications include treatises on comparing religions (1631), defending the existence of the Reformed church in France (1647), defending Reformed church government (1653), a four-volume work on Christian ethics (1652–1660) that deals with the Christian life and caring for souls, paraphrases on several New Testament books and the Psalms (1644–1653, 1662), and expositions on a wide range of theological topics.[30] Among these theological expositions is a pastoral discourse on the state of believers after death (1646), which he wrote following the death of his only daughter, Elizabeth, who was nineteen years old at the time. Amyraut frequently wrote in the common vernacular early-modern French and used many relatable illustrations to explain his points. Several stories reveal that Amyraut spent time walking with his students to address their questions on theology.[31] It is evident from his approach and some clear expressions in his writings that he desired for ordinary people to understand theology.[32]

THE CONTEXT OF AMYRAUT'S TEACHING
ON THE EXTENT OF THE ATONEMENT

The primary reason for the fame of Moïse Amyraut resulted from the first major work he published as a professor at the Saumur Academy in 1634.[33] Amyraut intended to address some of the expressed concerns regarding the Reformed doctrine of predestination. The immediate context apparently was following a dinner conversation with some Roman Catholics who "attacked Calvin's doctrine of predestination as harsh, narrow, and unworthy of God."[34] Amyraut intended to write a positive presentation of the Reformed doctrine of predestination that might convince Roman Catholics, Arminians, and other French readers.

---

30. For a more complete bibliography, see Nicole, *Moyse Amyraut: Bibliography*. Nicole enumerates 161 volumes and more than two hundred individual titles. See also Muller, "Beyond Hypothetical Universalism," 201–2.

31. Clifford, "A Quick Look," 28–29.

32. See Muller, "Beyond Hypothetical Universalism," 202. One example is the introduction to his *Brief Traitte*. Amyraut wrote, "My intention has solely been to render this doctrine that is commonly evaluated to be both difficult and thorny as capable to be understood by all and to take it back from the subtlety of controversy" (2b).

33. See below for analysis of this Brief Treatise.

34. Djaballah, "Controversy on Universal Grace," 171–72. See also Muller, "Beyond Hypothetical Universalism," 202.

However, his treatise actually ignited a new kind of debate within the Reformed world, specifically centered on his explanation of the "universal grace" God showed to all humanity. While Amyraut still held to the view that God's saving grace was limited *in application* to those whom God had unconditionally elected, he advanced this apparently divergent view that salvation through Christ's death was *intended* universally and equally for all people. The controversy that erupted from this publication would continue throughout Amyraut's career and beyond.

In response to the immediate attacks on his work, Amyraut wrote a seventy-five-page preface to a series of six sermons titled *Eschantillon de la doctrine de Calvin touchant la prédestination* [A Sample from the Doctrine of Calvin Addressing Predestination] (1636), a collection that contained many quotes and excerpts from John Calvin to defend his view.[35] This did not end the controversy, but rather eventually brought about an anonymously published treatise attacking Calvin's view on reprobation that led Amyraut to respond with a defense of Calvin's doctrine, first in 1641 and again in 1644.[36] Amyraut consistently and repeatedly contended, even from the pulpit, that his explanation of predestination and universal grace was completely consistent with John Calvin, and that Calvin's doctrine was consistent with Scripture.[37]

Some of the most significant opponents of Amyraut were Pierre Du Moulin (1568–1658), Andre Rivet (1572–1651), Friedrich Spanheim (1600–1649), and Francis Turretin (1623–1687).[38] They frequently charged him and his followers with Arminianism, even though Amyraut differentiated himself from Arminian teaching on many occasions, but especially in two major publications in 1646 and 1647.[39] Turretin had actually studied in Saumur when Amyraut was there as a professor. He eventually became a pastor and professor of theology in Geneva. His later systematic theology text, which included strong refutation of Amyraut's position, had significant influence on

35. Moïse Amyraut, *Eschantillon de la doctrine Calvin, touchant la predestination* (1636), a6v–ii1v. For background and some analysis of this publication, see Gootjes, "Calvin and Saumur," 204.

36. Anonymous, *De absoluto reprobationis decreto* (Amsterdam: Blaeu, 1640). Moïse Amyraut, *Doctrinae Joannis Calvini, de absolutio reprobationis decreto, defensio. Adversus scriptorem anonymum* (Saumur: D. Lesnier, 1641); *Defense de la doctrine de Calvin sur le sujet de l'election et de la réprobation* (Saumur: Isaac Desbordes, 1644).

37. Analysis and summaries of Amyraut's claims for consistency with Calvin can be found in Djaballah, "Controversy on Universal Grace," 194; Strehle, "Universal Grace," 351; Gootjes, "Calvin and Saumur," 204; Matthew S. Harding, "Atonement Theory Revisited: Calvin, Beza, and Amyraut on the Extent of the Atonement," *Perichoresis* 11, no. 1 (2014): 49–73.

38. For summaries of Amyraut's opponents' arguments, see Djaballah, "Controversy on Universal Grace," 190–95; Strehle, "Universal Grace," 349; David L. Allen, *The Extent of the Atonement: A Historical and Critical Review* (Nashville: B&H Academic, 2016), 166.

39. Moïse Amyraut, *Fidei Mosis Amyraldi circa errores Arminianorum declaratio* (Saumur: Lesnier, 1646); *Disputatio de Libero Arbitrio* (Saumur: Lesnier, 1647). Strehle observes that a significant reason for the charge of Arminianism is the similar tendency to isolate the mind as the instrument of faith rather than the whole of one's being as the Reformed did ("Universal Grace," 350–51).

Reformed theology into the late nineteenth century.[40] Amyraut's final major publications on the subject were responses to the polemics of Spanheim from the University of Leiden and previously professor of theology at the Genevan Academy.[41] Du Moulin, a pastor and professor at the Sedan Academy, followed Amyraut's response with his own account of the controversy and support of Spanheim's arguments against Amyraut.[42] Over the span of more than a decade, and in the face of much theological opposition, Amyraut articulated and explained his view on the extent of Christ's atonement, arguing its consistency with other tenets of Reformed theology and its distinction from Arminian views.

Amyraut was charged with serious doctrinal error at the national Synods of Alençon (1637), Charenton (1644–1645), and Loudon (1659). However, Amyraut and the other Saumur theologians received some support early on, and in each of these synods the charges against them were not upheld. One of the most important questions was whether Amyraut's teaching contradicted the Reformed confessions. The Canons of Dort (1619) predated Amyraut's first publication on the subject by fifteen years. But other earlier versions of unlimited or universal atonement existed and were developing at the time. The final committee at the Synod of Dort apparently modified some of the proposed language on the extent of the atonement to have enough ambiguity for those holding these positions to sign the Canons.[43] The later Amyraldians argued that their teaching was consistent with the respective articles in the Canons, and several scholars have documented that Amyraldianism and its hypothetical universalist counterparts did not go against the Canons of Dort.[44] Richard Muller further notes that the debates on the extent of the

---

40.   Allen, *Extent*, 166–72; J. Mark Beach, *Christ and the Covenant: Francis Turretin's Federal Theology as a Defense of the Doctrine of Grace* (Göttingen: Vandenhoeck & Ruprecht, 2007), 224–43. See Francis Turretin, *Institutes of Elenctic Theology*, 3 vols., ed. J. T. Dennison, trans. G. M. Giger (Phillipsburg, NJ: P&R, 1994), 2:458–59 [14.14.9].

41.   Moïse Amyraut, *Specimen animadversionum in Exercitationes de gratia universali* (Saumur: Lesnier, 1648). Initially Spanheim prepared disputation theses in 1644, which led to Amyraut's response, "Doctrinae de Gratia Universali, ut ab Orthodoxis Explicatur, Defensio," in *Dissertationes theologicae quatuor: de oeconomia trium personarum, de jure dei in creaturas, doctrinae de gratia particulari defensio, doctrinae de gratia universali defensio* (Saumur: Desbordes, 1645). Spanheim then produced a 2,600-page work, *Exercitationes de Gratia Universali* (Leiden, 1646), to which Amyraut's "sample" responded. Both Amyraut and Spanheim included lengthy historical surveys on the doctrines related to the atonement and universal grace.

42.   Pierre du Moulin, *Esclairissement des controverses Salmunennes* (Leyden, 1648); *De Mosis Amyraldi adversus Endencum Spanhemium libro judicium* (Rotterdam, 1649).

43.   Allen, *Extent*, 150–51.

44.   Crisp, *Deviant Calvinism*, 178–81; Muller, "Divine Covenants," 15; J. V. Fesko, *The Theology of the Westminster Standards: Historical Context and Theological Insights* (Wheaton, IL: Crossway, 2014), 189–203; Jonathan Moore, "The Extent of the Atonement: English Hypothetical Universalism versus Particular Redemption," in *Drawn into Controversie*, eds. Michael A. G. Haykin and Mark Johns (Göttingen: Vandenhoeck & Ruprecht, 2011), 144–48; Stephen Strehle, "The Extent of the Atonement and the Synod of Dort," *Westminster Theological Journal* 51, no. 1 (1989): 1–23; Allen,

atonement differed in kind from the previous debates with the Arminian Remonstrants. The debates surrounding Amyraut's theology had the potential to reach confessional status, but they never did, and therefore "his theology also arguably fell within the boundaries established by the Gallican Confession and the Canons of Dort."[45]

While the Synod of Dort happened before Amyraut's time, the Westminster Assembly (1643–1649) was called almost a decade after the controversy first began and was held during the same timeframe as many of the debates and major publications. Sometimes it has been assumed or claimed that the Westminster Confessions ruled out universal views on the atonement, like Amyraut's.[46] However, several scholars have identified numerous theologians at the Westminster Assembly who were Amyraldian or hypothetical universalists of some kind, and they have demonstrated that the language on the extent of the atonement in the confessions allows for at least some versions of universal atonement.[47] The primary condemnation of Amyraut's teaching did not come from the French Reformed or the main confessions, but from

---

Extent, 153–54, 160. The relevant article in the Canons of Dort that deals with the scope of the atonement is 2.8—*Christ's Death and Human Redemption through It*: "For it was the entirely free plan and very gracious will and intention of God the Father that the enlivening and saving effectiveness of his Son's costly death should work itself out in all the elect, in order that God might grant justifying faith to them only and thereby lead them without fail to salvation. In other words, it was God's will that Christ through the blood of the cross (by which he confirmed the new covenant) should effectively redeem from every people, tribe, nation, and language all those and only those who were chosen from eternity to salvation and given to him by the Father" (*Our Faith: Ecumenical Creeds, Reformed Confessions, and Other Resources* [Grand Rapids: Faith Alive, 2013], 127).

45. Muller, "Diversity in the Reformed Tradition," 18. See also Richard A. Muller, "Arminius and the Reformed Tradition," *Westminster Theological Journal* 70, no. 1 (2008): 19–48; and Muller, *Post-Reformation Reformed Dogmatics*, 2:15, where Muller notes in the preface that one of his subthemes is to demonstrate the "placement of Salmurian theology *within* the boundaries of confessional orthodoxy."

46. For various views on the relationship of Amyraldism and the Westminster Standards see Lee Gattis, "Shades of Opinion with a Generic Calvinism: The Particular Redemption Debate at the Westminster Assembly," *Reformed Theological Review* 69, no. 2 (2010): 101–18; J. V. Fesko, *Westminster Standards*, 170, 200–205. Scholars who argue that the WCF excludes hypothetical universalism include A. Craig Troxel, "Amyraut 'at' the Assembly: The Westminster Confession of Faith and the Extent of the Atonement," *Presbyterion* 22, no. 1 (1996): 43–55; Robert Letham, *The Westminster Assembly: Reading Its Theology in Historical Context* (Phillipsburg, NJ: P&R, 2009), 176–82.

47. See Lynch, "Confessional Orthodoxy and Hypothetical Universalism: Another Look at the Westminster Confession of Faith," in *Beyond Calvin: Essays on the Diversity of the Reformed Tradition*, eds. Bradford Littlejohn and Jonathan Tomes (Lincoln, NE: The Davenant Trust, 2017), 127–48; "Richard Hooker and the Development of English Hypothetical Universalism," in *Richard Hooker and Reformed Orthodoxy*, eds. W. Bradford Littlejohn and Scott N. Kindred-Barnes (Göttingen: Vandenhoeck & Ruprecht, 2017), 273–93; Allen, *Extent*, 204, 238; Muller, "Diversity in the Reformed Tradition," 23–25; "Cameron and Covenant Theology," 36–38; Lee Gatiss, "A Deceptive Clarity? Particular Redemption in the Westminster Standards," *Reformed Theological Review* 69, no. 3 (2010): 194; Their lists of those holding to universal atonement views include Davenant, Baxter, Bunyan, Charnock, Calamy, Preston, Hall, Howe, Hooker, and Henry. Allen also considers William Twisse (AD 1578–1646), the prolocutor and opening preacher of the Westminster Assembly, as a hypothetical universalist (244).

the Swiss Reformed in the *Geneva Theses* (1649) and the *Formula Consensus Helvetica* (1675), of which Francis Turretin was a contributing author.[48] In none of these cases was the view ever declared heretical or outside the bounds of orthodoxy. The Amyraldian view was opposed and censured, but remained within the confessional bounds and belonged to the diversity within the Reformed tradition.[49]

AMYRALDIANISM AND HYPOTHETICAL UNIVERSALISM

Amyraut's theology on the extent of the atonement was only one of several that expressed a universal aspect. The view that has become known as Amyraldism or Amyraldianism is sometimes equated with the term "hypothetical universalism."[50] However, Amyraldianism was only one form of the views developing during the seventeenth century that could be labeled "hypothetical universalism." And it was not the first nor the most typical version.[51] Although it became common to equate the views of those like John Davenant, James Ussher, Richard Baxter, and others with Amyraldianism, historically

---

48.   See Allen, *Extent,* 168; Djaballah, "Controversy on Universal Grace," 190–93. The most direct condemnation is from the *Formula Consensus Helvetica,* which does not even have "subordinate" confessional status in any Reformed community. Canon 6 of the *Formula Consensus Helvetica* (1675) states: "Wherefore, we can not agree with the opinion of those who teach: 1) that God, move by philanthropy, or a kind of special love for the fallen of the human race, did, in a kind conditioned willing, first moving of pity, as they call it, or inefficacious desire, determine the salvation of all, conditionally, i.e., if they would believe, 2) that he appointed Christ Mediator for all and each of the fallen; and 3) that, at length, certain ones whom he regarded, not simply as sinners in the first Adam, but as redeemed in the second Adam, he elected, that is, he determined graciously to bestow on these, in time, the saving gift of faith; and in this sole act election properly so called is complete. For these and all other similar teachings are in no way insignificant deviations from the proper teaching concerning divine election" (Martin I. Klauber, "The Helvetic Formula Consensus (1675): An Introduction and Translation," *Trinity Journal* 11, no. 1 [1990]: 103–23).

49.   Muller, "Diversity in the Reformed Tradition," 17–19; "Beyond Hypothetical Universalism," 197–200. Several other scholars draw the same conclusion. See, for example, Allen, *Extent,* 162; Thomas, *Extent of the Atonement Dilemma,* 164, 241. Gootjes gives the example of Jean Daillé being elected as moderator for the Synod of Loudon (1659) to demonstrate the allowance of supporters of Amyraut's theology among the French Reformed ("Calvin and Saumur," 214).

50.   David Wenkel surveys the use of the term Amyraldianism to conclude, "Current definitions of Amyraldianism acknowledge that it is a system larger than Moïse Amyraut, but for the most part, description is limited to Amyraut's life and his particular thought" ("Amyraldianism: Theological Criteria for Identification and Comparative Analysis," *Chafer Theological Seminary Journal* 11, no. 2 [2005]: 87–94). As an example of Amyraldianism as nearly equivalent to "hypothetical universalism," see Donald Macleod, "Amyraldus Redivivus: A Review Article," *Evangelical Quarterly* 81, no. 3 (2009): 210–29; *Christ Crucified: Understanding the Atonement* (Downers Grove, IL: InterVarsity Press, 2014), 124–27.

51.   See Muller, *Calvin and the Reformed Tradition,* 60–61, 76–78, 107–25, 126–60; "A Tale of Two Wills? Calvin and Amyraut on Ezekiel 18:23," *Calvin Theological Journal* 44, no. 2 (2009): 211–25; Crisp, *Deviant Calvinism,* 184–86; Lynch, "Hooker," 277; Djaballah, "Controversy on Universal Grace," 191; J. V. Fesko, "The Westminster Confession and Lapsarianism: Calvin and the Divines," in *The Westminster Confession into the 21st Century: Essays in Remembrance of the 350th Anniversary of the Westminster Assembly,* 3 vols., ed. J. L. Duncan III (Fearn, Scotland: Mentor, 2004), 2:477–525.

these are different views, particularly because many of these other "hypothetical universalists" rejected some of the distinctive elements of Amyraut's view, especially those that were particular to debates among the French Reformed.[52]

The label "hypothetical universalism" seems to have appeared first in the mid-seventeenth century as a pejorative term. The French Reformed theologian, Guillaume Rivet, one of the chief opponents of Amyraut's doctrine, referred to those associated with John Cameron and Moïse Amyraut as "les hypothétiques," or "the hypotheticals."[53] Additionally, by 1650 some of the Swiss Reformed were describing the Saumur theologians as "universalists."[54] The combination of these two references eventually led to the label, "hypothetical universalism." Use of this label is not commonly found during this time period, but developed in later history as a popular way for opponents of Amyraut and other Saumur theologians to denigrate them.[55] It likewise became the term to refer to other versions of theology which claimed that Christ made a satisfaction for sin on behalf of all human beings such that if all believed, all would be saved. The more common terms used during the seventeenth century to refer to the various forms of hypothetical universalism were "universal redemption" and "universal grace."[56]

The extent of the atonement was among the many debates that really did not arise within the Reformed tradition until the late-sixteenth and early-seventeenth century. Multiple views on the question already existed because previous exegetes had to explain the biblical passages which say that Christ died for the whole world along with the passages that also indicate a limitation

---

52. See, for example, Allen, *Extent*, 252; Jonathan D. Moore, *English Hypothetical Universalism: John Preston and the Softening of Reformed Theology* (Grand Rapids: Eerdmans, 2007), 217; "English Hypothetical Universalism," 124–61; Ian Hamilton, "Amyraldianism: Is It Modified Calvinism?," in *Confessing Our Hope: Essays Celebrating the Life and Ministry of Morton H. Smith*, eds. J. A. Pipa Jr. and C. N. Wilborn (Taylors, SC: Southern Presbyterian Press, 2004), 71–92.

53. Lynch, "Hooker," 276; Allen, *Extent*, 94. On the probable origin of the term, see Van Stam, *Controversy*, 277–78. Van Stam identifies a letter by Rivet in July 1645 as the first instance of this term. Lynch observes that the term became an epithet for the Salmurian School's teaching on the extent of the atonement "a half year after the national synod of Charenton" (1644).

54. Lynch, "Hooker," 276; Allen, *Extent*, 94. On the alternative term "Salmurianism," see Martin Klauber, *Between Reformed Scholasticism*, 26, and Wenkel, "Amyraldianism," 91.

55. Michael Lynch, "Early Modern Hypothetical Universalism: Reflections on the *Status Quaestionis* and Modern Scholarship" (presentation, Junius Institute at Meeter Center, Grand Rapids, Michigan, September 12, 2014). Lynch identifies examples of significant eighteenth- and nineteenth-century theological textbooks that categorized the "universalistae hypothetici" with the Amyraldians as Johann Lorenz von Mosheim, *Institutionum Historae Ecclesiasticae: Antiquae et Recentioris* (Helmstedt: Christianus Fridericus Weygand, 1755), 966–67; and William Cunningham, *Historical Theology: A Review of the Principal Doctrinal Discussions in the Christian Church since the Apostolic Age*, 2 vols. (1863; repr., London: Banner of Truth, 1960), 2:328.

56. Lynch, "Hooker," 278–79. In his works on non-Amyraldian forms of hypothetical universalism, Lynch identifies that the language of "universal redemption" can be found among Arminian, Reformed, Lutheran, and other theologians.

on those who benefit from Christ's death.[57] Neither the Amyraldians nor the Arminians were the first to suggest universal or unlimited atonement. Various scholars have identified sixteenth-century Reformed theologians such as Johannes Oecolampadius, Girolamo Zanchi, Ulrich Zwingli, Martin Bucer, Wolfgang Musculus, Peter Martyr Vermigli, Heinrich Bullinger, Rudolf Gwalther, and Zacharias Ursinus as holding to forms of universal atonement.[58]

Richard Muller provides a helpful taxonomy on the variety of views on the extent of the atonement among the Reformed.[59] We can categorize these with the following labels and Muller's explanations:

1. Extent: simple statement of the traditional medieval sufficiency-efficiency formula

2. Simple hypothetical universalism: simple statement of intentional sufficiency for all

3. Typical hypothetical universalism: a prior, absolute divine decree to save the elect followed by a subsequent universal will to save all who believe

4. Amyraldian hypothetical universalism: a prior, conditional divine decree to save all who believe followed by a subsequent, absolute decree to save the elect only

5. Definite atonement with hypothetical sufficiency: intentional sufficiency for all if God had intended to save all

6. Definite atonement with mere sufficiency: intentional sufficiency and efficiency for the elect only with the distinction between the accomplishment and the application of Christ's satisfaction

7. Definite atonement with limited sufficiency: intentional sufficiency only for the elect

---

57. Muller, *Calvin and the Reformed Tradition*, 60. See also Allen, *Extent*, 96–133; Raymond A. Blacketer, "Definite Atonement in Historical Perspective," in *The Glory of the Atonement: Biblical, Historical and Practical Perspectives: Essays in Honor of Roger Nicole*, eds. Charles E. Hill and Frank A. James (Downers Grove, IL: InterVarsity Press, 2004), 307–17.

58. David Allen presents many of these in their own words in *Extent of the Atonement*, 96–133. See also Muller, "Beyond Hypothetical Universalism," 208; Richard Muller, "Divine Covenants," 36–38.

59. Muller, *Calvin and the Reformed Tradition*, 77n22. Muller refers to these as "distinct patterns of formulation." David Wenkel also seeks to synthesize a "hypothetical universal" view by "developing an objective and history-sensitive set of [five] core criteria to form the basis for a method of comparison and identification" in "Amyraldianism," 92–95.

Based on this taxonomy, it is accurate to say that Amyraut's view is a form of hypothetical universalism, but not all forms of hypothetical universalism are Amyraldian. The key distinctions among these views are with regard to *intention* and *application*.[60] No matter what one's position on the extent of the atonement, Reformed theologians generally agreed that the infinite value of Christ's death *could have been* sufficient for all sinners and that the *application* of Christ's death for salvation was only given to the elect.[61] Where they disagreed was on the question, "For whose sins did God *intend* for Christ to make an objectively sufficient satisfaction for sins?"[62] The way Amyraut answered this and similar questions distinguished his view from the prevailing Reformed view and other developing versions of hypothetical universalism.

AMYRAUT'S VIEW ON THE EXTENT OF THE ATONEMENT
Amyraut's main line of reasoning on the extent of the atonement can best be identified from portions of his fourteen-chapter, 195-page *Brief Treatise on Predestination* (1634).[63] While he continued to teach and publish on the subject of "universal grace" with regard to the atonement, this text serves as the foundation for his position and includes the key distinctives of his view. It is quite evident from this work that he held to nearly all the common Reformed positions.

The opening chapters of the *Brief Treatise* address the state of the question on predestination, why God created the world and humanity, and why God permitted the first sin by humans. In chapters 4, 5, 8, and 9, he clearly rejected Arminian views on free will, foreseen faith, and prevenient grace.[64] Amyraut upheld the "double consequences" view of original sin with its unavoidable transmission of corruption and misery to all and the inability to self-recover from this corrupted state.[65] He explained that because of the resulting moral

60. Muller, *Calvin and the Reformed Tradition*, 72, 77; Allen, *Extent*, 249.
61. Lynch, "Early Modern Hypothetical Universalism," 8, 17. See also Muller, *Calvin and the Reformed Tradition*, 61, 279.
62. Lynch, "Early Modern Hypothetical Universalism," 4. Lynch later summarizes the question as "whether God in Christ made a satisfaction for *all* people's sins or *only* the elect's sins" (17).
63. Moïse Amyraut, *Brief traitté de la prédestination et de ses principales dépendances* (Saumur: Lesnier and Desbordes, 1634). An English translation of this treatise is available in Matthew Harding, *Amyraut on Predestination: The First Published Translation from the French* (Norwich: Charenton Reformed Publishing, 2017), 55–159. Additional English translations are R. Lum, "Brief Treatise on Predestination and Its Dependent Principles: A Translation and Introduction" (PhD diss., Dallas Theological Seminary, 1985) and Matthew Harding, "A Critical Analysis of Moise Amyraut's Atonement Theory Based on a New and Critical Translation of 'A Brief Treatise on Predestination'" (PhD diss., Southwestern Baptist Theological Seminary, 2014), 183–314. See also the summaries in Djaballah, "Controversy on Universal Grace," 173–90; and Strehle, "Universal Grace," 348–49.
64. Amyraut, *Brief Traitte*, 32–33, 37–38, 111–18; Harding, *Amyraut*, 73–81, 117–20; Djaballah, "Controversy on Universal Grace," 175, 176.
65. Amyraut, *Brief Traitte*, 47–60, 90–101; Harding, *Amyraut*, 83–89, 107–12; Djaballah, "Controversy on Universal Grace," 176.

inability, the only possibility for humans to respond in faith is if the Holy Spirit enables them to believe.[66] He further articulated that only those whom God alone chose will be given this faith, and that all to whom God gives this special grace *will* respond in faith and be saved.[67] To utilize later terminology, Amyraut adhered to the concepts of "total depravity," "unconditional election," "irresistible or effectual grace," and "perseverance of the saints." Of course, where he differed was on the extent of the atonement.

Amyraut most directly addressed the doctrine for which he later gets named in chapters 6 through 9. In his chapter titled, "What Was God's Purpose for Sending His Son to the World?," Amyraut echoed much of the logic that had already been established from the time of Anselm. According to Amyraut, God eternally decreed to create humans in the manner he did, foresaw that they would sin and require satisfaction that they could not provide themselves, and then Christ would "take the punishment of our offenses equal to their demerit, and by this means, to satisfy, by his infinite worth, God's perfect justice," and "to procure the salvation of the human race."[68] Few would take exception with these statements.

Amyraut began to depart from the prevailing view in the Reformed camp with chapter 7, "What Is the Nature of the Decree by Which God Has Ordained to Accomplish This Purpose, Both in Regard to Its Extent and for the Condition on Which It Depends?" Here Amyraut linked the universal misery of humanity with the desire for God to send the Redeemer to rescue them from that misery. He reasoned:

> And since they are equally still his creatures, the grace of redemption he offered to them and obtained for them must also be equal[69] and universal, on the condition that they find themselves equally disposed to receive it. . . . The sacrifice he offered for the propitiation of their offenses was equally for all; and the salvation that he received from his Father to communicate to humanity through the sanctification of the Spirit, and the glorification of the body, is intended equally for all, provided, I say, that the necessary disposition to receive it is also equal.[70]

This statement is a prime example of Amyraut's "universal grace" with its "hypothetical" condition. While God intended the grace of redemption

66. Amyraut, *Brief Traitte*, 72–76; Harding, *Amyraut*, 95–98.
67. Amyraut, *Brief Traitte*, 80–86, 131–46; Harding, *Amyraut*, 101–5, 127–34.
68. Amyraut, *Brief Treatise*, 72–73; Harding, *Amyraut*, 96.
69. At the requirement of some of the early French synods, Amyraut removed the words "equal" and "equally" in later editions of this work. See Jean Aymon, *Tout les Synodes Nationaux* (Netherlands: Chez Charles Delo, 1710), 2:575–76; John Quick, *Synodicon in Gallia Reformata: Or, the Acts, Decisions, Decrees and Canons of the Seven Last National Councils of the Reformed Churches in France,* 2 vols. (London: J. Richardson, 1692), 2:354–57, 2:573–74. See also Harding, *Amyraut*, 99.
70. Amyraut, *Brief Treatise*, 77–78; Harding, *Amyraut*, 99–100.

universally for all and the atonement to be equally for all, the condition exists
that they have "the necessary disposition to receive" the salvation intended,
purchased, and provided at the cross.

In Amyraut's view, God's goodness and compassion extends to all who
are in misery, which he established is, in fact, all humanity. Therefore, God's
grace to save them through the sacrificial propitiation of Christ's death is
presented to all universally and with "not even a single person excluded by
the will of God from the salvation that he has acquired for the human race."[71]
Yet the *application* of this saving grace is only received "provided that one
takes advantage of the testimonies of the mercy that God has given to him."[72]

Numerous times throughout this section Amyraut reiterates that God
intended this saving grace for all humanity, but the "principle condition" must
still be met that "one does not show oneself to be unworthy" or "not neglect
the mercy of God."[73] Amyraut even concluded this chapter by stating:

> God's grace is universal and presented to all humanity. But if you consider
> the condition that is inescapably appointed, which is to believe in his Son,
> you will find . . . this love does not exceed the following limit, to give
> salvation to humanity provided that they do not refuse it. If they refuse it,
> he deprives them of hope and by their own unbelief they aggravate their
> condemnation.[74]

This is an important element that distinguishes Amyraut's view from
Arminian or Calvinist views on the extent of the atonement. God intended
that Christ's life and death would atone for the sins of every human, but
included the condition that they believe in the Son, otherwise "the grace of
salvation universal and common to all human beings" would be "entirely inefficacious without the fulfillment of the condition."[75] This way Amyraut can
maintain God's universal goodness such that he does not turn anyone away
who would come to him, since their sins would have been atoned for at the
cross, while also still adhering that salvation is only for those who trust in
Jesus because they were elected before the creation of the world.

Further exploration of Amyraut's reasoning demonstrates how Amyraldian
hypothetical universalism differs from other forms of hypothetical universalism. Amyraut's contemporaries identified that his view on the extent of the
atonement was very reminiscent of John Cameron's, especially with its distinc-

---

71. Amyraut, *Brief Treatise*, 80; Harding, *Amyraut*, 101.
72. Amyraut, *Brief Treatise*, 80–89; Harding, *Amyraut*, 101–6. See also the summary analysis in Djaballah,
     "Controversy on Universal Grace," 183; and Nicole, *Amyraut: A Bibliography*, 3, 4.
73. Amyraut, *Brief Treatise*, 82, 84, 85; Harding, *Amyraut*, 103, 104, 105.
74. Amyraut, *Brief Treatise*, 89; Harding, *Amyraut*, 106.
75. Amyraut, *Brief Treatise*, 89; Harding, *Amyraut*, 106. See also Amyraut, *Brief Treatise*, 66, 68, 70, 75–
     76, 104.

tive elements.[76] The three main unique features that distinguish Amyraut's own view are (1) the order of divine decrees, (2) a twofold will of God, and (3) a threefold covenant.

ORDER OF DECREES

Some scholars have observed that the primary distinctive of Amyraut's (and Cameron's) view on the extent of the atonement is their ordering of the logical decrees by God before creation.[77] The more common views in the seventeenth century regarding the order of decrees were supralapsarianism and infralapsarianism. The order of decrees for these views can be summarized in the following way:

Supralapsarianism (Election Before the Fall)	Infralapsarianism (Election After the Fall)
Elect some and condemn others	Create free human beings
Create the elect and the reprobate	Permit the fall
Permit the fall	Elect some and leave others condemned
Provide salvation for the elect through Christ's death	Provide salvation for the elect through Christ's death

Supralapsarianism orders the eternal decrees of election, creation, fall, and salvation such that God's unconditional decision of who to save came *before* his decision to permit the fall. Infralapsarianism orders the eternal decrees of creation, fall, election, and salvation such that God's unconditional decision of who to save came *after* his decision to permit the fall. The infralapsarianism view seems to be the one expressed in the Canons of Dort, although the Synod of Dort did not explicitly reject those who held to a supralapsarian position.[78] English theologians such as John Davenant "conceived of hypothetical universalism as a doctrine that sits within a conventional infralapsarian scheme."[79] Amyraut's view, however, differed.

---

76. Gootjes provides a helpful delineation of the Saumur doctrine of universal grace from Cameron to Amyraut and beyond in "Claude Pajon (1626–1685) and the Academy of Saumur" (PhD diss., Calvin Theological Seminary, 2012); "Pajon and the Academy of Saumur," 29–33. See also Stephen Strehle, "Universal Grace," 345–48; Allen, *Extent*, 163; Muller, "Beyond Hypothetical Universalism," 197, 199.

77. For example, Djaballah, "Controversy on Universal Grace," 191; Thomas, *Extent of the Atonement Dilemma*, 203.

78. *Our Faith*, 120. The relevant article is 1.7: "Before the foundation of the world, by sheer grace, according to the free good pleasure of his will, [God] chose in Christ to salvation a definite number of particular people out of the entire human race which had fallen by its own fault from its original innocence into sin and ruin" (*Our Faith*, 120).

79. Crisp, *Deviant Calvinism*, 189.

In both supralapsarianism and infralapsarianism, the logical decree of election comes *before* the decree of salvation. The distinctive for Amyraut is that the logical decree of election comes *after* the decree of salvation. Although Amyraut does not specifically delineate his order of decrees in his writings, his opponent Frederic Spanheim provided a helpful and accurate summary.[80] Amyraut held that logically following the decree to permit the fall, God decreed to send the Son to die for all humanity, making salvation possible for all universally.[81] The consequent decree followed that since God foreknew that humanity would reject this provision for salvation, he willed to elect some whom he would save by granting them in the future the necessary effectual grace through the Spirit.[82] When we add the Amyraldian view to the more common seventeenth-century views on the order of eternal decrees, then a summary can be portrayed in the following way:

Supralapsarianism (Before the Fall)	Infralapsarianism (After the Fall)	Amyraldianism
Elect some and condemn others	Create free humans	Create free humans
Create the elect and the reprobate	Permit the fall	Permit the fall
Permit the fall	Elect some and leave others condemned	Provide salvation for all through Christ's death
Provide salvation for the elect through Christ's death	Provide salvation for the elect through Christ's death	Elect some to receive effectual grace

This unique ordering of decrees necessitated that Amyraut identify and specify how these decrees differed from one another. Muller states: "to clarify his position, Amyraut argued that God's will to save all who would believe was an *antecedent hypothetical* divine decree, standing logically prior in God to a *consequent, absolute,* and infralapsarian decree to save the elect."[83]

These final two divine decrees did not have the same intent or outcome as each other. The decree to provide salvation was hypothetical, and therefore

---

80. Frederic Spanheim, *Exercitationes de gratia universali* (Leyden, 1646), 683–84. Since Amyraut's view follows Cameron, see also John Cameron, *Ioannis Cameronis Scoto Britanni Theologi Eximij [Ta sōzomena] sive Opera partim ab auctore ipso edita*, ed. Frederic Spanheim (Geneva: Jacob Chouet, 1642), 529.

81. It is important to recognize that these pre-creation decrees are logical and not sequential or chronological. Amyraut emphatically denies a sequential view of the divine decrees. See Clifford, *Calvinus: Authentic Calvinism: A Clarification* (Norwich: Charenton Reformed Publishing, 1996), 15, 29.

82. See also Crisp, *Deviant Calvinism*, 188–89; *God Incarnate: Explorations in Christology* (London: T&T Clark, 2009), 44.

83. Muller, "Beyond Hypothetical Universalism," 205.

would only result if the condition to believe was met. The decree to elect, however, was absolute, and would definitively result in salvation for those whom God had chosen. Amyraut's reasoning for the difference in these decrees connects to the second distinctive feature of Amyraut's view.

TWOFOLD DIVINE WILL

Amyraut made the distinction that the prior logical decree of salvation was conditional (or hypothetical) as an expression of God's "revealed" will, whereas the consequent, absolute decree to save the elect was according to God's "secret or hidden" will.[84] Djaballah comments that the "bifurcation of God's will (revealed and secret) is the key to understanding Amyraut's doctrine of predestination and atonement."[85] Again Amyraut's view on the distinction within the divine will is similar to his mentor, John Cameron.[86] This has sometimes resulted in Amyraut being characterized as teaching two wills in God. However, he maintained that there is a single divine will with two distinctions. This "twofold will" of God distinguishes between his revealed, universal will to save all humans upon the condition of faith, and his absolute, unconditional, irresistible will which leads people to that necessary faith.[87] Amyraut contended: "If they do not believe, He does not desire it. This will to make the grace of salvation universal and common to all men is in this way conditional that without the accomplishing of the condition, is entirely ineffectual."[88]

This is Amyraut's way to address the biblical texts such as Ezekiel 18:23, 1 Timothy 2:4, and 2 Peter 3:9, which reveal God's universal desire for all humans to be saved while still also holding to Reformed doctrines of unconditional election and effectual grace. While others similarly held to a differentiation between God's revealed and hidden will, the uniqueness for Amyraut was that he used this to explain God's intention that Christ's death universally provided salvation for all on the condition of faith.

THREEFOLD COVENANT

The third distinctive, and closely related, feature of Amyraut's view is his articulation of covenant. Technically speaking, Amyraldiansim is based on a

---

84. Amyraut, *Brief Traitte*, 131–38; Harding, *Amyraut*, 127–30.

85. Amar Djaballah, "Controversy," 190.

86. Strehle, "Universal Grace," 346. Strehle notes that Cameron proposed "a dichotomy in the divine will, between God's conditional and unconditional will." Muller observes that Amyraut modified and supplemented "Calvin's argument with a concept of two wills in God—a scholastic distinction not found in Calvin's reading of the text and related, probably, to Amyraut's own training under John Cameron" ("A Tale of Two Wills: Calvin and Amyraut on Ezekiel 18:23," *Calvin Theological Journal* 44 [2009]: 224).

87. Amyraut, *Breif Traitte*, 144. Amyraut explained that in Scripture God reveals two ways of "willing" something, though seemingly paradoxical. One will simply makes its desire known (as in God's revealed will), while the other type of will effectively provides the necessary means to make its desire actual. See further analyses in Muller, "Two Wills," 211–25; Strehle, "Universal Grace," 348; Allen, *Extent*, 164.

88. Amyraut, *Brief Treatise*, 78.

specific view of covenant theology.[89] Again, Cameron's earliest writings laid the groundwork for Amyraut's development of a threefold covenant. Similar to the way they articulated the order of decrees, the Saumur theologians used the language of primary, antecedent, and conditional covenants.[90] Cameron had added to the traditional Reformed covenant theology another subservient covenant.[91] This threefold covenant structure included (1) the covenant of nature between God and Adam that required obedience to the divine order, (2) the covenant of law between God and Israel that required obedience to the law of Moses, and (3) the covenant of grace between God and all humanity that requires faith in Christ. Each of these covenants has conditions that must be met, making them "hypothetical" rather than absolute.

For Amyraut, Jesus died to put into effect the covenant of grace, which is hypothetical in the sense that all may be saved *if* they obey the covenant stipulation to believe in Christ. Amyraut further separated the "covenant of grace" into two parts. The first part of the covenant of grace is universal and conditional. The second part of the covenant of grace is particular in that God not only requires faith and repentance, but also grants the grace to create that necessary faith and repentance.[92] This position on the threefold covenant allowed Amyraut to affirm that all humanity is under the covenant of grace such that God intended Christ's death to be for all without exception, while still also maintaining that only those who fulfill the conditions of this "hypothetical covenant" will actually receive salvation. Other forms of hypothetical universalism did not include this unique explanation of a threefold covenant.

THE LEGACY OF AMYRALDIANISM

Both the Amyraldian and the English versions of hypothetical universalism spread at the end of the seventeenth century. For the Amyraldian versions,

---

89. Gootjes, "Pajon and the Academy of Saumur," 28; Strehle, "Universal Grace," 348; Allen, *Extent*, 164; Armstrong, *Calvin and the Amyraut Heresy*, 47–59.

90. Amyraut was similar to other covenant theologians of his day by making the distinction between "absolute" covenants with unconditional guarantees of blessing (e.g., Noahic) and "hypothetical" covenants that conditioned blessing upon human obedience (e.g., Mosaic). An absolute covenant is what God determined by his pure will and for his good pleasure, and the conditional covenant of salvation is what God grants to all in Christ's death on the condition of faith (*Brief Treatise*, 131–47). See also the observations by Djaballah, "Controversy on Universal Grace," 176, 185.

91. Cameron maintained that a primary, conditional covenant proceeded from the antecedent love of God, and a secondary, absolute, and consequent covenant of God fulfills the former's condition, bringing about the blessings offered in the former conditional promises. See John Cameron, "Certain Theses, or Positions of Learned John Cameron, concerning the Threefold Covenant of God with Man," in *The True Bounds of Christian Freedome*, ed. Samuel Bolton (London: Golden-Lion in Paul's Church-yard, 1656), 353–401.

92. Bird offers a brief summary: "The intracovenant of universal grace required the condition of faith in order to be effective, while the intracovenant of particular grace did not simply call for faith; rather, in God's good pleasure, he created faith in the elect" (*Evangelical Theology*, 2nd ed. [Grand Rapids: Zondervan, 2020], 485).

the revocation of the Edict of Nantes in 1685 compelled many French Protestants to flee to other locations throughout Europe, which contributed to the spread of Amyraut's view in a way that differed from the way the views of Davenant and Ussher spread.[93] In many cases, these various versions of hypothetical universal atonement were not received with favor, especially among the Reformed communities influenced by theologians like Francis Turretin.[94] French theologians after Amyraut, such as Claude Pajon, modified elements of Amyraut's view, as Amyraut had done with Cameron's view.[95] Likewise, opponents of Amyraut's view sometimes conflated it with Arminian unlimited atonement or with other versions of hypothetical universalism, causing confusion about the use of the term "Amyraldianism."

Over the centuries, numerous theologians have expressed views similar to that of Amyraut's hypothetical universal atonement without necessarily including the distinctive elements of his own theology. Some have explicitly referred to their view as Amyraldianism, while others have not. There are likely very few, if any, examples of those who affirmed all of Amyraut's distinctives or who contended to be faithfully consistent with him the way Amyraut had claimed to be with John Calvin. Some of the most recognizable names among those considered to hold forms of hypothetical universalism include John Bunyan, Jonathan Edwards, David Brainerd, Andrew Fuller, J. C. Ryle, D. Martyn Lloyd-Jones, Millard Erickson, and Bruce Demarest.[96] Other scholars, of course, argue about the legitimacy of certain historical figures being included in these lists, especially where they do not identify themselves this way. Undoubtedly many unnamed people have held to a version of Amyraldianism whether they would articulate it that way or not.

CONCLUSION

Moïse Amyraut contributed to the development of theology on the extent of the atonement in unique and profound ways. The label "Amyraldianism" reveals the level of fame and importance he had. In the face of much theological opposition from fellow Reformed theologians and amidst the turbulence of religious conflicts in France, Amyraut championed a view from the Saumur

---

93. See Gootjes, *Pajon and the Academy of Saumur*, 34; "John Cameron and the French Universalist Tradition," in *The Theology of the French Reformed Church: From Henri IV to the Revocation of the Edict of Nantes*, ed. Martin I. Klauber (Grand Rapids: Reformation Heritage, 2014), 169–96; Allen, *Extent*, 296–97.

94. Allen, *Extent*, 167.

95. Gootjes, *Pajon and the Academy of Saumur*, 90–91; "Calvin and Saumur," 211–13. See also Klauber, *Between Reformed Scholasticism*, 20; Wenkel, "Amyraldianism," 92–94.

96. David Allen's very extensive list uses the label of "Classic/Moderate Calvinism." Throughout his work he also identifies the following as Calvinists who reject a strictly limited atonement: T. Cranmer, H. Latimer, M. Coverdale, J. Daillé, J. Preston, R. Baxter, E. Calamy, R. Vines, L. Seaman, S. Charnock, J. Howe, W. Bates, J. Humfrey, J. Truman, G. Swinnock, T. Chalmers, R. Wardlaw, A. Strong, N. Douty, C. Daniel, B. Ware (*Extent of the Atonement*). Clifford also names several Calvinists "expressing also a quasi-Amyraldian view of the Gospel" ("Amyraldian Soteriology"), 173.

Academy that God intended before creation that Christ's death would atone universally for the sins of all people on the condition that they receive it by faith, which they can only possess by the effectual grace of the Holy Spirit given to them by the unconditional sovereign election of God.

Amyraldianism emerged from within the Reformed tradition with the full intent to stay true to Calvinism and arguably Calvin's own views. It had many similarities and significant overlap with views developing in England prior to and during the time of Amyraut. The uniqueness of the view of Amyraut and the Saumur theologians includes their specific explanations of an ordering of the divine decrees that has the provision of salvation logically prior to election, a twofold distinction of the revealed and hidden will of God applied to the atonement, and a threefold covenant structure with the covenant of grace as partially hypothetical, since all may be saved if they meet the condition to believe in Christ, and as partially absolute, since God grants effectual grace to the elect to create the required faith. Amyraut and those holding similar positions on the extent of the atonement faced significant questioning, criticism, opposition, and censure, but Amyraldianism and its hypothetical counterparts were never determined to be heretical or officially outside the bounds of the Reformed confessions. Rather, the position that God intended Christ's death to atone for the sins of all humanity on the condition that they believe has long been an alternative position to both Calvinist limited atonement and Arminian unlimited atonement views.

CHAPTER EIGHT

D. B. KNOX

A Twentieth-Century Proponent of Hypothetical Universalism

Rory Shiner

Permit me to begin autobiographically. My first encounter with Calvinistic soteriology came through a full-throttled exposition of Romans 9. It was an event for which I was hopelessly unprepared. I was on a gap year travelling through Africa at the tender age of nineteen and was, on that Sunday, in a church in Lusaka, Zambia. I was horrified by what I heard, having never knowingly encountered anything remotely Calvinistic in my Christian upbringing. Like many who encounter Reformed theology for the first time, I mustered all the limited theological arsenal at my disposal to ward off this threat to human freedom, moral agency, and God's character. My supplies ran out at an alarming rate. Eventually, through a series of animated discussions, personal Bible studies, and reading Eugene Palmer's *The Five Points of Calvinism*, I admitted defeat and embraced all five petals of the Reformed flower.

Returning to Perth, Western Australia, I went to university and joined the Christian Union. It was 1994. There I discovered the Reformed tradition to be alive and kicking, but in a different key. Less Lloyd-Jones, more John Stott; less covenantal theology, more biblical theology; less doctrine, more exegesis. There was also, to my surprise, an ambivalent attitude to the *limited atonement* of the TULIP acronym. Limited atonement, I had been led to believe, was a nonnegotiable, necessary corollary of the whole system. But here was a four-point Calvinism, in an otherwise robustly Reformed and theologically conservative context.

This rejection of limited atonement is, it turns out, a common feature on the Australian Reformed landscape. And it can be traced fairly directly to the influence of Australian theologian D. B. Knox (1916–1994).

Knox, principal of Moore College, Sydney, from 1959 to 1985, rejected limited atonement and taught his version of "Amyraldianism" or hypothetical universalism to generations of students. These students in turn transmitted the tradition orally, through preaching and instruction, to churches and student ministries across Australia. It was this phase of the *paradosis* I encountered in Perth in 1994.

Then, from the year 2000, the tradition took a written form through the publication of Knox's *Selected Works*. From this point on, the *dramatis personae* of evangelical debates about the atonement began to include posthumous appearances from D. B. Knox. In this phase, Knox's position became one which warranted respect, though it was increasingly cited as an example of friendly fire: a well-meaning but faulty take on the issue, coming from within the Reformed family.

It is this story I wish to tell here. What was the nature and shape of Knox's position? Against which background did it emerge? How was it transmitted, and where can its influence be seen and felt?

To anticipate my conclusion, I will argue that Knox's position on the extent of the atonement is a cogent one, best understood against the background of a distinctively Australian biblical theology which emerged mid-century. Its transmission has occurred in two distinct phases: an oral phase in which it was widely embraced by those who taught it, and a written phase in which it was more often cited in respectful disagreement. It was first taught by Knox in the mid-twentieth century to head off what he perceived as a threat to the rebirth of Reformed theology; in the early decades of the twenty-first century his position has itself been cast as a threat to the full flowering of that same theology.

WHO WAS D. B. KNOX?

D. B. Knox was the principal of Sydney's Moore College from 1959 to 1985. He has been described as the father of modern Sydney Anglicanism. From his position at Moore he taught and profoundly shaped several generations of Sydney Anglican clergy, biblical scholars, and Christian leaders both within and beyond the Anglican tradition.

He was born in 1916 in Adelaide, South Australia, the son of well-known Anglican rector David Knox. The family moved to Sydney in 1922, where he attended Knox Grammar School before studying Greek and Latin at Sydney University. Though a convinced evangelical, he did not join the then newly formed Evangelical Union, preferring to start an apologetics group with a small circle of friends.[1] He was by nature independent and contrarian.

---

1.   Donald Robinson, "David Broughton Knox: An Appreciation," in *God Who Is Rich in Mercy: Essays Presented to D. B. Knox*, eds. Peter T. O'Brien and David Peterson (Homebush West: Lancer, 1986), xi–xiii, xi.

In 1939 Knox travelled to England to study theology at St John's College, Highbury. He was ordained by the Bishop of Ely in 1941 and served a curacy at St. Andrew the Less in Cambridge. There he formed a lifelong friendship with T. H. L. Parker. Parker was to dedicate his first book on Calvin to Knox.[2]

At Cambridge he began the Theological Tripos. He was greatly impressed by C. H. Dodd, who was then conducting his New Testament seminars. But war interrupted study. In 1943 he enlisted as a chaplain in the Royal Navy, a position in which he served until he was discharged in 1947 and returned to Australia.

While in London and Cambridge, Knox had come into close contact with the men who formed (in 1938) the Biblical Research Committee. Through this circle Knox would attend the 1941 conference at Kingham Hill School, Oxfordshire. This conference began the Tyndale Fellowship, eventually resulting in the establishment of Tyndale House, Cambridge, and the publication of the *New Bible Dictionary*. This movement represented the efforts of postwar evangelicals to develop a scholarly approach to Scripture, and to distance themselves from the anti-intellectualism they perceived to be rife in evangelical culture.

Returning to England for the years 1951 to 1953, Knox went on to complete a DPhil at Oxford on the doctrine of faith in the reign of Henry VIII. He returned to Moore College in 1954 and taught there continually until his retirement in 1985. In retirement he went to South Africa to establish George Whitefield College, where he served as principal from 1989 until 1992. He died in Sydney in 1994.

POSTWAR CALVINISM IN AUSTRALIA

Reformed theology experienced a significant revival in Australia in the postwar period. The *Reformed Theological Review* (founded in 1942) became the journal of Calvinistic ecumenism, the place where Presbyterians and Anglicans joined hands in exploring Reformed theology.[3] Presbyterian Calvinists gathered strength in Victoria, and the Reformed Theological College in Geelong was founded in 1954. The cause received a boost from the postwar migration of Dutch Calvinists to Australia.

The place of Calvin's theology at Moore College was only emerging at this time. Archbishop Marcus Loane (1911–2009), a student at Moore in the 1930s, recalled that Calvin's *Institutes* were "virtually *terra incognita*."[4] He did not know a single Moore College student or Sydney cleric who had read Calvin.

T. C. Hammond, possibly the most distinguished conservative evangelical scholar in the Anglican world at that time, came out from Ireland to be

2.   Robinson, "David Broughton Knox," xiii.
3.   Rowland S. Ward, "Aspects of the Revival of Calvinism in Australia, 1938–1978," *Church Heritage* 16, no. 2 (2009): 94–200.
4.   Marcia Cameron, *An Enigmatic Life: David Broughton Knox, Father of Contemporary Sydney Anglicanism* (Brunswick East: Acorn, 2006), 135.

principal of Moore College in 1936. Hammond's theological idealism shaped the theological ethos of the diocese. It was "a structured Anglican Evangelical College" rather than what would become in the 1960s "a more broadly based Reformed College."[5] The basic texts used by Hammond, W. H. Griffith Thomas's *The Principles of Theology* (1930) and later E. J. Bicknell's *The Thirty-Nine Articles of Religion* (1940), tied students to a close examination of the Anglican Church's theological formularies, understood in their most Protestant terms. In order to ward off critique of penal substitution from without evangelicalism, and to correct poor accounts from within, Hammond focused on the *quality* of Christ's personhood rather than the *quantity* of his suffering. Hammond says, "The work of Christ is not merely a substitute for an equivalent unfulfilled work of the sinner. It has in itself an intrinsic value. . . . The value of Christ's sacrifice consisted in the infinite worth of his person."[6]

Hammond's theology of atonement was not one that lent itself to the language of limitation. This is important background to Knox's own formulation.

Knox began teaching at Moore in 1954 and became principal in 1959. Under him and his vice principal Donald Robinson (1922–2018), the College was to undergo a profound theological shift. Hammond's reading list was replaced by Gustav Aulén, B. B. Warfield, and John Calvin.[7] As a student at the time, Moore College lecturer William Lawton recalls people reading and discussing the work of Joachim Jeremias, Karl Barth, Emil Brunner, and Søren Kierkegaard. The effect was to move the college in a more Reformed (as opposed to specifically Anglican) direction. They left the white cliffs of Dover and ventured, theologically, to the continent.

The continent also ventured to Australia. The postwar migration of Dutch Calvinists to Sydney was an opportunity Knox embraced. Along with Lawton, Knox brought together a meeting of the Australian Reformed pastors at Moore College to set up what was called the Reformed Association. Their purpose was to "explore Calvinism as a common theology."[8] They went so far as to set up a college in the inner-city suburb of Leichhardt for men preparing for ministry in the Reformed or Free churches. Teaching and enrolment required signing off on the Synod of Dort, the Heidelberg Catechism, and the Westminster Confession.[9] It is very likely that this context provided the anvil against which Knox was to hammer out his own distinctive take on particular redemption, and the context in which he discerned limited atonement to be an Achilles' heel for Reformed theology.

5.   William Lawton, "'That Woman Jezebel'—Moore College after 25 Years," Moore College Library Lecture, Sydney, 1981, 3.
6.   T. C. Hammond, *In Understanding Be Men: A Handbook on Christian Doctrine for Non-Theological Students* (London: Inter-Varsity Fellowship, 1936), 154.
7.   Lawton, "That Woman Jezebel," 4.
8.   Cameron, *An Enigmatic Life*, 203.
9.   Cameron, *An Enigmatic Life*, 203–4.

This is the background to Knox's rejection of limited or particular atonement. The Sydney diocese and postwar British evangelicalism shaped him in the mild Simeonite Calvinism of that world. Hammond's idealism, with its patristic emphasis on the divinity of Christ and his sharing in our nature, is important background to Knox's own account of the atonement. And the engagement with contemporary continental theology raised the question of the extent of the atonement for Knox. It was in the context of this background, I submit, that Knox was required to grapple with, and ultimately to reject, the idea of a limited or definite atonement.

KNOX'S "SOME ASPECTS OF THE ATONEMENT"
The main written record of Knox's thought on the extent of the atonement is a paper titled "Some Aspects of the Atonement."[10] Undated and until 2000 unpublished, it was originally addressed to the Tyndale Fellowship of Australia. Two pieces of internal evidence point to a date in the late 1950s or early 1960s. First, the paper deals with the *Report of the Lambeth Conference of Anglican Bishops,* published in 1958, as if that report is of contemporary concern. Second, Knox hints at the paper's *Sitz im Leben* as he expresses his anxiety that the doctrine of limited atonement "introduces unscriptural concepts into the doctrine of God's relation to the world, and may prove an Achilles' heel for the revival of Reformed theology."[11]

In this statement Knox takes the revival of Reformed theology as an uncontroversial fact, perceiving limited atonement as a threat to its continued rise. His reference to "the writings of seventeenth century Calvinists and their modern successors" is likely a reference to the Dutch migrants with whom Knox was involved in the establishing of the Reformed College. This points to a date in the early 1960s.

The context, if correct, is also significant. In the first half of the paper (where Knox deals with the Lambeth report), he plays the part of an evangelical and Reformed Anglican, seeking to tie his communion to a more Reformed atonement theology in its eucharistic liturgy. In the second half, he is a Reformed and evangelical (and indeed evangelistic) theologian, seeking to liberate the wider Reformed world from a doctrine he judges to be theologically untenable, biblically unsupported, and evangelistically restrictive.

KNOX'S THEOLOGICAL CASE FOR HYPOTHETICAL UNIVERSALISM
Knox rejected limited atonement and put forward the case for an atonement universal in scope. It was a position that would become known (though not so labeled by him) as Knox's Amyraldianism. We will refer to it here (somewhat anachronistically) as Knox's hypothetical universalism. This was

10. D. B. Knox, "Some Aspects of the Atonement," in *D. Broughton Knox: Selected Works,* ed. Tony Payne, vol. 1, *The Doctrine of God* (Kingsford: Matthias, 2000), 253–66.
11. Knox, "Some Aspects of the Atonement," 266.

not his term but is a more felicitous label for the actual content of his position, as I hope to demonstrate.

Knox's position was framed against two explicit concerns: a concern for the successful rebirth of Reformed theology on the one hand, and a concern for evangelistic preaching on the other. As a Calvinist, he wanted to see the Reformed faith flourish, and perceived the early 1960s as a fertile moment. As an *evangelical* Calvinist, he wanted to see the lost saved. He was, for example, a firm supporter of the hugely successful 1959 Billy Graham Crusade in Australia—a project about which many others in the Reformed camp were more circumspect. It mattered to Knox that the preacher could present Christ's death to the audience (as Graham did) without qualification. He says, "*From the point of view of the preacher,* Christ has died for all his audience."[12] Knox wanted the resurgent postwar Calvinism to be evangelical, and to be evangelical, it needed to be evangelistic.

How then did Knox make his theological case? In the paper "Some Aspects of the Atonement," Knox's reasoning is sometimes elliptical and terse, reflecting the occasional nature of the paper itself. Nevertheless, four key theological weight-bearing pillars can be clearly identified. I label these the patristic, the soteriological, the confessional, and the biblical pillars.

First, the patristic pillar. Knox argues that Christ's atonement is coextensive with humanity because, in line with the patristic emphasis on the incarnation, all of Christ's work is coextensive with humanity. In Christ's incarnation, his perfect righteousness, his victory over Satan, and his bearing of the curse, Christ stands for all of humanity, and not the elect only.[13] It is an emphasis that was a mainstay of Knox's theology. In his 1982 book *The Everlasting God,* he puts it in these terms:

> Our Lord's obedience was unique and its effect was coextensive with humanity. . . . Our Lord bore every man's penalty, the punishment that every man deserves. It is impossible to conceive of the limitation of our Lord's work on the cross, as though he would have borne more suffering, more punishment had his merits been applied in the mind and purpose of God to more sinners. The atonement is not quantitative, as though God added up the sins of the elect and placed the penalty for these and these only on Jesus; but the atonement is qualitative. Our Lord experienced fully the penalty for sin.[14]

Atonement theology, in other words, must proceed from the person and nature of Christ.

12. Knox, "Some Aspects of the Atonement," 262. Italics original.
13. Knox, "Some Aspects of the Atonement," 260–61.
14. Knox, "One Lord, Jesus Christ," in D. B. Knox, *D. Broughton Knox Selected Works,* ed. Tony Payne, vol. 1, *The Doctrine of God* (Kingsford: Matthias, 2000), 109.

Second, Knox teases out a soteriological argument. God, he says, "in intending to reconcile the elect only" had chosen to "make all men reconcilable." In this, both Calvinists and Arminians are right in what they affirm, and wrong in what they deny. Arminians affirm that Christ made all men savable, and Calvinists that Christ saves the elect. But Arminian soteriology in effect denies that Christ saves anyone, the work of Christ merely making them in principle savable. Knox, however, also criticizes Calvinistic soteriology as "inclined to speak as though the atonement in no wise affects the savableness of any others."[15] This Knox denies. For him, it does not follow that Christ's effective salvation of the elect requires denying any benefit of Christ's death to the nonelect. On the contrary, "All men receive benefits from Christ's death. This is agreed. It should be further agreed that one of those benefits is savableness—which no fallen angel has received."[16]

Third, Knox argued that at least some significant Reformed confessional theology favors hypothetical universalism. The Church of England Catechism, for example, states that "Christ redeemed me, and all mankind."[17] For Knox, this is in harmony with the Synod of Dort's affirmation that he efficaciously redeemed only the elect.[18] That is, Dort limits the atonement at the point of application, not intention. He faults the Westminster Confession as having gone beyond the Synod of Dort and beyond Scripture in confining Christ's redemptive work *only* to the elect.[19] For Knox, if Reformed confessional theology did not univocally welcome his position, it at least made space for it.

Fourth, on the biblical front, Knox argues that limited atonement is a "textless doctrine" that constitutes a "fatal defect for any doctrine for which a place in Reformed Theology is sought."[20] Passages with wording that affirm an intentionality in Christ's death—such as Christ dying for his sheep, or purchasing the church with his own blood—do not imply that his death was only for them. Moreover, 2 Peter 2:1 represents something of a smoking gun. Here is a text where, Knox argues, the positive is in fact affirmed—namely, that apostates are among those whom God has in some sense purchased through atonement.[21]

Knox's formulation did not specifically draw on Amyraldus, nor was Knox self-consciously developing an Amyraldian position.[22] His shared with Amyraldus a penal substitutionary account of satisfaction characteristic of Reformed atonement theology, as well as the more distinctive view that "the

---

15. Knox, "Some Aspects of the Atonement," 261.
16. Knox, "Some Aspects of the Atonement," 261.
17. Knox, "Some Aspects of the Atonement," 262.
18. Knox, "Some Aspects of the Atonement," 262.
19. Knox, "Some Aspects of the Atonement," 263.
20. Knox, "Some Aspects of the Atonement," 263.
21. Knox, "Some Aspects of the Atonement," 263.
22. Knox had not read Amyraldus and was himself coy about the label. See discussion below.

decree of election is logically after the decree of atonement."[23] However, Amar Djaballah is right to say that Knox's formulation is, by shape and affinity, a species of British hypothetical universalism.[24]

This, then, is the shape of Knox's case for hypothetical universalism. The patristic emphasis on the incarnation prevents a limitation of Christ's work to the elect, but extends it to all of humanity. Reformed soteriology errs by assuming Christ's atonement has no impact on those who are, in the end, not saved. Reformed confessions, such as Dort and the Church of England Catechism, allow for hypothetical universalism. And the biblical witness does not limit the atonement to the elect, and in at least one case explicitly extends it beyond them.

KNOX AND CONTEMPORARY THEOLOGY

Knox has sometimes been accused of failing to bring his theology into conversation with other contemporary theologians. This may be a fair criticism of his overall corpus. However, the paper we are considering here evinces a reasonably wide range of theological reference: Karl Barth, B. B. Warfield, Eugene Palmer, and C. F. D. Moule all make it into the conversation.

Barth and Warfield are caught, Knox argues, on the horns of a dilemma. Knox rejects Warfield's contention that Christ's substitution for all logically entails universalism. Warfield argues that if Christ substituted for all, then logically all are saved. But, because all are not saved, Warfield is constrained to reject the premise that Christ substituted for all.[25] Barth, on the other hand, accepts the premise that Christ substituted for all, and at least leaves open the conclusion that all are indeed saved. For Knox, both Warfield and Barth are at fault for excluding paradox from the heart of atonement theology. Both Warfield and Barth's conclusions "prove too much" and exclude the paradox of a death that is simultaneously for all and salvific only for the elect. When Edwin Palmer makes a similar argument from substitution to affirm limited atonement, Knox dismissed the line of thinking as "pecuniary."[26] There is room in Knox's atonement theology for a degree of mystery, for an account of atonement that doesn't count out to the decimal point.

For historical conversation partners, Knox engaged John Owen, nineteenth-century Scottish theologian William Cunningham, and John Calvin himself.[27] In the latter he finds an ally. In the former two he finds fault. Owen comes in for particularly harsh treatment. Owen's notion that the decree of

---

23. Knox, "Some Aspects of the Atonement," 265.

24. Amar Djaballah, "Controversy on Universal Grace: A Historical Survey of Moïse Amyraut's Brief Traitté de La Predestination," in *From Heaven He Came and Sought Her: Definite Atonement in Historical, Biblical, Theological, and Pastoral Perspective*, eds. David Gibson and Jonathan Gibson (Wheaton, IL: Crossway, 2013), 165–99, 198.

25. Knox, "Some Aspects of the Atonement," 264.

26. Knox, "Some Aspects of the Atonement," 265.

27. Knox, "Some Aspects of the Atonement," 263.

redemption, if antecedent to the decree of election, is purposeless is a *non sequitur.* "This appears to be his only argument," says Knox. Not only is it a logical fallacy, it also "smacks of anthropocentrism (i.e., Arminianism)" for "God is glorified even in those who are perishing." William Cunningham is guilty of the same error.[28]

It is instructive to compare Knox with other then-contemporary evangelical atonement theologies. Almost at the same time Knox was defending hypothetical universalism, J. I. Packer published his famous defense of limited atonement as the preface to Banner of Truth's republication of Owen's *The Death of Death in the Death of Christ.* The revival of Reformed theology in the UK included a warm embrace of Puritan theology, especially through the circle around Martyn Lloyd-Jones, transmitted to at least some Anglicans through J. I. Packer. Meanwhile, in the US, the influence of the old Princeton theologians, J. Gresham Machen, and institutions such as Westminster Seminary ensured that Presbyterianism was a prominent shaper of the Reformed revival on that side of the Atlantic.

Australia was different. Knox, despite having a radical and iconoclastic attitude toward Anglicanism's liturgy and polity, was in his theology a true son of the Church of England. The more broadly Reformed and circumspect formularies of the Elizabethan Church were also Knox's. Neither Puritanism nor Protestant Scholasticism were significant sources for the theology emerging from Moore College in the 1950s and 1960s. Rather, patristic theology, the Anglican reformers, and modern theology were prominent and combined, above all, with a direct engagement with scriptural exegesis in the Cambridge exegetical tradition.

Knox concludes his paper with a clarion call: "Limited atonement as commonly propounded, introduces unscriptural concepts into the doctrine of God's relation to the world, and may prove an Achilles' heel for the revival of Reformed theology."[29]

The judgment is complete. Limited atonement is unbiblical, untheological, and a potential roadblock to the wider acceptance of Reformed theology. Such was Knox's assessment. It was an assessment which many in his sphere of influence would come to share.

RECEPTION AND INFLUENCE

Perhaps the most remarkable aspect of our story is the extent of Knox's influence. For the better part of three decades (from the 1960s to the 1980s) Knox's ideas were transmitted in the classroom, the pulpit, and through his students. A written account of his position on the extent of the atonement only became available to a wider audience when the undated Tyndale Fellowship paper of the early 1960s was published by Matthias Media in the

28.   Knox, "Some Aspects of the Atonement," 262.
29.   Knox, "Some Aspects of the Atonement," 266.

year 2000. Through his teaching, Knox's position became a widely accepted one in Australian Reformed thought. Then, as conservative evangelicals renewed their defenses of penal substitutionary atonement in the period roughly from 2005 to 2015, Knox's paper began to warrant critical interaction internationally.

The first, oral phase of transmission ran from roughly 1960 until Knox finished teaching at Moore in 1985. Glenn Davies (until recently archbishop of Sydney) recalls hearing Knox speak on Calvinism at Sydney University in 1969. Knox on that occasion described himself as a "four-and-a-half" point Calvinist.[30] New Testament scholar Paul Barnett—a student at Moore in the early 1960s—also recalls Knox to have been "a four-pointer." Evidently, both within the college and in other teaching contexts, Knox was commending and defending his position in Sydney.

In 1994 Glenn Davies wrote an unpublished conference paper titled "A Response to D. B. Knox's Critique of Limited Atonement."[31] Knox's position was well-enough known at that time to warrant a detailed response and (in this case) a refutation from the Westminster-seminary trained Davies. The Moore College library has a paper in its catalogue dated as 1970 and labeled "Radio Broadcast Transcript." It is the text of the second half of the Tyndale Fellowship paper. This indicates that Knox broadcast a version of the material on his radio show "The Protestant Faith."

In summary, Knox exploited various opportunities—in the classroom, on the radio, and in symposia—to commend his position of hypothetical universalism. He taught it repeatedly. Through these contexts, several generations of students were taught, and many embraced, his account.

It is worth noting, however, that Knox's teaching method was Socratic, and his custom was to provoke students to thought, often by arguing for minority positions. Alongside hypothetical universalism, Knox also disputed the imputation of Christ's righteousness, questioned whether the great commission referred to Christian water baptism, and argued for the subjective genitive understanding of "the faith of/in Jesus Christ." At the same time, Knox continued to encourage and employ faculty who disagreed with him on all of these matters. Knox was not so much concerned to pass on particular positions so much as to pass on a critical and somewhat adventurous approach to the task of theological thinking itself.

In popular discourse, Knox's position became known as his "Amyraldian" position. This was not his own nomenclature. In a letter to Archbishop Marcus Loane, Knox says, "I think it a little too definite to describe me as a

---

30. Glenn N. Davies, "Personal Reflections and Experiences," in *The Legacy of David Broughton Knox*, ed. Edward Loane (London: Latimer Trust, 2018), 129–34, 130.

31. Glenn N. Davies, "A Response to D. B. Knox's Critique of Limited Atonement" unpublished conference paper, 1994.

follower of Amyraldus. I have never read anything by Amyraldus; in fact, I don't think there is anything available in English by Amyraldus."[32]

Within the Tyndale Fellowship paper, Knox does not nominate a label. He understands himself to be within the historic mainstream of Reformed thought. Andrew Leslie has cogently argued that Knox's position is better understood as a form of British hypothetical universalism, genealogically connected with John Davenant (1572–1641). For Leslie, this is an explicitly Reformed hypothetical universalism, one rarely explicitly excluded by Reformed confessions.[33]

Phillip Jensen, the influential preacher and evangelist, accepted and taught Knox's position. Through his teaching ministry at the University of New South Wales, many students were taught a robustly evangelical and Reformed atonement theology, with a Knoxian twist. Jensen, whose influence was also significant in British evangelical circles, recruited a substantial number of men and women for full-time Christian ministry. These recruits went on to pastor churches, lead student ministries, and teach in theological colleges across Australia. Many of them inherited the Knoxian take as part of their catechism into Reformed faith, including those I encountered at university in Perth in 1994. By this means Knox's influence spread across Australian evangelicalism.

Robert Forsyth, later the bishop of North Sydney, also taught Knox's basic position across seventeen years of student ministry at Sydney University. He recalls no pushback on the issues in those years, reflecting perhaps the reach Knox's teaching has achieved in evangelical circles in Sydney.

PUBLICATION AND WIDER INFLUENCE

In the first two decades of the second millennium, conservative evangelicals returned to the theme of penal substitutionary atonement. On the one hand, challenges from emergent church theology to traditional penal substitutionary accounts of atonement pushed conservative evangelicals to restate this evangelical essential. And, on the other hand, the embrace of Calvinistic soteriology among the so-called "new Calvinists" (or the "Young, Restless, and Reformed") energized a conversation around Calvinistic soteriological categories.[34]

---

32. Typed note to Marcus Loane, D. B. Knox Archive, Samuel Marsden Archives, Moore College, Sydney, Box 16. F. I; cited in Andrew Leslie, "Was Broughton Knox an Amyraldian?," in *The Legacy of David Broughton Knox*, ed. Edward Loane (London: Latimer, 2018), 1–25.

33. Andrew Leslie, "Was Broughton Knox an Amyraldian?," 9. Leslie notes the *Formula Consensus Helvetica* 1675 as an exception. Knox, in his essay, understands his position to be at odds with the Westminster Confession. Leslie argues that Knox is here mistaken, and that the Westminster Confession does not, as Knox suggests, exclude hypothetical universalism.

34. See Collin Hansen, *Young, Restless, Reformed: A Journalist's Journey with the New Calvinists* (Wheaton, IL: Crossway, 2008).

Meanwhile, in the year 2000, the Sydney publisher Matthias Media (founded by Phillip Jensen) began publishing a three-volume series of the selected works of D. B. Knox. The first volume was to include Knox's paper "Some Aspects of the Atonement." Here for the first time Knox's views were made available to a wider audience. The timing was propitious. The emergent church theology's discomfort with penal substitutionary atonement on the one hand, and the new Calvinists' enthusiasm for Reformed soteriology on the other, meant that Knox's position became available at a time when the issues it raised were of contemporary concern. It was picked up in a number of contexts.

In 2007, British conservative evangelicals Steve Jeffery, Michael Ovey, and Andrew Sach published *Pierced for Our Transgressions: Rediscovering the Glory of Penal Substitution.* In the introduction the authors note that evangelicals such as Steve Chalke, Alan Mann, and Brian McLaren were bringing criticisms of penal substitutionary atonement to a wider audience. The disquiet was enough for the Evangelical Alliance to host a public debate in London in 2004. Positions were aired, but resolution proved elusive.[35]

The book is positioned as a robust restatement of the doctrine in the context of controversy, much as Leon Morris's *The Apostolic Preaching of the Cross* (1955), J. I. Packer's lecture "What Did the Cross Achieve?" (1973), and John Stott's *The Cross of Christ* (1986) had done in previous decades. Interestingly, limited atonement was not a prominent theme in Morris, Packer, or Stott's interventions. However, in *Pierced for Our Transgressions,* the question is addressed head-on. This perhaps reflects the then-rising influence of the new Calvinists, a movement in which the theology of the Westminster Confession was more prominent than in the largely Anglican-led interventions of the previous decades (Packer, Morris, and Stott all being Anglican).

In *Pierced for Our Transgressions,* the authors consider the objection that penal substitution "implies universal salvation, which is unbiblical." The objection is answered by an appeal to the doctrine of particular redemption. Penal substitution, the authors argue, does not imply universal salvation because the intent of Christ's substitution was not in fact universal.

Having put forward this argument, the authors state that they "must address several arguments against particular redemption set forth in an influential essay by D. Broughton Knox."[36] It is noteworthy that Knox's essay, published only seven years prior to *Pierced for Our Transgressions*, is described as "influential" and warrants its own particular refutation. The authors are careful to frame Knox as "a faithful and godly scholar" who is "held in esteem by many," but who at this point is "mistaken."[37] This language, focused as it

---

35.   Steve Jeffery, Michael Ovey, and Andrew Sach, *Pierced for Our Transgressions: Rediscovering the Glory of Penal Substitution* (Wheaton, IL: Crossway, 2007), 25.

36.   Jeffery, Ovey, and Sach, *Peirced for Our Transgressions,* 276.

37.   Jeffery, Ovey, and Sach, *Peirced for Our Transgressions,* 276.

is on Knox's reputation rather than his essay as such, may reflect that Knox's position was still primarily being carried by the preaching and teaching of his students, rather than the essay as such. (It is worth noting that two of the three authors—Ovey and Sach—had both studied at Moore.) Clearly, they felt the weight of Knox's challenge and saw in his position some friendly fire that needed its own treatment.

Six years later, David and Jonathan Gibson edited a major volume defending particular redemption itself. *From Heaven He Came and Sought Her: Definite Atonement in Historical, Biblical, Theological, and Pastoral Perspective* (2013) is a substantial, 650-page treatment of the topic. Chapters by Jonathan Gibson, Amar Djabllah, and Donald Macleod all cite Knox's paper, interacting appreciatively but critically with his thought.

The most sustained treatment comes in Garry Williams's chapter on "The Definite Intent of Penal Substitutionary Atonement." In this chapter, Williams considers two historical accounts of hypothetical universalism: that of James Ussher (1581–1656) and D. B. Knox's. Williams correctly understands the heart of Knox's position to be grounded in a qualitative rather than quantitative account of the nature of Christ's atonement. Despite being someone who "unequivocally affirms penal substitutionary atonement,"[38] Knox is equally emphatic that the extent of the atonement is universal.

Williams agrees that Christ's death was of infinite value considered in itself. His critique is that it does not follow from the infinite value of Christ's death that it can only be limited at the point of application. Rather, for Williams, a "properly covenantal ontology" is the way forward. "The sufferings of Christ were what they were because of God's eternal intention for them in the covenant of redemption," says Williams.[39]

This is an interesting insight. In the 1950s and 1960s, Donald Robinson and D. B. Knox were developing a biblical-theological approach to Scripture. This was an approach that had affinities with, but was not the same things as, the biblical theology movement of the mid-twentieth century. Robinson and Knox had both been impressed by a J. I. Packer article on the importance of the idea of covenant in the Bible's story.[40] The covenantal approach was suggestive to Robinson of a way in which the Bible's disparate parts could be integrated. However, in what would become one of the distinguishing features of biblical theology at Moore College, "covenant" came to assume a

38. Garry J. Williams, "The Definite Intent of Penal Substitutionary Atonement," in *From Heaven He Came and Sought Her: Definite Atonement in Historical, Biblical, Theological, and Pastoral Perspective*, eds. David Gibson and Jonathan Gibson (Wheaton, IL: Crossway, 2013), 468.
39. Williams, "The Definite Intent of Penal Substitutionary Atonement," 470.
40. Robinson mentions the existence of this article in both Donald Robinson, "Origins and Unresolved Tensions," in *Interpreting God's Plan: Biblical Theology and the Pastor* (Carlisle: Paternoster, 1998), 1–17; Donald Robinson, "'The Church' Revisited: An Autobiographical Fragment," in *Donald Robinson: Selected Works*, vol. 2, *Preaching God's Word* (Sydney: Australian Church Record/Moore College, 2008), 259–71. In neither article can he recall the name and provenance of the piece by Packer.

smaller place than was typical of other Reformed approaches. Covenant was subsumed under wider ideas such as the kingdom of God. The slight place of the covenants in the integration of the Testaments relative to other Reformed accounts helps to explain Knox's reluctance to appeal to any sort of "covenant of redemption" or "covenantal ontology" in his work on the atonement.

For Williams, covenantal theology would have allowed Knox to simultaneously affirm an intentionality in Christ's death while also affirming the infinite and unquantifiable nature of his atonement as such.[41] However, the explanatory power of the covenants was an aspect of traditional Reformed theology with which Knox had early dispensed. The biblical theology approach had won the day with Knox, and the covenants had been relegated in the process.

Williams is at pains to affirm Knox's orthodoxy and his trenchant defense of penal substitution. Knox, along with Ussher, is an example for Williams of "how the Lord graciously protects us from the logical consequences of those errors that we all undoubtedly hold somewhere in our own theological systems."[42]

Williams casts Knox in a similar role to that given him in the early *Pierced for Our Transgressions*. He is an ally, a member of the Reformed fraternity, and a firm defender of penal substitutionary atonement. His position, however, is an inadvertent threat to the very Reformed theology he was known to uphold. In the early 1960s, Knox fretted that limited atonement could be an Achilles' heel to the rebirth of Reformed theology. Ironically, in the first two decades of the twenty-first century, his hypothetical universalism was itself cast as a potential Achilles' heel to the full-flowering of Reformed theology, and to a robust defense of penal substitution itself.

CONCLUSION

In 2018, a group of scholars produced a book exploring Knox's influence. Titled *The Legacy of David Broughton Knox*, the first chapter addressed the question "Was Broughton Knox an Amyraldian?"[43] It is noteworthy that the volume begins here, suggesting Knox's position on this matter was indeed a major (and contested) aspect of his legacy.

Knox's position, commonly referred to as his Amyraldianism, but better understood as a Reformed species of hypothetical universalism, has been a significant twentieth- and early twenty-first century influence. Originally, from the 1960s to the 1990s, it was an orally transmitted tradition influencing Sydney Anglicans and the theology of the evangelical student world. In those contexts it was often pressed into service of the causes for which Knox had originally intended it. It smoothed the path for evangelistic preaching, and

---

41. Williams, "The Definite Intent of Penal Substitutionary Atonement," 480.
42. Williams, "The Definite Intent of Penal Substitutionary Atonement," 481.
43. Leslie, "Was Broughton Knox an Amyraldian?"

removed what was perceived to be an objectionable aspect of Reformed theology, with a view to making its other treasures more readily available.

Then, as international evangelical debates responded to challenges from emergent theology, Knox's position became cast in another role. In these debates Knox's position was framed as a significant, well-intentioned, but ultimately faulty rejection of particular redemption. It represents a deviation from, rather than a path toward, the full embrace of Reformed theology. To discard the doctrine of particular redemption in the manner Knox proposed, it was argued, left evangelicalism's defense and proclamation of penal substitutionary atonement exposed and vulnerable. It has not been the purpose of this chapter to arbitrate between these claims, but rather to provide some of the historical context in which they have arisen.

CHAPTER NINE

UNLIMITED ATONEMENT IN THE TWENTY-FIRST CENTURY

Joshua M. McNall

I n Zadie Smith's bestselling novel, *White Teeth*, she chooses what might seem like a rather tired line from Shakespeare as her overarching epigraph.[1] But as one of the twenty-first century's most astute literary voices, Smith adds a wry twist to the Bard's famous quotation. The attribution reads as follows:

> WHAT IS PAST IS PROLOGUE
> —Inscription in Washington, DC, museum

Why do that? Why alter Shakespeare's sentence slightly (extending the contraction "What's"), and then fail to trace its ancestry? Smith knows precisely what she is doing. Her entire novel plays upon the complex ways in which the past influences the present, even if the present makes some subtle tweaks to the received tradition. So too in many twenty-first-century treatments of unlimited atonement (UA).

My assigned task in this chapter is to engage with a selection of contemporary theologians who espouse versions of UA: the belief that Christ died for all humans without exception, rather than for only a select portion of humanity. The most difficult part of this task is, of course, determining which voices to include. The representatives I have chosen are meant neither to exhaust the available versions of UA, nor to be seen as the most influential theologians

---

1.   Zadie Smith, *White Teeth* (New York: Vintage, 2000).

169

of our century (though each one is important). I have selected them for their connections to traditions from the past, and in order to note the subtle decisions ("tweaks") that mark their own twenty-first-century inscriptions on the monument of atonement doctrine. After all, "what is past is prologue."

My interlocutors are taken from a recent book on the subject: *Five Views on the Extent of the Atonement*.[2] Of the perspectives surveyed there, four of the five views are versions of UA:

1. the Orthodox perspective of Andrew Louth;

2. the Roman Catholic position of Matthew Levering;

3. the Wesleyan theology of Fred Sanders; and

4. the Christian universalism of Tom Greggs.

None of these authors make special appeal to the work of Moïse Amyraut. And only one of the book's contributors, the Reformed theologian Michael Horton, rejects UA—though even Horton's demurral comes with certain caveats. This basic agreement between the other contributors illustrates what David Allen calls the relative "unity" between "all moderate Calvinists, Arminians, and non-Calvinists on the specific issue of the extent of the atonement."[3] As I will show, however, that unity does not imply a uniformity.

ANDREW LOUTH: AN ILL-FRAMED
DISCUSSION OF UNLIMITED LOVE

"From the perspective of Orthodox theology," writes Andrew Louth, the atonement must be conceived as "unlimited." Yet Louth quickly notes that to employ the language of "extent" at all is to leave behind the idiom of the East to engage in a uniquely Western debate.[4] For this reason, Louth's contribution is to challenge what he takes to be the faulty Latin, rationalistic, and forensic presuppositions that often undergird this discussion.

Born in England in 1944, Louth studied at Cambridge and Edinburgh, where (at the latter) he wrote a thesis on Karl Barth. He began vocational ministry as an Anglican priest before converting to Eastern Orthodoxy in 1989. A long teaching career followed, and he now holds the post of Emeritus Professor of Patristic and Byzantine Studies at Durham University.[5] With the

2. Adam J. Johnson, ed., *Five Views on the Extent of the Atonement* (Grand Rapids: Zondervan, 2019).

3. David L. Allen, *The Extent of the Atonement: A Historical and Critical Review* (Nashville: B&H Academic, 2016), xviii.

4. Andrew Louth, "Eastern Orthodox View," in *Five Views on the Extent of the Atonement*, ed. Adam J. Johnson (Grand Rapids: Zondervan Academic, 2019), 38.

5. See the biographical sketch to be found on Durham's website: https://www.durham.ac.uk/staff/andrew-louth.

zeal of a convert, Louth approaches what he sees as the unfortunate juridical presuppositions behind much Western theology. And he seeks to counter these imbalances not merely by looking East, but by paying particular attention to Christian mysticism. All these themes converge in his essay on the extent of the atonement.

Since God is limitless love, Louth claims that it would be a grave error to consider that reconciliation might have a limited extent. This mistake stems from what he takes to be three deeper problems. First, he highlights an undue favoring of forensic categories (after Anselm especially) that view atonement as a quantitative "making amends" rather than a mystical union.[6] Second, Louth bemoans a focus on individual predestination that results in a God who chooses some people from eternity instead of others for salvation. Third, he critiques the early Christian supposal that a select number of humans will be redeemed to make up for a specific number of fallen angels. Taken together, Louth sees these errors as leading to a misguided discussion regarding the limited scope of the atonement. But, in his view, the entire conversation is an adventure in missing the point.

Louth recommends three corrections to address the prior problems: first, a retrieval of the Middle English meaning of atonement as a "oneing" by way of mystical union; second, an unabashed affirmation of ongoing human freedom as rooted in the image of God; and third, a hopeful universalism that views salvation as something that *may* remain possible for those who have rejected God's unlimited atoning love in this lifetime. Any other position would allegedly place limits on the mysterious and powerful scope of divine grace.[7]

While space precludes a full evaluation of Louth's theology, the most helpful result of his essay is a reminder that discussions on the atonement's extent remain somewhat foreign to significant portions of the global church—not just in the East but also across the centuries. Likewise, his reminder that atonement requires an emphasis upon union or participation is echoed by theologians and biblical scholars, both past and present.[8] Indeed, it is always helpful to ask what linguistic and cultural assumptions we have brought to our understanding of redemption. But, as I will now note, that critique cuts both ways.

Important weaknesses stand out in Louth's argument. First, he adopts what I have elsewhere called a *reductionistic* articulation of God's saving work.[9] From this posture, other images and models of atonement (say, liberation,

---

6. Louth, "Eastern Orthodox View," 26.
7. Louth, "Eastern Orthodox View," 43.
8. In recent Pauline studies, see especially Michael Gorman, *Inhabiting the Cruciform God: Kenosis, Justification, and Theosis in Paul's Narrative Soteriology* (Grand Rapids: Eerdmans, 2009). And in analytic theology, see Oliver Crisp, *Approaching the Atonement: The Reconciling Work of Christ* (Downers Grove, IL: IVP Academic, 2020), chap. 10.
9. See Joshua McNall, *The Mosaic of Atonement: An Integrated Approach to Christ's Work* (Grand Rapids: Zondervan Academic, 2019), 19–21.

substitution, moral influence, triumph) are not merely downgraded in a hier-
archy of value, but seemingly left out entirely.[10] Instead, Louth devotes almost
the whole of his attention to the single theme of *theosis* by which God will
ultimately draw all things into mystical union with himself. The problem here
is not so much what Louth includes (since a proper understanding of deifica-
tion belongs in the discussion) but what he leaves out in a reductionist focus
on a single aspect of atonement.

Second, Louth's endorsement of UA proceeds largely in detachment from
the Scriptures. This allows him to acknowledge that while, yes, passages like
Ephesians 1 and Romans 9–11 speak of predestination, we can be quite sure
that Reformed readings of these texts are wrong because, after all, "Freedom is fundamental to being human," and Chrysostom was not a Calvinist.[11] Although I agree with Louth's claim that certain Reformed conclusions
on these passages deserve to be questioned, that verdict requires a more
substantial engagement with the biblical texts that some Calvinists (like
Horton) believe to support the corollary theme of definite/limited atonement. It is not enough to make assertions and aspersions devoid of careful
biblical argumentation.[12]

Third and finally, Louth's treatment of "Western theology" deals often in
caricatures and questionable generalizations. To blame limited atonement
on Augustine's tentative speculation about the number of fallen angels is
certainly the oddest argument in the chapter. But other caricatures are no less
problematic for being well-worn. Anselm is blamed yet again for all manner
of horrors, despite a wealth of recent scholarship to suggest that he was not
nearly as *limited* to the forensic and feudalistic assumptions that his critics
allege. In fact, Anselm's prayerful and aesthetic concern for God's restoration
of the beauty of all creation might qualify as downright mystical and pleas-
ing to some Eastern ears.[13] In the end, even proponents of UA may be left
wondering if Louth hasn't played too loose with both the Western sources and
the legacies ascribed to them—as if Shakespeare (or was it Anselm?) could be
blamed for every ill-played pun upon the Western stage.[14]

10. Michael Horton levels this critique in his "Response to Andrew Louth," 52.
11. Louth, "Eastern Orthodox View," 30.
12. In fairness to Louth (and the other contributors), one chapter is not sufficient to address all the
     thorny passages and arguments surrounding issues like predestination and human freedom. It is
     important, however, for scholars to show an appreciation that these debates are complex and not
     reducible to dismissive generalizations.
13. See especially David Bentley Hart, "A Gift Exceeding Every Debt: An Eastern Orthodox Appreciation
     of Anselm's *Cur Deus Homo*," *Pro Ecclesia* 7, no. 3 (Summer 1998): 330–49.
14. Louth's caricatures and sweeping generalizations would be more forgivable if he were approaching
     the Western tradition as a complete outsider, separated from the sources by language and a lack of
     prior engagement. But Louth is an Englishman, a former Anglican priest, and a student who wrote a
     master's thesis on Barth. For these reasons, the excuse of unfamiliarity is not open to him.

MATTHEW LEVERING: A TENSION WITHIN
SCRIPTURE AND CATHOLIC TRADITION

Our second contemporary articulation of unlimited atonement comes from the Roman Catholic theologian Matthew Levering. For Levering, the challenge in affirming UA has two facets. First, there is the "nonuniversal extent of predestination." And second, there is Christ's knowledge in the Gospels of those, like Judas, who would permanently reject him.[15] Hence the fate of UA may be seen to hang upon a single question: Did Jesus *truly* die for Judas? Levering's answer is "Yes," but he acknowledges that this response reveals a *tension* within Scripture and Catholic tradition. In this way, his verdict (both biblically and historically) is far more nuanced than that of Louth—but also far less clear.

Let's begin with tradition. Levering notes that the most official Catholic affirmation of UA comes in the constitution *Cum occasione* (1653). There one finds a rejection of the idea that it would be semi-Pelagian to assert that "Christ died or shed his blood for all men without exception." On the contrary, Pope Innocent X claims that it is both "blasphemous" and "heretical" to say that "Christ died only to save the predestined."[16] As a good Catholic, Levering concurs, and he concludes with a strong statement of unlimited atonement: "God enters the world truly to save it, not merely to act and pray for the elect."[17]

So where is the tension? Levering claims that it can be glimpsed in the work that occasioned the verbal intensity of *Cum occasione*: Cornelius Jansen's *Augustinus* (1640). This treatise attempted to acknowledge the full implications of Augustine's doctrine of predestination, built, in Jansen's view at least, upon the Scriptures.

Levering concedes that recent Catholic theologians have often softened the doctrine of predestination that is found in the likes of Augustine, Aquinas, and the Scriptures themselves.[18] In his view, God predestined some (and not others) to salvation before the foundation of the world (Eph. 1:4–5). Hence Aquinas claimed that when Jesus prayed "Father forgive them" from the cross, he was not interceding for all those who crucified him, but only for those predestined to be saved among that number.[19] Statements like this in the Catholic tradition raise a question: Would not the same logic apply to Christ's *work* as well as his *words* on the cross?

---

15. Matthew Levering, "Roman Catholic View," in *Five Views on the Extent of the Atonement,* ed. Adam J. Johnson (Grand Rapids: Zondervan Academic, 2019), 67.

16. Heinrich Denzinger, *Compendium of Creeds, Definitions, and Declarations on Matters of Faith and Morals,* 43rd ed., eds. Peter Hünermann and Helmut Hoping (Latin-German), eds. Robert Fastiggi and Anne Englund Nash (Latin-English) (San Francisco: Ignatius, 2012), 2005–6. Cited in Levering, "Roman Catholic View," 87.

17. Levering, "Roman Catholic View," 83.

18. Levering, "Roman Catholic View," 67.

19. Thomas Aquinas, *Summa Theologica,* trans. Fathers of the English Dominican Provence (New York: Benzinger, 1947–48), III, q. 21, a. 4, ad. 2. Cited by Levering, "Roman Catholic View," 74.

Levering does not attempt to resolve the tension. And this move leaves at least one respondent (Horton) to ask if what he actually upholds is a "contradiction."[20] It is best, however, to allow Levering to speak for himself. In his view, some biblical texts "indicate that God abundantly loves only the elect (while permitting others to fall away due to their own free sin), while other passages indicate that God loves all humans and desires the salvation of all." Nonetheless,

> The two biblical portraits of God cannot be squared by subordinating one to the other, as theologians throughout the centuries have tried to do. It seems to me, instead, that we must hold two affirmations in tension without being yet able to see how they can be integrated: from eternity God efficaciously predestines some rational creatures to salvation and permits the free everlasting rebellion of others, and from eternity God superabundantly loves without any constriction or narrowness each and every rational creature.[21]

To the extent that Levering attempts to address the tension, he looks to Francis de Sales. There he finds the suggestion that although God has not deprived anyone of his love, some have deprived God of their cooperation.[22]

In all of this, Levering takes more seriously than Louth the varied themes of Scripture and tradition as they relate to predestination and the extent of the atonement.[23] If Louth's conclusion flows confidently from "first principles" (God is limitless love, *ergo*: UA), Levering gives deference to the Catholic consensus (e.g., in *Cum occasione*), while admitting that he doesn't understand how this conclusion can be fully "squared" with (1) God's eternal predestination of some and not others, and (2) Christ's foreknowledge of those, like Judas, who would reject salvation.

This means, second, that Levering's approach grants more weight to mystery and magisterium. Perhaps the lesson to be learned is that when exegesis, Augustine, and Aquinas leave you baffled, take shelter in a clear and infallible pronouncement like *Cum occasione*. On the one hand, Levering's honest admission of the vexing nature of Scripture's various statements seems praiseworthy. He is careful and conversant with both the biblical text and diverse voices from tradition. And indeed, the ability to say "I don't know" is a discipline that all Christians should cultivate.[24] But for those not already

---

20.   Horton, "Response to Matthew Levering," 98.
21.   Levering, "Roman Catholic View," 89.
22.   Levering, "Roman Catholic View," 87.
23.   See also his careful, book-length treatment of both Scripture and tradition. Matthew Levering, *Predestination: Biblical and Theological Roots* (Oxford: Oxford University Press, 2011).
24.   See my own treatment of what I call the "sacred IDK" that is often needed when pondering things that are indeed "too lofty for us to understand" (Ps. 139:6). Joshua M. McNall, *Perhaps: Reclaiming the Space Between Doubt and Dogmatism* (Downers Grove, IL: IVP Academic, 2021).

convinced of the Magisterium's infallible authority, the secure fortress of *Cum occasione* will not seem like a "bulwark never failing." For Protestants especially, the move may appear like granting authority to Zadie Smith's "Inscription in Washington, DC, museum," over the inspired author (Shakespeare), simply because the later verdict was, at some point, etched in stone.

Finally, it is unclear how Levering's appeal to Francis de Sales offers any help in resolving the tension in Scripture's "two portraits of God." If anything, it seems to heighten the disparity. Recall de Sales's contention was that God superabundantly loves every rational creature, and that God gives each rational creature more than enough grace to be saved. In turning to the damned (and even Lucifer himself), his suggestion was that "God did not deprive thee of the operation of his love, but thou didst deprive his love of thy co-operation."[25] By this logic, creaturely cooperation becomes a deciding factor in salvation or damnation; it echoes Louth's insistence that human freedom (gifted either at creation or later) is important to UA, and it fits well within the orbit of Catholic thought.

Unfortunately, it is unclear how de Sales's emphasis upon human cooperation fits with Levering's *prior* insistence upon "the eternal God efficaciously predestining and causing the unmerited salvation of *some* while allowing others to remain permanently in their sins."[26] One solution might be to assert with other Catholic thinkers that God *foreknew* who would cooperate with his unlimited grace. But Levering rejects this path.[27] In his words, the predestination of some individuals rather than others is "not an eternal response to [God's] foreknowledge of how humans will exercise their free will."[28]

If this is true, how then can one affirm de Sales's *via media* between the likes of Augustine, Jansen, and Calvin on one side, and the alternatives that supposedly undermine God's eternal predestination on the other? Unfortunately, this particular tension—if not outright contradiction—between Levering's two "portraits of God" is not resolved by an appeal to mystery and magisterium.

FRED SANDERS: SALVATION ACCOMPLISHED VERSUS SALVATION APPLIED

In Fred Sanders we finally have a version of UA that attempts to account for *both* the universal and particular claims of Scripture regarding atonement and salvation. If Louth ignores the tension and Levering fails to resolve it, then Sanders reveals a solution that borrows heavily from the grammar of

---

25. Francis de Sales, *Treatise on the Love of God,* trans. Henry Benedict Mackey, OSB (Rockford, IL: Tan, 1997), 91. Cited by Levering, "Roman Catholic View," 87.

26. Levering, "Roman Catholic View," 85–86. Italics added.

27. See also his rejection of Molina's proposed solution (and that of others) for not giving enough weight to God's eternal providence and election. Levering, *Predestination,* 196–97.

28. Levering, "Roman Catholic View," 89; see also his treatment of Augustine's own rejection of this option (73).

Trinitarian theology. His chapter is dubbed a "Wesleyan View" of unlimited atonement, but as with much of Sanders's irenic and (small "c") catholic theology, the argument has little about it that is exclusively Wesleyan. Indeed, most of it could easily be adopted or adapted by Reformed theologians, as Sanders readily acknowledges.[29]

Drawing upon the doctrine of the Trinity, Sanders's account of UA hinges on the distinction between "nature" and "persons." Although Christ's death reconciles human nature to God, this universal accomplishment still needs to be specifically *applied* to specific persons by the Holy Spirit when individuals respond to the gospel. In this way, Sanders utilizes three doctrinal distinctions:

1. between nature and person;

2. between salvation accomplished and applied; and

3. between the Son and Holy Spirit.[30]

When Scripture says that Christ is the atoning sacrifice not only for our sins "but also for the sins of the whole world" (1 John 2:2), it speaks of how the Son took up and reconciled human nature to God. But when we read Scripture's command for particular persons to "Be reconciled," we have turned to the need for salvation to be specifically *applied* to individuals, despite the simultaneous insistence that "God was reconciling the world to himself in Christ" (2 Cor. 5:18–21).

Sanders acknowledges that the concepts of "nature" and "person" are not particularly "thick" (or content-bearing): "It is not the case that these terms bring extra content to the subject matter."[31] Rather, the words serve as "concise labels that are useful for picking out things we already know" from divine revelation.[32] Though Sanders is speaking here of the doctrines of the Trinity and Christology, the same goes for his nature/person distinction when it comes to atonement *accomplished* versus atonement *applied*.

Support is drawn from the ranks of Reformed theologians, both past and present. Calvin himself spoke of the Spirit as "the bond by which Christ effectively unites us to himself."[33] So while the work of salvation is accomplished by Christ, it must be applied by the Spirit. Likewise, Kevin Vanhoozer affirms that although the incarnation unites the Son to human nature in general, it

---

29. See Sanders, "Wesleyan View," in *Five Views on the Extent of the Atonement*, ed. Adam J. Johnson (Grand Rapids: Zondervan Academic, 2019), 172–73.

30. Sanders, "Wesleyan View," 158.

31. Sanders, "Wesleyan View," 161.

32. Sanders, "Wesleyan View," 160.

33. John Calvin, *Institutes of the Christian Religion*, ed. John T. McNeill, trans. Ford Lewis Battles (Louisville: Westminster John Knox, 2011), 3.1.1.

does not follow that the incarnation unites the Son to *me* in particular. This specific application of Christ's work takes place when the Spirit draws the believer into union with Christ by faith.[34] With reference to these theologians, and by drawing on these same distinctions, Sanders believes he has found a way to articulate the biblical notion that Christ has indeed acted for all humans, despite the fact that not all humans will be saved.

The strength of this argument is threefold: First, it provides a way to account for both the universal and particular statements in Scripture without ignoring or sublimating one or the other. Second, this harmonizing result comes by way of language that is already enshrined in creedal formulas on Christ and the Trinity (in other words, Christians have long accepted both its orthodoxy and its utility). And third, Sanders's approach proceeds in a way that is amenable to many Christian traditions—not just Wesleyans. Indeed, as with much of his work, the chapter is ecumenical, irenic, and well-tethered to what one might call the great tradition of Christian orthodoxy.

If there is a weakness, it lies in what Sanders acknowledges to be the relative "thinness" of a concept that occupies a crucial place in his argument: human nature. After all, the *unlimited* aspect of atonement is said to be "accomplished" with respect to human nature. But it is never really spelled out what this means. We know what it looks like for a particular person (Jose or Sally) to profess faith in Christ by the Holy Spirit. But what is meant by the claim that Christ accomplished salvation for human nature? If the concept does not bring any content to the conversation (as Sanders admits), then what is gained by the argument other than the addition of a grammatical placeholder?[35]

It bears noting that John Wesley had more specific things to say regarding the universal benefits of Christ's atoning work. Wesley's claim was that Christ dealt universally with the guilt incurred by Adam's sin. This Adamic guilt—which was quite real in Wesley's opinion—was wiped away for all humans at the cross. But this did not mean that all humans would be saved. Instead, it meant the important fact that no one (not least unbaptized infants!) will ever be damned for Adam's sin.[36] For Wesley at least, this specific benefit (the abolition of original guilt) was not just "accomplished" but also "applied" to all humans because of Christ's work on our behalf.

---

34. See Kevin J. Vanhoozer, "The Origin of Paul's Soteriology: Election, Incarnation, and Union with Christ in Ephesians 1:4 (with Special Reference to Evangelical Calvinism)," in *Reconsidering the Relationship between Biblical and Systematic Theology in the New Testament: Essays by the Theologians and New Testament Scholars,* eds. Benjamin E. Reynolds, Brian Lugioyo, and Kevin J. Vanhoozer (Tübingen: Mohr Siebeck, 2014), 198.

35. As when Augustine admits that he says three "persons" [*personae*] in the Trinity only as a way to keep from being silent. See *De Trinitate* 5.8.9.

36. See John Wesley, *The Letters of John Wesley,* ed. John Telford, vol. 6 (London: Epworth, 1931), 239. See also T. A. Noble, "Original Sin and the Fall: Definitions and the Proposal," in *Darwin, Creation and the Fall: Theological Challenges,* eds. R. J. Berry and T. A. Noble (London: Apollos, 2009).

A second universal benefit of Christ's atoning work was what Wesley called the prevenient grace that restores to all humans "a measure of free-will" so that each person may accept or reject God's saving grace.[37] Unlike Louth, who located human freedom as a corollary of the *imago Dei*, or Levering who connected it ambiguously to cooperation, Wesley saw prevenient grace as resulting from Christ's universal work on our behalf. He saw it as restoring a kind of equilibrium so each person might accept or reject salvation without being banned by fate or forced by grace. Of course, one may challenge (as I have) Wesley's articulation of this point, along with its exegetical underpinnings (I prefer to speak of the prevenient work of the Spirit).[38] But prevenient grace is, from a Wesleyan perspective, another universal benefit that is bestowed upon all humans by virtue of Christ's work and the Spirit's application. For his own part, Sanders hints at something like this when he acknowledges that the Spirit is responsible for "awakening" the "free human response to the gospel."[39] And it is this gracious reality that reveals why Sanders's Wesleyan account of atonement is not at all a Pelagian (or semi-Pelagian) one.

TOM GREGGS: UNLIMITED ATONEMENT AS UNIVERSAL SALVATION

In the fourth and final version of UA, Tom Greggs offers what he takes to be a combination of Calvinist and Wesleyan-Arminian assumptions in the form of Christian universalism. This view "combines the Arminian position that God *wills* the salvation of all people with the Calvinist position that God's sovereign will cannot be resisted."[40] Greggs is clear that his version of universalism is particularist rather than pluralistic in nature. In other words, salvation is seen as coming only through the work of Jesus the Christ. In this way, his universalism is distinguished from the pluralistic universalism of John Hick, in which salvation *solo Christo* is seen as problematic in a multireligious and multicultural environment.[41]

Greggs admits that his view is a minority report in Christian history. But he claims that Christian universalism in and of itself was never specifically condemned by an ecumenical council. It was Origen (or perhaps more accurately, Origenism) that was renounced at the Second Council of Constantinople, and here the anathemas pertained to other aspects of Origen's supposed theology: for instance, to the preexistence of souls rather than to *apokatastasis* in general. What's more, Scripture uses this much-maligned Greek word with

---

37. John Wesley, "Predestination Calmly Considered," in *The Works of John Wesley* (Grand Rapids: Zondervan, 1958), 10:229–30.

38. See McNall, *Mosaic of Atonement*, 303–5.

39. Sanders, "Wesleyan View," 173.

40. Greggs, "Christian Universalist View," in *Five Views on the Extent of the Atonement*, ed. Adam J. Johnson (Grand Rapids: Zondervan Academic, 2019), 197.

41. For more detail on these two kinds of universalism, see Trevor Hart, "Universalism: Two Distinct Types," in *Universalism and the Doctrine of Hell: Papers Presented at the Fourth Edinburgh Conference in Christian Dogmatics, 1991*, ed. Nigel M. de S. Cameron (Grand Rapids: Baker, 1993).

approval in Acts 3:21, when speaking of the "universal restoration" announced long ago through the prophets (NRSV).[42]

Greggs cites a familiar bevy of biblical passages that reference Christ's saving work in unlimited terms. Colossians proclaims that "God was pleased to reconcile to himself all things, whether on earth or in heaven, by making peace through the blood of his cross" (1:20 NRSV).[43] And as Paul writes in relation to the universal implications of Adam's sin, "just as one trespass resulted in condemnation for all people, so also one righteous act resulted in justification and life for all people" (Rom. 5:18).

By this point in my chapter, questions of how to relate these universal-sounding passages to the particular ones will be familiar. In addition, my goal is not to provide a full evaluation of Greggs's universalism,[44] since that task is both too large and somewhat disconnected from an engagement with recent versions of UA. Instead, we should find Greggs's universalism to be revealing insofar as it brings together certain themes, traditions, and doctrinal imbalances seen previously.

Like Louth, Greggs prioritizes the universal emphases of Scripture over and against the particularist ones, without devoting much attention to *how* we should understand those "damning" texts. He mentions Trevor Hart's claim that we should preach a "kerygmatic hell," but he does not clarify either what that means or if it is his own position.[45] Is Greggs's own view that some humans experience a hell on earth because of sin and suffering, or is it that the kerygma is meant merely to scare the "hell" out of wayward individuals to draw them to Christ? Or is it that there remains a postmortem judgment that, although real, will not be eternal or will not be experienced because all will ultimately repent? Perhaps the best conclusion is that Greggs remains open to more than one possibility, and in this way he leans into the mystery without the magisterium of Levering.

Greggs also follows Louth in relying strongly upon *first principles* about God's nature to form his argument for UA as universal salvation. He asks rhetorically, "What does it say about God's nature that God should elect to damn the majority of the world (or even a part of it) in God's sovereign foreknowledge?"[46] The point here is that while certain Scriptures, and the vast majority of Christian tradition, might seem to teach something contrary to universalism, our presupposition about God's nature as holy love must overrule those interpretations.

---

42. Greggs, "Christian Universalist View," 201.
43. See also Rom. 5:18–19; Eph. 1:9–10; 2 Cor. 5:19.
44. For the lengthiest recent response to universalism, see Michael J. McClymond, *The Devil's Redemption: A New History and Interpretation of Christian Universalism*, 2 vols. (Grand Rapids: Baker Academic, 2018).
45. See Hart, "Universalism: Two Distinct Types," 21–22. In fact, Hart's meaning is derived from J. A. T. Robinson. The idea for Robinson was that hell remains the only real alternative to rejecting Christ forever. Hart's supposal is therefore that no one may actually *choose* this very real alternative, if given enough opportunity. See J. A. T. Robinson, *In the End God* (London: James Clark, 1950), 118.
46. Greggs, "Christin Universalist View," 203.

It is precisely at this point, however, that Greggs leaves Louth, Levering, and Sanders to their non-Reformed ways. In effect, he sides with Horton and a certain strand of Calvinistic thought when he rejects the idea that creaturely freedom should ever be cited as a factor in whether one accepts salvation—either as God's abiding gift in the *imago Dei* (Louth), through creaturely cooperation (Levering), or as a restoration that occurs through the prevenient work of the Spirit (Sanders). For Greggs, each of these escape hatches result in an impotent deity and a misguided definition of what liberty is.[47] True freedom is "to be for (not against) God."[48] All humans will therefore be *set free* by the sovereign work of Christ that will ultimately be efficacious without exception.[49] Having now engaged with these four versions of UA in contemporary theology, it is now time to reiterate some of the lessons learned.

CONCLUSION

Perhaps the closest biblical analogue to Shakespeare's famous line, "What's past is prologue," comes from 1 Corinthians. There Paul tells the church that "these things" from the past "occurred as examples" so we might learn from Israel's history and avoid her missteps (10:6). In a similar fashion, we may extract some helpful cautions from these four versions of UA.

First, when wrestling with the biblical material, one should resist the urge to ignore or favor either the universal-sounding passages or the particular ones. Both sets of texts are in the Scriptures—sometimes in close proximity!—and one set of passages should not be privileged over the other. This weakness was found in both Louth and Greggs at certain points, despite their helpful reminders that traditional objections to universalism should not keep us from recognizing the many universal references to God's love and Christ's atoning work.

Second, it is not enough to recognize the tension between these two sets of passages without seeking reasonable ways to address it. This weakness was noted in Levering, despite his rightful emphasis upon the need to look for help within church tradition. In the face of age-old questions regarding predestination and God's universal love, much mystery will no doubt remain, but we can do more than merely acknowledge it in ways that seem closer to a contradiction than a conundrum. As Sanders illustrates, the great tradition itself has given us the resources to do as much, however imperfectly.

Finally, we should be open to specific ways in which Christ's work does something *for* all humans, even if the application of this unlimited atonement is not final salvation for all individuals without exception. At this point, we see the possibility that Sanders's Wesleyan perspective could be, perhaps, a bit

---

47. Greggs, "Christian Universalist View," 208.
48. Greggs, "Christian Universalist View," 204.
49. In this way, Greggs's version of UA makes more explicit a line of thinking in the Reformed theology of Karl Barth as well as others.

more Wesleyan—despite the insightful and irenic way in which he accounts for Scripture's universal and particularlist emphases by referencing the grammar of the Trinity and Christology. To affirm unlimited atonement need not mean that one is left with either universalism or an entirely hypothetical benefit to all people.

In the end, however, it would be deeply unfair to mine these four approaches to UA only to highlight their potential flaws—as if the only thing to be learned from the distant or the recent past is that everyone was wrong until *I* stepped on the stage five minutes ago: "surely to tell these tall tales," writes Zadie Smith, "would be to speed the myth, the wicked lie, that the past is always tense and the future perfect."[50] Indeed, a final benefit to be gained from these four authors is the helpful reminder that UA is, in one form or another, the consensus viewpoint of the Christian tradition. So if we look askance at Greggs's universalism because it represents a minority report (and a small one at that), we might consider looking at "limited" (or definite) atonement with the same wariness. A near consensus does not make a view correct, but it does matter. Because in spite of our contemporary tweaks, "What's past *is* prologue" in theology.

---

50. Smith, *White Teeth*, 448.

PART THREE

AMYRALDISM AND TRADITION

CHAPTER TEN

UNLIMITED ATONEMENT

Anglican Articles and an Analytic Approach

James M. Arcadi

Christian theories of salvation pull toward poles that represent universalizing extremes on one end and particularizing extremes on the other. One sees explications of salvation in the Christian tradition drawn all the way to the universalizing pole by arguing for full-blown universalism. On the other hand, there are explications that tend toward the particularizing by proffering that Christ's work is limited to some segment of humanity significantly less than the total amount of humans. The unlimited atonement theory, typically construed, attempts to find a *via media* of sorts between these poles. By, again typically construed, emphasizing the "sufficiency-efficiency" distinction, the unlimited atonement theorist attempts to hold together a universalizing proclivity regarding the sufficiency of Christ's work for all humans, together with a particularizing tendency regarding the efficiency of Christ's work for only some humans.

The Anglican tradition is often held up—or marketed—as the Christian tradition uniquely in pursuit of *via media* between a plethora of theological topics regarding doctrine, liturgy, and polity. Many of the early theological formularies of this tradition reflect an attempt to find a middle ground between competing extremes. One such formulary is the Thirty-Nine Articles of Religion, which offer the (or *an*) Anglican angle on a number of issues particularly controversial in that most theologically controversial of centuries in the Christian tradition: the sixteenth. Some of the Articles clearly attempt to find a middle path between, for instance, Roman Catholicism and

Anabapatism, or Lutheranism and Reformed thought, or even intra-Anglican positions as well. The Articles's view of salvation—and specifically the scope of the work of Christ—likewise, so I will show, attempts to find a soteriological *via media* that might best be described as unlimited atonement. Hence, this chapter explores the early Anglican views on the scope of the atonement by probing the teaching of the Articles themselves and by surveying the tradition of commentating on these Articles. In the process, I will argue (1) that unlimited atonement well characterizes the teaching on the atonement from the Articles; (2) the manner in which the Articles describe faith functioning in achieving the efficacy aspect of the sufficiency-efficiency model can be understood utilizing the conceptual framework of dispositional properties from contemporary metaphysics; and (3) contrary to a recent attempt to characterize unlimited atonement in the Anglican tradition, faith is the only stimulus condition for this efficacy for all humans who are saved.[1]

UNLIMITED ATONEMENT IN THE THIRTY-NINE ARTICLES

As noted, the Thirty-Nine Articles of Religion were the early Anglicans' attempt at staking out views on various theological positions that would come to be the hallmark of the Church of England. The Articles emerged over the course of a few decades in the mid-sixteenth century as the newly independent Church of England sought to articulate its positions on some of the more controversial theological topics of the day. They reached something of their final form in 1571 when they were included in the *Book of Common Prayer*. In no wise were the Articles as comprehensive or exhaustive as other Protestant formularies of the day—such as the Augsburg Confession—or subsequent ones—such as the Westminster Confession of Faith. However, they do address such theological, and specifically soteriological, issues as one might expect would arise from the sixteenth century. Given that the Articles of Religion were officially incorporated into the life of the Church of England some two decades before the birth of Moïse Amyraut, any points of contact between the theologies expressed by both is simply coincidental. Indeed, the unlimited atonement perspective emerged independently in England, even if Amyraut came to be known by later Anglicans.[2] In what follows, I survey some of the issues wherein the Articles

---

1.   My purpose in this chapter is not to legislate for Anglicans which view on the scope of the atonement Anglicans *ought* to have or which is *the* authentic Anglican position. There are, have been, and will be Anglicans who favor limited atonement, just as there are, have been, and will be Arminian Anglicans. I do contend that the unlimited atonement position is most harmonious with a straightforward read of the Articles, but Anglicans have long been comfortable with less straightforward reads of these Articles on nearly every topic they discuss.

2.   For discussion, see especially Michael J. Lynch, *John Davenant's Hypothetical Universalism: A Defense of Catholic and Reformed Orthodoxy* (New York: Oxford University Press, 2021); Alan Ford, *James Ussher: Theology, History, and Politics in Early-Modern Ireland and England* (New York: Oxford University Press, 2007); and Jonathan D. Moore, *English Hypothetical Universalism: John Preston and the Softening of Reformed Theology* (Grand Rapids: Eerdmans, 2007).

speak most clearly on the issue of the scope of the atonement, along with some engagement with the tradition of theological commentaries on these Articles.[3]

ORIGINAL AND ACTUAL SIN

In two locations in the Articles, a distinction is drawn between original sin and actual sin.[4] Both Article II and Article XXXI indicate that Christ's work is applicable to both categories of sin. Moreover, not only is Christ's work applicable to both categories—in support of the unlimited atonement position—Christ's work is applicable to *all* sins that fall into these categories, not just the sins of the elect.

This first place in the Articles where Christ's atoning work crops up comes in Article II, which deals specifically with the "Word, or Son of God, which was made very man." The focus of this article is a simple expressing of creedal Christology. Regarding this, the article states that Christ is God "of one substance with the Father" and a human being, the nature of which the Word took "in the womb of the blessed Virgin, of her substance." A clearly Chalcedonian influence comes when the article specifies that "the Godhead and the manhood were joined together in one person, never to be divided."

Then, in explicating the work of Christ, the article turns to outline that Christ suffered, was crucified, died, and was buried (alluding to the Apostles' Creed), "to reconcile His Father to us, and to be a sacrifice, not only for original guilt *but also for all actual sins of men*" (emphasis added). This latter clause is identical to the statement on the Son of God found in the Augsburg Confession. I take it that the primary objective of framers of the Articles for these clauses is to ensure that the faithful understood that no other means than Christ's work were required to cover the sins of humans. Many of the Articles ought to be read as responses to (popular, if not official) Roman Catholic theological positions. The worry the framers seem to have in mind is a perspective that would say, "Well, Christ's work deals with original guilt, but we need something extra like penance or pardons or indulgences to deal with the ongoing problem of the execution of actual sins." W. H. Griffith Thomas comments, "The Article is thus intended to cover all forms of moral evil, whether those associated with the sin of Adam, or those due to man's personal action. The Bible clearly distinguishes between 'sin' and 'sins,' the root and the fruit, the principle and the practice, and the Article teaches that our Lord's Atonement covers both of these."[5] Hence, there is a universalizing pull in this article: Christ's work is not just a solution

---

3. Many editions of the Articles of Religion are available. For this chapter, I have used the version found on the Church of England's website at https://www.churchofengland.org/prayer-and-worship/worship-texts-and-resources/book-common-prayer/articles-religion, accessed June 4, 2021.

4. Original sin is in Article II referred to as "original guilt." Although principled distinctions are made in theological discourse between original sin and original guilt, in this context these terms appear to be synonymous.

5. W. H. Griffith Thomas, *The Principles of Theology: An Introduction to the Thirty-Nine Articles* (London: Longmans, Green, 1930), 50.

for a particular aspect of the problem of sin (original guilt), but is the solution for the entirety of the sin problem—original and actual sin.

These comments reflect the Articles's teaching that all *classes* of sin are addressed in Christ's work, but the Articles—and their commentators—also indicate that all *members* of all classes of sins are covered. In fact, it is the case that at times in the history of the dissemination of the Articles the effort was made to particularize the universalizing tendency of the understanding of Christ's work by removing the universal quantifier in "for all actual sins of men." As E. T. Green comments:

> The omission of the word "all" in some modern copies is entirely with-out authority. The wording is important because strongly anti-Calvinistic, Calvinism teaching that Christ did not die for all sins, but for those of the elect only. That the Calvinistic party considered the word "all" hostile to their doctrine is proved by the fact that in the text as revised by the West-minster divines it is wanting.[6]

By "Calvinist" here, I take it that Green means the five-point variety with its emphasis on limited atonement. Moreover, Edgar Gibson too makes note of the importance of the preservation of "all" in the article. Gibson writes,

> Attention is drawn to this assertion of the universality of redemption, because in various editions of the Articles the important word "all" has been, without the slightest authority, omitted in order to force the article into agreement with the Calvinistic theory of "particular redemption," i.e., the doctrine that Christ died not for all but only for "the elect."[7]

Clearly, much is made by these Anglican commentators on the Articles that Christ's work is for all sins is the proper interpretation of the Articles.

In fact, the commentators wish to go so far as to emphasize that the Articles specify that Christ's work is for *all* sins of *all* humans. As with many theological or scriptural statements, the meaning of the statement turns significantly on the identification of the antecedent to a pronoun: Who is "us" in "to reconcile His Father to *us*"? Or the specific members included in a general term: Who are "men" in "for all actual sins of *men*"? A similar issue arises in Article III when it states, "Christ died for *us*." Again, Gibson writes, "For the *universal* character of redemption and the fact that it was for *all* men that Christ died, appeal may be made to S. John iii.16. . . . The breadth of such language is quite inconsistent with narrower theories that would limit the saving work of Christ to 'the elect.'"[8]

---

6.   E. Tyrrell Green, *The Thirty-Nine Articles and the Age of the Reformation: An Historical and Doctrinal Exposition in the Light of Contemporary Documents* (London: Wells Gardner, Darton, 1896), 34.

7.   Edgar C. S. Gibson, *The Thirty-Nine Articles of the Church of England* (London: Methuen, 1898), 149.

8.   Gibson, *Thirty-Nine Articles*, 151, emphasis original.

Hence, "all" ought to be understood in the simplest and most straightforward manner as indeed all humans, not just all the elect.

Whereas a particularization of the work of the atonement to only the elect is found in such places as the Westminster Confession of Faith, the term "the elect" is nowhere to be found in the Anglican Articles. Rather, as Thomas states, "The Atonement means that God in the Person of His Eternal Son took upon Himself in vicarious death the sin of the whole world. The offer of mercy is made to everyone, since there is no sinner for whom Christ did not die, and every sin, past, present, and future, is regarded as laid on and borne by Him."[9] Thomas here clearly expresses the position that the Articles teach that the scope of Christ's work is unlimited; all the sins of all humans are sufficiently atoned for by Christ's death.

SUFFICIENCY-EFFICIENCY

As just alluded to, the Lombardian sufficiency-efficiency distinction—and related characterizations—is even noted by some of the commentators on the Articles. R. L. Cloquet juxtaposes the language found in Article II with that found in Article XXXI when he writes, "But if we compare the analogous and indeed almost synonymous words of the thirty-first Article . . . unless we adjust Scripture teaching to our own narrow theories, we must conclude that Christ's Death was an Atonement for the sins of all mankind—*sufficient* for all, *efficient* for some."[10] This is a hallmark phrase of the unlimited atonement position: Christ's work is sufficient for all humans, but only efficient for some segment less than the total number of humans. Cloquet further specifies the sufficiency-efficiency distinction by describing another contrast, this one between "objective universality" and "subjective individuality." Cloquet comments on 2 Corinthians 5:14–15,[11] "Here we have plainly set out the *objective universality* of Christ's death or atonement, in 'that he died for all'; and the *subjective individuality* of the living power of that death, in 'they which live unto him which died for them.'"[12] From an objective angle, Christ's work is sufficient for the redemption of all humans—this is a pull toward the universalizing pole. But from the subjective angle of the individual human, Christ's work is only efficiently applied to those who have faith, of which the tradition is clear that this is not all humans—and hence the pull toward the particularizing that results in a *via media* position.

The universal objective value of Christ's work is also an emphasis of Gibson's reflections on Article II. He states:

---

9. Thomas, *Principles of Theology*, 58–59.
10. Robert Louis Cloquet, *An Exposition of the Thirty-Nine Articles of the Church of England* (London: James Nisbet, 1885), 26, emphasis original.
11. "For the love of Christ urges us on, because we are convinced that one has died for all; therefore all have died. And he died for all, so that those who live might live no longer for themselves, but for him who died and was raised for them" (NRSV).
12. Cloquet, *Exposition*, 26, emphasis original.

Language such as that [of Article II] is surely incompatible with any theory that denies the objective value of the Atonement. To maintain that the whole value of the death of Christ lies in its effect upon the minds and hearts of men by the supreme revelation which it makes of the love of God is to evacuate the words of Scripture of their plain meaning, and to introduce a method of interpretation which, if permitted, will enable men to evade the force of the clearest declarations.[13]

For Gibson, denial of this universal objective scope of Christ's work is to distort the plain reading of Scripture, which he takes the Articles to reflect, and thus open the door to all manner of reinterpretations of doctrine. Rather, the *via media* position of unlimited atonement with limited application best characterizes the scriptural position, as interpreted by these Anglicans.

This *via media* comes across when characterizing the Articles' position between five-point Calvinism and Arminianism. This is a particular concern of E. A. Litton's theological commentary on the Articles. His reflections on the manner in which the sufficiency-efficiency distinction preserves the *via media* of Anglicanism is worth quoting at length:

The death of Christ placed mankind as a whole in a new and favourable position as regards God, though by many this position may never be realised or made their own; it was a propitiation not for our sins only, but also for the sins of the whole world (1 John ii. 2). A public advantage was thereby secured, which however may become a savour of death unto death or of life unto life according as it is used (2 Cor. ii. 16). And is not this substantially the meaning of the assertors of particular redemption when they admit, as they do, the sufficiency of the Atonement for the sins of the world, or ten thousand worlds? And on that sufficiency ground the right and the duty of ministers or missionaries to proclaim to all men that if they repent and believe they will be saved? This proclamation could not be made if there had not been effected by the death of Christ a general expiation for our fallen race. And thus the combatants may not be in reality so much at variance as they had supposed. The most extreme Calvinist may grant that there is room for all if they will come in; the most extreme Arminian must grant that redemption, in its full scriptural meaning, is not the privilege of all men.[14]

Litton holds that the *via media* of unlimited atonement best preserves the evangelistic mandates found in Scripture. All humans are potentially redeemed, but not all humans are ultimately actually redeemed. Yet, the honest proclamation of the gospel, for Litton and others, is dependent on the

---

13.   Gibson, *Thirty-Nine Articles*, 152.
14.   E. A. Litton, *Introduction to Dogmatic Theology on the Basis of the XXXIX Articles of the Church of England* (London: Elliot Stock, 1882), 285–86, emphasis original.

conception of potentiality that unlimited atonement affords, and of which more will be said in this chapter.

Although the distinction between the sufficiency and efficiency of the work of Christ goes back to Peter Lombard, the Anglican Articles and the commentators on them put forth this perspective in order to articulate a middle way between the universalizing and particularizing pulls of Christian theories of salvation. Before we probe the thread regarding the potentiality of all to be saved, in the next subsection I turn to examine the Articles's concern for the *solus Christus* of Reformation theology.

THE SUFFICIENT SACRIFICE OF CHRIST

The context for many of the Articles—and especially Article XXXI—is clearly a polemic against a certain interpretation of Roman Catholic sacramentalism pertaining to the notion of Eucharistic sacrifice. I say "a certain interpretation" because it is not clear to me that there is not great divergence between (a) an official Roman doctrine of Eucharistic sacrifice, (b) popular conceptions within Roman circles concerning Eucharistic sacrifice, (c) the early Anglican understanding of the Roman position on this issue, or (d) early Anglican caricatures of either (a) or (b). What is at issue in Article XXXI is the attempt to secure the sole sufficiency of Christ's work on the cross for the remission of sins. This article is as anti-Pelagian as it is anti-Roman, although likely in the minds of many early Anglicans, these two are one and the same.

Regarding Christ's "one oblation . . . finished upon the cross," Article XXXI states,

> The Offering of Christ once made is that perfect redemption, propitiation, and satisfaction, for all the sins of the whole world, both original and actual; and there is none other satisfaction for sin, but that alone. Wherefore the sacrifices of Masses, in the which it was commonly said, that the Priest did offer Christ for the quick and the dead, to have remission of pain or guilt, were blasphemous fables, and dangerous deceits. (emphasis added)

As we have seen previously, the distinction between original and actual sin is not relevant to limit the scope of Christ's salvific work. But likewise does the inclusion of the universal quantifier regarding the sin of "the whole world" serve to push against the particularizing draw of the limited atonement theory. Thomas here comments on this article and refers to the Latin version of the first line, "*Oblatio Christi semel facta*": "The force of 'once' should be particularly noted as meaning 'once for all' (*semel*), answering to the New Testament words ἅπαξ, and ἐφάπαξ (Rom. 6:10; Heb. 7:27; 9:12, 26, 27, 28; 10:10; 1 Pet. 3:18)."[15] I take it that this phrase and his comments on it have an eye both to the chronological and the anthropological in their focus on the universal quantifier. Christ's sacrifice

---

15. Thomas, *Principles of Theology*, 414

is "once for all" in that it occurred at one time and yet is sufficient for all times. But, moreover, Christ's sacrifice occurred once by one individual and yet is sufficient for all humans and all sins committed by all humans. This is expounded in the next line where the article specifies that all the sins of the whole world are addressed in the satisfying work of Christ's one sufficient sacrifice.

This theme also comes to the fore by means of some phrases in Article XV. Continuing with the theme of finding indirect atonement doctrine within expressions pertaining directly to Christology, Article XV likewise conveys a universal sufficiency of Christ's work. After reiterating the notion that Christ is of the same nature as other humans, and specifying in Chalcedonian fashion that Christ is "like unto us in all things, sin only except," the article states that Christ "came to be the lamb without spot, Who by sacrifice of Himself once made, should take away the sins of the world." The limited atonement position takes it that Christ's sacrifice is not sufficient to take away the sins of the whole world, but only the sins of the elect. On the contrary, these articles stress the universal sufficiency of Christ's sacrifice to be "the propitiation for our sins, and not for ours only, but also for the sins of the whole world," as the quoting from 1 John 2 expresses.

LITURGICAL CORROBORATION

This liturgical note can briefly transition us away from the Articles to turn to the Anglican liturgy as a means of corroborating the unlimited atonement perspective in the Anglican formularies. The Anglican tradition has long been conceived of as a Protestant tradition influenced heavily by the maxim *lex orandi, lex credendi*. It is sometimes quipped that when the Lutherans and Reformed were forging their identities in the sixteenth and seventeenth centuries, they wrote confessions and catechisms, and when the Anglicans were forging theirs, they wrote a prayer book. This, of course, is not entirely fair, for the Lutherans and Reformed also composed liturgies and, as this chapter shows, the Anglicans also attempted to express their theology in propositional form. Here I offer a brief foray into liturgical theology in order to corroborate the reading of the Articles of Religion presented. This specifically concerns the universalizing trend in the Articles's conception of the extent of the work of Christ.

I quote here from the Communion office from the first Edwardian Prayer Book published in 1549. In this liturgy, the priest would say prior to the Eucharistic blessing:

O God heavenly father, which of thy tender mercie diddest geve thine only sonne Jesu Christ to suffre death upon the crosse for our redempcion, who made there (by his one oblacion once offered) a full, perfect, and sufficient sacrifyce, oblacion, and satysfaccyon, for the sinnes of the whole worlde, and did institute, and in his holy Gospell commaund us, to celebrate a perpetuall memory of that his precious death, untyll his comming again.[16]

---

16. Emphasis added. Many editions of the Book of Common Prayer can be found here: http://justus.

The phrase "by his one oblation once offered" is clearly connected to Article XXXI's language of "The Offering of Christ once made is that perfect redemption, propitiation, and satisfaction, for all the sins of the whole world." Again, while anti-Roman Catholic rhetoric regarding the sufficiency of Christ's sacrifice is likely primarily in sight, the universalizing pull of unlimited atonement is also characterized by the "perfect" and "sufficient" sacrifice of Christ. Moreover, this liturgical element includes the reminder that this work is for the "sins of the whole world" with no qualification or restriction.

The unqualified application of Christ's work on all the sins of all humans is brought again to the fore later in the same liturgy. Near the climax of the Eucharistic blessing the priest says: "Christ our Pascall lambe is offred up for us, once for al, when he bare our sinnes on hys body upon the crosse, for he is the very lambe of God, that taketh away the sines of the worlde: wherfore let us kepe a joyfull and holy feast with the Lorde."

The allusion to John the Forerunner's proclamation about Christ conveys the sufficiency of Christ's sacrifice that it is offered "once for all" whereby he "takes away the sins of the world." This conception is, of course, repeated just a bit later in the liturgy during the *Agnus Dei*: "O lambe of god, that takeste away the sinnes of the worlde: have mercie upon us."

One can find key expressions of Anglican theology in its early articles and its liturgy. When one probes these formularies for their teaching on the scope of the atonement, it is clear that the unlimited atonement perspective best fits data. Moreover, this has been the interpretation of a number of commentators on the Articles in the Anglican tradition. The Articles's focus on the manner in which Christ's work addresses all sins—original and actual—of all humans expresses well the sufficiency-efficiency distinction that is the trademark of the unlimited atonement standpoint. Furthermore, the Articles and liturgy emphasize the sole and total sufficiency of the sacrifice of Christ for all these sins. Yet, these formularies do not teach a full-blown universalism. Rather, I argue, a *via media* can be plotted by attending to the role that faith plays in making actual the potentially universally effective work of Christ.

SALVIFIC EFFICACY AS A DISPOSITIONAL PROPERTY

The picture painted by the Articles on the scope of Christ's work, I think, can be further probed by showing the application of this work to be akin to the manner in which dispositional properties function within the powers metaphysics conceptual scheme.[17] What I will argue here is that in the unlimited atonement model portrayed by the Articles, all humans are potentially saveable, for the scope of the atonement is sufficient for all. What is required for this potentiality

---

anglican.org/resources/bcp/england.htm. For the Communion service in uses here, see http://justus.anglican.org/resources/bcp/1549/Communion_1549.htm, accessed June 4, 2021.

17. A very helpful encyclopedia entry is Sungho Choi and Michael Fara, "Dispositions," *The Stanford Encyclopedia of Philosophy* (2021), https://plato.stanford.edu/archives/spr2021/entries/dispositions.

to become actual is the presence of faith in the individual. I here first sketch the notion of dispositional properties and then apply this idea to the salvific context. The next section addresses a potential objection to the sole requirement of faith as the means for making effective the sufficient work of Christ.

Properties are features of objects. For instance, a porcelain teapot might have such properties as *being made from porcelain*, or *being 16 ounces in weight*, or, on some occasions, *being full of tea*. A dispositional property is certain kind of property or feature of an object that refers to the object's ability to change in ways that are specific to that kind of object. We might say an object has a disposition or capacity or tendency to change in certain ways in certain contexts. These contexts are sometimes referred to as stimulus conditions—as in, these conditions stimulate the change in an object. For example, we would typically think that a porcelain teapot has the property of *being fragile*. But "being fragile" just means that in a certain context—like being smashed with a mallet—the teapot would shatter. Hence, we can say that the teapot has the dispositional property of *being such that it would shatter when struck with a certain amount of force*. We can imagine a porcelain teapot on a counter, and this teapot has this dispositional property, even though the teapot is resting undisturbed. If, however, the stimulus condition noted in the conditional of the dispositional property is activated—say, I strike the teapot with a mallet—then the state of affairs noted in the first part of the property description (i.e., shattering) obtains (and I have a mess to clean up!).

Here is another example: think of simple table salt. Salt, as we learn in school, is *soluble*. Yet this property is a dispositional property. It is more specifically stated that salt is *being such that were it immersed in liquid it would dissolve*. Hence, while in the saltshaker on the table, the salt is only potentially dissolved (it is *dissolvable*), once I catalyze the appropriate stimulus conditions—say, sprinkling it onto my soup—then this property comes to actualization. The point of both of these illustrations is to point out that noting dispositional properties helps us to specify where, when, and what changes occur that can so radically alter a particular object.

A similar analysis can be had for the actualization of salvation in an individual human on the unlimited atonement scheme. Because Christ's sacrifice is sufficient for "all the sins of the whole world," all that is needed for individual humans is that they are placed in the appropriate condition to receive the benefits of Christ's sacrifice. I quoted Litton earlier, and do so again, on just this point, "The death of Christ placed mankind as a whole in a new and favorable position as regards God, though by many this position may never be realised or made their own."[18] On the unlimited atonement theory according to the Anglican variety sketched above, faith is the stimulus condition requisite for "making their own" Christ's work in the lives of some segment less than the total number of humans. In this manner, one can hold to the universality of the objective

---

18.   Litton, *Dogmatic Theology*, 285.

work of Christ without being compelled to embrace universalism. Rather the subjective individuality of faith makes effective Christ's work for particular humans. Thus, in good Reformational *sola fide* fashion, faith is the only ingredient, so to speak, that differentiates the saved from the damned.

This dispositional analysis, I think, fits well with another Article of Religion, Article XI on justification. This article states, "We are accounted righteous before God, *only* for the merit of our Lord and Saviour Jesus Christ by Faith . . . that we are justified by Faith *only* is a most wholesome Doctrine" (emphasis added). Note that these clauses state that it is *only* by faith that the merit of Christ's work applies to those individuals to whom it applies. Simply put, faith is *the* stimulus condition to make effectual the work of Christ for an individual. In the next section, I will argue that it is best to hold fast to the singularity of this conception, even in the face of a potential objection.

SOLA FIDE NOT JUST NORMALLY, BUT ALWAYS

The view of the scope of Christ's work sketched in this chapter has been that Christ's sacrifice is sufficient to atone for all sins of all humans. However, it is also the teaching of the Christian tradition that not all humans receive the benefit of this sacrifice. In the previous section, I showed how one could think of faith as that stimulus condition within which the universal objectivity of Christ's work is made subjectively individual. Yet, might we not ask a question about those who potentially do not have faith? If faith is the sole ingredient needed to effect salvation for individuals, does that not mean that those who are unable to exercise faith due to cognitive limitations are also unable to tap into the benefits of Christ's work? Just such questions arise from a recent discussion of unlimited atonement in the English or Anglican tradition.

CRISPIAN ENGLISH HYPOTHETICAL UNIVERSALISM

In his *Deviant Calvinism: Broadening Reformed Theology*, Oliver Crisp attempts to show that there is more diversity of theological positions within the Reformed tradition than is often considered.[19] One such effort at broadening Crisp takes is to show that limited atonement is not the only perspective on the scope of Christ's work in the Reformed tradition. In order to show this, he probes the work of some English Reformed theologians in order to present a view he calls "English Hypothetical Universalism."[20] For this scheme, Crisp

---

19. Oliver Crisp, *Deviant Calvinism: Broadening Reformed Theology* (Minneapolis: Fortress, 2014), chap. 7.

20. I note that in this volume we are using the term "unlimited atonement" as opposed to "hypothetical universalism," but the same conceptual scheme is targeted. I also note that whereas in *Deviant Calvinism* Crisp refers to this position as "English Hypothetical Universalism," more recently he has taken to calling the view "Anglican Hypothetical Universalism." In both instances, Crisp is largely expositing and expanding upon the thought of John Davenant, an Anglican I have avoided discussing in this chapter due to the thorough treatments of him elsewhere. For Crisp's more recent work on this topic, see *Freedom, Redemption and Communion: Studies in Christian Doctrine* (London: Bloomsbury, 2021), chap. 5.

describes the following flow to the state of affairs of humans coming to be reconciled with God:

1. The atonement is sufficient for all of humanity, upon the condition of faith.

2. God intends the work of Christ to bring about the salvation of all those who have faith.

3. Faith is a divine gift.

4. Normally, fallen human beings obtain salvation through Christ by means of the interposition of divine grace logically prior to salvation, producing faith.

5. God provides faith for the elect.[21]

Regarding (1) we can understand this as the dispositional character of the atoning work of Christ. The work of Christ is *sufficient* for all, that is, all humans are potentially savable. However, any human that is actually saved requires the condition of faith, that is, we might say, given the stimulus condition of the exercise of faith, making the atonement *efficient* for this class of humans. Now, what appears to be a universal statement in (1) is then shown, on Crisp's view, to be not universal in (4). Rather what is shown in this description is that (1) is the normal or typical state of affairs for salvation, but (4) admits of exceptions to this rule. In a footnote to proposition (4), Crisp writes, "The caveat 'normally' is inserted because there may be classes of fallen humans who are saved *without* faith, such as the severely mentally disabled and infants who die before the age of discernment."[22] Hence, for Crisp, *most* humans who are saved have the universally sufficient work of Christ applied to them by faith, but there "may" be some humans who are not saved in this standard manner.

To my mind, however, the atonement situation need not be so complicated, and we can Ockham this situation (to coin a verb) to make it simpler and more consistent. On the Crispian interpretation, God has to provide one means of stimulating atonement in one class of humans—faith—and another means of stimulating atonement in another class of humans, those who are "severely mentally disabled and infants who die before the age of discernment." Call the first class ordinary humans (OH) and the subsequent class special humans (SH). OH are "saved by faith," and SH presumably are saved by some other means. However, an Ockhamly simpler way to construe the

---

21. Crisp, *Deviant Calvinism*, 201 (emphasis added).
22. Crisp, *Deviant Calvinism*, 201 (emphasis added).

situation is hold that OH and SH are both saved by the same means, which is faith; *sola fide* always, not just normally.

The clue for advancing this simpler conceptual framework is in Crisp's own proposition (3), "Faith is a divine gift." I see no reason to hold that any divine gift is necessarily predicated upon a prior or natural quality, feature, or property of any individual human. According to the scriptural witness, God has no problem making an ineloquent shepherd like Moses God's mouthpiece, enabling a man who was born blind to see, or bringing a dead person back to life. Rather, God gives God's gifts to whom God wishes and the exercise of those gifts is due to the—at times—cooperative power of the human with God's fundamental empowerment. But how this looks, how the divine power is manifest, how the gift is exercised, is and will be as individually unique as the individual human is unique. Simply put, it does not seem to me required to say that God normally provides one way to apply the atonement to OH and another to apply the atonement to SH. Not only does this strain the *sola fide* principle of the theology of the Articles, it is a less simple situation as well.

INFANT BAPTISM AS TEST CASE

One way to probe the consistency of the *sola fide* ingredient is through a test case of a standard Anglican and Reformed liturgical practice, infant baptism. Regarding this ancient practice Article XXVII says,

> Baptism is not only a sign of profession, and mark of difference, whereby Christian men are discerned from others that be not christened, but it is also a sign of Regeneration or new Birth, whereby, as by an instrument, they that receive Baptism rightly are grafted into the Church; the promises of forgiveness of sin, and of our adoption to be the sons of God by the Holy Ghost, are visibly signed and sealed; Faith is confirmed, and Grace increased by virtue of prayer unto God. The Baptism of young Children is in any wise to be retained in the Church, as most agreeable with the institution of Christ.

One might wonder how it is that infants or those without the cognitive abilities of adult humans would be able to have their faith "confirmed." Would it not seem as though an individual is first to profess faith and then to have that faith confirmed in the waters of baptism? In fact, just such a scenario is envisioned by Crisp.

However, John Calvin is instructive on this point, wherein he argues that we do not know that infants—or any SH—do not have faith. In the *Institutes* Calvin argues against the Anabaptists who would require that those who are baptized be of a certain age. He writes, somewhat colorfully:

> Therefore, if it please him, why may the Lord not shine with a tiny spark at the present time on those whom he will illumine in the future with the full splendor of his light—especially if he has not removed their ignorance

before taking them from the prison of the flesh? I would not rashly affirm that they are endowed with the same faith as we experience in ourselves, or have entirely the same knowledge of faith—this I prefer to leave undetermined—but I would somewhat restrain the obtuse arrogance of those who at the top of their lungs deny or assert whatever they please.[23]

Note that Calvin here is not so bold as to declare definitively that infants do have faith, as Luther before him had. Rather, Calvin takes the epistemically humble stance of asserting that we cannot know that those SH are without faith. Given the logic of unlimited atonement and attention to the Crispian (3), I would be inclined to argue that any member of SH has the work of Christ applied to them in the same manner as those in OH. Consequently, it seems to me, one can hold that the only stimulus condition necessary in order for the dispositional property of being saved by Christ is faith—for the members of OH and SH alike.

CONCLUSION

This chapter has explored unlimited atonement in the Anglican tradition by attending to the Articles of Religion, an early Eucharistic liturgy from this tradition, and some historical commentaries on both. Although emerging independently from Amyraut and continental Amyraldism, from this data set it appears that unlimited atonement is the best way to characterize the teaching of these early formularies regarding the scope of Christ's salvific work. What these formularies teach regarding the scope of the atonement is that every individual human is potentially a human that could be saved. In this regard, humans have the dispositional property of *being saved* if they are found to be in the proper stimulus condition. Hearkening to the Reformation staple of *sola fide*, I averred that faith is that only missing ingredient that need be added to the human condition in order to make Christ's sufficient work efficient for a particular individual. Despite Crisp's suggestion that some segments of the human population might be saved in another manner, I argued that it is simpler and more consistent with other Christian practices—namely, infant baptism—to hold that all humans who are saved possess the divine gift of faith, albeit in manner that are as individually unique as there are unique individuals. Hence, while Christ's work is universally sufficient for salvation, it is efficient by only faith for some particular humans.

---

23.   John Calvin, *Institutes of the Christian Religion*, vol. 2, trans. Ford Lewis Battles, ed. John McNeill (Philadelphia: Westminster, 1960), 1342.

CHAPTER ELEVEN

AMYRAUT AND THE BAPTIST TRADITION

David L. Allen

From their beginning in the early seventeenth century, Baptists have been an eclectic group with respect to soteriology. The earliest group, the General Baptists, were mostly Arminian in theology and acquired the designation "General" because they held to a "general" or "unlimited" atonement. The "Particular" Baptists arose about thirty years later, so designated because most of them held to "particular" atonement, where "particular" refers specifically to the extent of the atonement—Jesus died for the sins of the elect only.[1] But here we must speak carefully and with proper nuance, because as I have demonstrated in *The Extent of the Atonement: A Historical and Critical Review*, some Particular Baptists held to an unlimited atonement,[2] and this fact will play a significant role in evaluating Amyraut's connection with Baptist history.

In the succeeding generations of Baptists, a variety of views on soteriology can be observed—non-Calvinism, moderate Calvinism, high Calvinism, and hyper-Calvinism. Some Baptists are Arminian or non-Calvinistic. Some are moderate Calvinists in that they affirm all aspects of mainstream

---

1. For a survey of General and Particular Baptists in English Baptist History, see Roger Hayden, *English Baptist History and Heritage*, 2nd ed. (Oxfordshire: Nigel Lynn, 2005).
2. See David L. Allen, *The Extent of the Atonement: A Historical and Critical Review* (Nashville: B&H Academic, 2016), 459–514; David Wenkel, "The Doctrine of the Extent of the Atonement among the Early English Particular Baptists," *Harvard Theological Review* 112, no. 3 (2019): 358–75. In the case of these Particular Baptists, they held to a sense of particular redemption wherein Christ is determined to save the elect alone through his death, but he also purposed that his death provide a satisfaction for the sins of all humanity.

Calvinism except limited atonement. Some Baptists are high-Calvinists in that they affirm all aspects of mainstream Calvinism, including limited atonement. Some Baptists, at least historically, are hyper-Calvinists, in that they deny one or more of the following: common grace, duty faith, God's universal love, God's universal saving will, and/or the well-meant gospel offer.

When Southern Baptists were founded in 1845 in Augusta, Georgia, they too continued in the eclecticism of their forefathers with respect to soteriology. Two eighteenth- and early-nineteenth-century tributaries fed the Southern Baptist stream: the Charleston tradition and the Sandy Creek tradition. The Charleston tradition was Calvinistic in theology. The Sandy Creek tradition softened their Calvinism to include unlimited atonement along with other modifications.[3]

Although most early Southern Baptists were Calvinistic in some sense, they were certainly not all "five-pointers," to use today's modern lingo. Many affirmed an unlimited atonement along with unconditional election while others affirmed unlimited atonement and a modified form of unconditional election, corporate election, or conditional election. Most all adhered to total depravity and perseverance of the saints. Today, the majority of Baptists, including Southern Baptists, are non-Calvinists strictly speaking, though most would adhere to total depravity (though not necessarily defined to include total inability) and perseverance of the saints.

Amyraut and Amyraldianism are not normally associated with Baptists. Is there any connection between Amyraut and Baptists, past or present? Before we answer that question, we must first consider the connection between Amyraldianism and hypothetical universalism. Sometimes these two terms are considered synonymous. In reality, Amyraldianism is a subset of hypothetical universalism.

DEFINITIONS OF HYPOTHETICAL UNIVERSALISM: ITS ORIGIN AND CONTEMPORARY APPLICATIONS

What is hypothetical universalism? The theological label "hypothetical universalism" surfaced for the first time in a letter written by Guillaume Rivet in July 1645 and was intended pejoratively. Rivet was likely the first to employ the term as a label for the theologians of Saumur, including Amyraut. Van Stam identified the source of the label "hypothetical universalism":

Another sign of the hardening of the conflict is the rise, a half year after the national synod of Charenton, of a designation for the adherents of Saumur that was intended to be unfavorable. The expression in question is "les hypothetiques," the "hypotheticals." In the later history of dogma the theology of Saumur would be known as "hypothetical universalism," a phrase in which the pejorative element occurs as adjective. The Reformed in France adopted

---

3.   H. Leon McBeth, *The Baptist Heritage* (Nashville: Broadman, 1987), 227–35.

the concept "les hypothetiques" as a fixed designation for the theologians of Saumur while the Swiss Reformed before 1650 described them as "universalists." . . . Amyraut's intent was to make plain that whoever believes may rest assured that God will save him or her and has in fact elected that person.[4]

The idea of "hypothetical universalism" is basically that God, desiring to save humanity, intended to give Christ to be a satisfaction for the sins of all humanity, such that, if all were to believe, all would be saved. By virtue of Christ suffering for the sins of the entire human race, God has thereby rendered all people saveable. Although hypothetical universalism was a label first used in a narrow sense for the Saumur theologians, there were other equivalent labels used in the early modern period, especially for the English Reformed theologians. As Michael Lynch has noted, there were

> two terms that were regularly used to identify a position much like hypothetical universalism among the early English Reformed theologians: "universal redemption" and "the middle way." These terms often denoted a theology that taught a conditional or hypothetical decree; thus, "universal redemption" taught that Christ died for all human beings in such a way that if all believed, all would be saved. . . . By the middle of the seventeenth-century the term ["universal redemption"] became commonplace among Arminian, Reformed, Lutheran and other theologians who claimed that Christ made a satisfaction for sin on behalf of all human beings such that if all believed, all would be saved.[5]

Amyraut's doctrine was called "hypothetical universalism," but, like "universal redemption," as E. F. Karl Müller noted,

> the term is misleading, since it might be applied also to the Arminianism which he [Amyraut] steadfastly opposed. His main proposition is this: God wills all men to be saved, on condition that they believe—a condition which they could well fulfill in the abstract,[6] but which in fact, owing

---

4. See Frans Pieter van Stam, *The Controversy over the Theology of Saumur, 1635–1650: Disrupting Debates among the Huguenots in Complicated Circumstances* (Amsterdam: APA-Holland University Press, 1988), 277–78.

5. Michael J. Lynch, "Richard Hooker and the Development of English Hypothetical Universalism," in *Richard Hooker and Reformed Orthodoxy*, eds. S. N. Kindred-Barnes and W. B. Littlejohn (Göttingen: Vandenhoeck & Ruprecht, 2017), 278.

6. By "in the abstract," he probably meant *hypothetically* or *theoretically*, in the sense that all people, in Amyraut's view, have the *natural* ability to believe, but not the *moral* ability. Amyraut likely picked up this distinction from his mentor, John Cameron (c. AD 1579–1625), even though the distinction was not unique to him. This distinction is also crucial with respect to Christ's satisfaction in the theology of hypothetical universalists in the sense that they maintain that Christ has removed all the legal (or natural) barriers to man's salvation.

to inherited corruption,[7] they stubbornly reject, so that this universal will for salvation actually saves no one. God also wills in particular to save a certain number of persons, and to pass over the others with this grace. The elect will be saved as inevitably the others will be damned.[8]

The other label, "the middle way," was often used as a synonym for universal redemption in the Calvinistic sense, and is also potentially misleading. As Lynch notes:

> When Reformed theologians used this term, it highlighted the distinctiveness of their approach to the thorny question of the extent of Christ's satisfaction from other approaches to the doctrine. In the latter part of sixteenth century—with the rise of what the Reformed deemed as unorthodox Lutheran views (such as the teachings of Samuel Huber) and what might be called proto-Remonstrant opinions—certain Reformed theologians were interested in preserving what they (at least) perceived to be the status quo: the catholic and Reformed doctrine of universal redemption. The use of the term "middle-way" coincides with the increase of Reformed theologians who denied that Christ was appointed as mediator for both elect and non-elect, often explicitly teaching that Christ died for [the sins of] the elect alone.[9]

Robert Godfrey also correctly described both the concerns of the moderate Calvinists at the Synod of Dort, as well as what it meant to advocate for the middle way:

> For the moderates, catholicity encompassed more than a clear rejection of the Remonstrant heterodoxy. All the moderates did join in a fundamental rejection of the Remonstrant position, yet they felt that the threat to the Reformed faith was not exclusively the threat of the heterodox. They feared that the strict orthodox erred in using some novel theological expressions which tended to cut them off from the tradition of Christendom.[10]

In summary, historically speaking, hypothetical universalists are (1) Calvinists with both (2) a concern for "the universal significance of the death of Christ" in the sense described above, that is, Christ died for the sins

---

7. "Inherited corruption" from Adam, on Amyraut's view, renders mankind *morally* unable to believe, and so they "stubbornly reject" God's offer of life in Christ.
8. Ernst F. Karl Müller, "Amyraut, Moïse," in *The New Schaff-Herzog Encyclopedia of Religious Knowledge,* eds. S. M. Jackson, et al., 13 vols. (New York: Funk and Wagnalls, 1908–1914), 1:161.
9. Lynch, "Richard Hooker and the Development of English Hypothetical Universalism," 279.
10. W. Robert Godfrey, "Tensions within International Calvinism: The Debate on the Atonement at the Synod of Dort, 1618–1619" (PhD diss., Stanford University, 1974), 231–32.

of all humanity, and (3) for a middle way position between the Remonstrants and the stricter Reformed orthodox.

While there is diversity among hypothetical universalists, the crucial area that all of them in the Calvinist tradition have in common is the view that *Christ substituted himself on behalf of all humanity, not merely for those appointed to eternal life (the elect).* Although the terminology to describe this unlimited-imputation-of-sin-to-Christ category changes throughout the history of moderate forms of Calvinism, the fundamental concept is the same for them all: Christ suffered *for the sins* of all humanity.

Today, the term "hypothetical universalism" is applied to all Calvinists who assert unlimited atonement. The legal barriers prohibiting God from saving sinners have been removed by the death of Christ. Christ substituted for the sins of all humanity in such a way that if anyone meets the condition of salvation—faith in Christ—he or she can be saved. All humanity is "savable" because there is an atonement for the sins of all humanity. What is "hypothetical" in "hypothetical universalism" is the condition "if anyone believes," not the atonement as a payment for all sins. Anyone who believes in Christ will be saved. However, as Calvinists, all hypothetical universalists also believe that only the elect will receive the gift of faith in order to believe. It should be noted that this understanding of atonement and its relation to the sins of all people is essentially that of historic Christianity from the church fathers until the Reformation, regardless of how election is defined.

Given this history of usage, and the fact that there is nothing "hypothetical" in the satisfaction for all sin according to all Calvinists who affirm such, "hypothetical universalism" is an unhelpful term. Some in the Reformed tradition have even inaccurately associated "hypothetical universalism" (at least the Saumur variety) with Pelagianism and Arminianism.[11]

VARIETIES OF HYPOTHETICAL UNIVERSALISM

Scholars have recognized different historical streams of hypothetical universalism since the beginning of the Reformation period, and within these groups there are still more differences and distinctions, as the universality of the death of Christ is packaged within various theological systems. These include (1) the early Reformers (2) the seventeenth-century English Puritan variety, and (3) the Saumurian school.[12]

First, there are the early Reformation hypothetical universalists on the continent and England in the sixteenth century. Continental reformers include Zwingli, Luther, Calvin, Bullinger, and Bucer, along with many others. Second-generation reformers on the continent who were hypothetical universalists include Girolamo Zanchi, Zacharias Ursinus, Casper Olevianus,

---

11. See Allen, *Extent of the Atonement*, 172–73.
12. See the helpful chapter "Hypothetical Universalism" in Oliver D. Crisp, *Deviant Calvinism: Broadening Reformed Theology* (Minneapolis: Fortress, 2014), 175–211.

David Paraeus, and Jacob Kimedoncius. Early English reformers who were hypothetical universalists include William Tyndale, Hugh Latimer, Thomas Cranmer, John Hooper, and John Jewel, among others.

Second, seventeenth-century English hypothetical universalists include James Ussher,[13] the archbishop of Armagh, whose influence on John Davenant (of the Synod of Dort fame) and John Preston, both of whom were hypothetical universalists, is well known. Many Puritans, including the celebrated Richard Baxter, were hypothetical universalists.[14]

Third, another branch of hypothetical universalists was the Salmurian variety in France, including John Cameron, Moise Amyraut, Paul Testard, John Daille, and others.[15] The Salmurians believed that Christ died *equally* for the sins of all people, but with the intent to apply the atonement only to the elect. Many have misunderstood Amyraut on this point. When he spoke of Christ dying "equally" for all, it is clear he meant that his death was equally sufficient for all as an actual satisfaction for sin, not in the sense of intention or purpose.[16] Amyraut believed Christ died for the sins of all people, but with the special *intent* of saving only the elect.

DEFINING AMYRALDIANISM

Defining Amyraldianism has been difficult for scholars. In an excellent article, "Amyraldianism: Theological Criteria for Identification and Comparative Analysis,"[17] David Wenkel attempted to provide criteria to properly define

---

13. The seventeenth-century English variety of hypothetical universalism may have begun with James Ussher. He knew the patristics and schoolmen well. His influence was primarily disseminated through John Davenant.

14. Baxter makes some references to Amyraut in his writings. One such reference occurs in his *Universal Redemption*, where he acknowledges his agreement with Amyraut on the extent of the atonement: "Here Amyraldus and Dalleus (Dallie) coming forth stop [support] me." Baxter, *Universal Redemption*, 198.

15. For a survey with specific respect to Amyraut, see Lawrence Proctor, "The Theology of Moise Amyraut Considered as a Reaction against Seventeenth-Century Calvinism" (PhD diss., University of Leeds, 1952); Brian Armstrong, *Calvinism and the Amyraut Heresy: Protestant Scholasticism and Humanism in Seventeenth-Century France* (1969; repr., Eugene, OR: Wipf & Stock, 1999); and F. P. van Stam, *The Controversy over the Theology of Saumur 1635–1650: Disrupting Debates among the Huguenots in Complicated Circumstances* (Amsterdam: APA-Holland University Press, 1988). For Amyraut's views, see Matthew Harding, *Amyraut on Predestination* (Norwich: Charenton Reformed Publishing, 2017). See also Allen, *Extent of the Atonement*, 163–69.

16. See Proctor, *The Theology of Moïse Amyraut*, 376n78; Jean Daillé, *Apologia pro duabus Ecclesiarum in Gallia Protestantium Synodis Nationalibus*, 2:632; and M. Amyraldo [Amyraut], *Specimen Animadversionum in exercitationes de gratia universali* (Saumur: Jean Lesnier, 1648), 223. As Proctor said, "In the statement that Christ died *pro omnibus equiliter* (explained Daillé, *Apologiae* ii 632), the theologians of Saumur meant the adverb to signify that there is none for whom Christ did not die; it does not mean that all are equal in affection or will of God in giving Christ to die. Cf. Drost, *Specimen* 25: Amyraut and Testard explained the death of Christ for all equally in terms of sufficiency. . . . Amyraut explained the two uses of the adverb in *De Grat* (Gen) 223." Proctor, *The Theology of Moïse Amyraut*, 376n78.

17. David Wenkel, "Amyraldianism: Theological Criteria for Identification and Comparative Analysis," *Calvin Theological Journal* 11 (2005): 83–96.

Amyraldianism. Wenkel perceptively noted that Roger Nicole and John Davenant both share five similar core criteria for analysis of Amyraldianism (Nicole) and its near kin hypothetical universalism (Davenant).[18] Wenkel proposed adding a third source to identify the key themes of Amyraldianism: the *Formula Consensus Helvetica* of 1675. This confession was designed and constructed specifically to be an anti-Amyraldian document. As a direct response to Amyraldianism, it provides a third source for an objective criterion noting the main points of contention high Calvinists had with Amyraldianism. As Wenkel states: "This document provides a window into how Calvinists who were involved in the disputations at the time defined Amyraldianism."[19]

A consideration of these three sources results in five core criteria in a definition of Amyraldianism:

1. Sin affects men in such a way that it removes all moral ability regarding salvation yet leaves all natural ability (i.e., understanding, will, emotions) intact.

2. God, moved by an earnest love and desire to save all mankind, decided to give in ransom His Son, Jesus Christ, who died equally for all men and makes a universal offer of salvation to all men.

3. Remission of sins and eternal life are offered to all on the conditions of faith and repentance.

4. Christ himself, through his goodness and love, intercedes for the elect by supplying faith in the hearts of the elect via the Holy Spirit.

5. The death of Christ satisfied God the Father for the entire human race, yet actual reconciliation does not take place until an individual believes.[20]

This definition and description does not include the speculative ordering of the decrees which allegedly characterized Amyraut and many Amyraldians.[21] The key point in Amyraldianism, and the point of greatest contention

---

18. The connection between Amyraut and Davenant has also been noticed by others. Louis Berkhof, *The History of Christian Doctrines* (Edinburgh: Banner of Truth, 1985), 190, states, "The views of the School of Saumur were practically shared by Davenant, Calamy, and especially Richard Baxter, in England."

19. Wenkel, "Amyraldianism," 93. Of crucial importance also is Amyraut's and Testard's response to their critics during the Synod of Alançon. See John Quick's record of it in *Synodicon in Gallia Reformata*, 2 vols. (London: T. Parkhurst and J. Robinson, 1692), 2:352–57.

20. Wenkel, "Amyraldianism," 94–95. Wenkel also draws from Mark Shand, "John Davenant: A Jewel of the Reformed Churches or a Tarnished Stone? Pt. 2," *Protestant Reformed Theological Journal* 32, no. 1 (1998): 20–28, particularly Shand's comparison of Amyraut and Davenant.

21. Quick, *Synodicon*, 2:355.

among the Reformed in history, was the issue of the extent of the atonement. These five statements do seem to encapsulate the gist of Amyraldianism with respect to soteriology and the extent of the atonement. Amyraldianism is not idiosyncratic but systematic; and it is Calvinism and not Arminianism.

Richard Muller has argued that non-Amyraldian (or "non-speculative") hypothetical universalism antedated Amyraldian hypothetical universalism and that both were understood by their proponents to be within the Reformed confessional tradition. He noted the debates over hypothetical universalism "manifest a kind of diversity and variety of formulation not suitably acknowledged in the older scholarship on Reformed orthodoxy.[22]

Muller also rightly asserted that there was a hypothetical universalist trajectory in Reformed theology well before Amyraut.

> A question can be raised here concerning Moore's description of the non-Amyraldian trajectory of hypothetical universalism as a "softening" of a Reformed tradition that was "on the whole" particularistic and resistant to such softening. Given that there was a significant hypothetical universalist trajectory in the Reformed tradition from its beginnings, it is arguably less than useful to describe its continuance as a softening of the tradition. More importantly, the presence of various forms of hypothetical universalism as well as various approaches to a more particularistic definition renders it rather problematic to describe the tradition as "on the whole" particularistic and thereby to identify hypothetical universalism as a dissident, subordinate stream of the tradition, rather than as one significant stream (or, perhaps two!) among others, having equal claim to confessional orthodoxy.[23]

Richard Muller's comments on Bullinger, Musculus, and Dort are especially important:

> Clear statements of nonspeculative hypothetical universalism can be found (as Davenant recognized) in Heinrich Bullinger's *Decades* and commentary on the Apocalypse, in Wolfgang Musculus' *Loci communes*, in Ursinus' catechetical lectures, and in Zanchi's *Tractatus de praedestinatione sanctorum*, among other places. In addition, the Canons of Dort, in affirming the standard distinction of a sufficiency of Christ's death for all and its efficiency for the elect, actually refrain from canonizing either the early form of hypothetical universalism or the assumption that Christ's sufficiency serves only to leave the nonelect without excuse . . . and that in the course of seventeenth-century debate even the Amyraldians were able to argue that their teaching did not run contrary to the Canons. In other words, the nonspeculative, nonAmyraldian form of hypothetical

---

22. Muller, "Diversity in the Reformed Tradition," 23–24.
23. Muller, "Diversity in the Reformed Tradition," 24–25; emphasis mine.

universalism was new in neither the decades after Dort nor a "softening" of the tradition: The views of Davenant, Ussher, and Preston followed out a resident trajectory long recognized as orthodox among the Reformed.[24]

Muller's statement that the Amyraldian view is compatible with Dort and the Westminster Confession is significant.[25] This means that there are, according to Muller, *at least three* branches *within* the Calvinistic position, a notion that has only begun to take hold in Reformed historiography over the past twenty-five years, yet many popular Calvinist books take virtually no notice of this understanding and continue to operate from an outdated historiography.

Dort did not take sides on the "imputation of sin to Christ" debate, but it only took sides on the issue of the effectual purpose of God to save his elect through the work of Christ and the effectual application of the Spirit, contrary to Remonstrant thinking on those points.[26]

From these facts we may draw several conclusions. First, the oft-held belief that it was the Arminians and the Amyraldians who first promulgated the notion of unlimited atonement among the Reformed is false. Hypothetical universalism was well represented among the Reformed from the beginning of the Reformation. There was no such thing as a Reformed consensus on the extent question unbroken until Amyraut and the Amyraldians. After surveying the Reformed debates on the extent of the atonement during the sixteenth and seventeenth-centuries, Thomas's conclusion appears undeniable: neither Cameron nor Amyraut can be blamed for introducing universal atonement into Reformed theology since the majority of first-generation Reformed theologians held it.[27] This effectively blows the lid off all attempts to suggest that Amyraut was somehow the deviant, drunk uncle who showed up at the family picnic and compromised the "true" Reformed doctrine of limited atonement.

Second, hypothetical universalism was the majority position among the Reformed in the sixteenth century, at least prior to Beza in 1586. In fact, it was virtually the *only* position of the Reformed as there was no one who advocated limited atonement in any clear, incontrovertible way until 1586.[28]

---

24. Muller, "Review of Jonathan Moore's *English Hypothetical Universalism*," 150.
25. Richard Muller, *Post-Reformation Reformed Dogmatics: The Rise and Development of Reformed Orthodoxy, ca. 1520 to ca. 1725*, 4 vols. (Grand Rapids: Baker, 2003), 1:76–80. See also Quick, *Synodicon*, 2:353.
26. See Allen, *The Extent of the Atonement*, 149–62, for the situation at Dort.
27. G. Michael Thomas traced the concept of unlimited atonement and related doctrines of Amyraldianism in Reformed thought from Calvin and Bullinger to the English hypothetical universalists Davenant and Ward, and finally to Cameron and Amyraut. Thomas, *The Extent of the Atonement*, 250. Thomas also mentioned the connection between Amyraldianism and John Davenant in his assertion that Davenant was a "forerunner of the theology of Saumur." Thomas, *Extent of the Atonement*, 152. "It seems fair to conclude that the question of the extent of the atonement, already handled ambiguously by the Synod of Dort, was never satisfactorily answered by the Reformed Churches throughout their early and classical period." Thomas, *Extent of the Atonement*, 241.
28. See Allen, *Extent of the Atonement*, 103.

THE INFLUENCE OF THE ENGLISH VARIETY OF HYPOTHETICAL UNIVERSALISM IN BAPTIST THOUGHT

The earliest Baptists in England, General Baptists, subscribed to an unlimited atonement. To the surprise of some historians and theologians, early English Particular Baptists did not subscribe univocally to limited atonement (known also as particular redemption or strict particularism). A careful study of the writings of these men coupled with analysis of the two London Baptist Confessions of 1644 and 1646 demonstrates this.[29]

Among those English Particular Baptists who held to unlimited atonement, we can include Paul Hobson (d. 1666), Thomas Lamb (d. 1672 or 1686), John Bunyan (d. 1688), Robert Hall (d. 1831), and Andrew Fuller (d. 1815). These Baptists were essentially hypothetical universalists.[30]

But the question arises, what early stream of hypothetical universalism influenced them? It is not just the Saumur stream that influenced moderate Calvinistic Baptists, but the early Reformational and English varieties as well. For example, Robert Oliver, in his book on English Particular Baptists, lists Daniel Turner as a "Particular Baptist" in the 1700s, and Turner said he is one "with the good Mr Polhill, Mr How[e], Dr. Watts and many others who hold the doctrine of Particular Election and general Redemption as it may be called."[31] These three men, in turn, were influenced by the earlier and contemporary hypothetical universalists, especially within the early Reformational and English streams.

Some Puritans, such as Charnock, do evidence some influence by the Saumurian school of thought, but most do not.[32] They are just a part of the large group of "classic Augustinians" who held to an unlimited atonement coupled with unconditional election—hypothetical universalists in the early Reformational and English hypothetical universalist tradition—well before Amyraut and Amyraldianism developed.

Richard Baxter is often regarded as an Amyraldian and/or the chief exponent of Amyraldianism in England.[33] Baxter and Amyraut certainly agreed that the extent of the atonement was unlimited. Yet it should be noted that Baxter was committed to unlimited atonement "long before he had heard of Amyraut."[34]

---

29. See Allen, *Extent of the Atonement*, 459–514; and David Wenkel, "The Doctrine of the Extent of the Atonement," 359.

30. Allen, *Extent of the Atonement*, 459–514.

31. Oliver referenced Daniel Turner, "Daniel Turner to Mr Mumm, Watford, 14 June 1782," Angus Library, Regent's Park College, Oxford, in Robert W. Oliver, *History of the English Calvinistic Baptists 1771-1892* (Edinburgh: Banner of Truth, 2006), 62. See Allen, *Extent of the Atonement*, 474.

32. Stephen Charnock quotes the Saumurians extensively. "In his *Works* he cited Moise Amyraut 130 times and Jean Daille 79 times." Larry Daniel Siekawitch, "Stephen Charnonck's Doctrine of the Knowledge of God: A Case Study of the Balance of Head and Heart in Restoration Puritanism" (PhD diss., University of Wales, Bangor, 2007), 70.

33. Alan Clifford, "Amyraldian Soteriology and Reformed-Lutheran *Rapprochement*," in *From Zwingli to Amyraut: Exploring the Growth of European Reformed Traditions*, eds. Jon Balserak and Jim West (Göttingen: Vandenhoeck & Ruprecht, 2017), 170.

34. Alan Clifford, "Amyraldian Soteriology and Reformed-Lutheran *Rapprochement*," 170.

Turning to the Baptists, there is variety *within* the group of people who describe themselves by the "particular redemption" label. John L. Dagg (1794–1884), Southern Baptists's first systematic theologian and a strict particularist himself, knew about this diversity in his own day. In addition to those Calvinists who maintain a strictly limited extent for the atonement, he spoke of some "people who maintain the doctrine of particular redemption," that "distinguish between redemption and atonement, and because of the adaptedness [of Christ's death to every man] referred to, consider the death of Christ an atonement for the sins of all men."[35]

There are at least three particular redemption positions within Calvinism (and among Baptists who are Calvinists), and this is something which is seldom clearly recognized. One of these particular redemption positions affirms that Christ died for the sins of all people. All Calvinists affirm Christ's *intent* or *effectual purpose* is to save the elect alone, and they *all* also agree that this results in an eventual limited *effectual application* of the benefits of the atonement to the elect alone. These categories necessarily relate to one another and are essential to their view of a pretemporal, intra-Trinitarian, unconditional election of some to faith. Where Calvinists differ is over the *extent* of the atonement, as Dagg himself observed.

The first category of so-called particular redemption is Dagg's own position. Christ's atonement is viewed as "so much suffering for so much sin." This is often labeled the "commercial" or "equivalentist" view. There is a quantifiable amount of suffering that Christ underwent that corresponds to the exact number of sins of the elect alone. The just suffering due for this quantifiable amount of elect sin corresponds to the degree of Christ's suffering and literal payment for sin on the cross. Few hold this position today.

A second category of particular redemptionists is the majority view among Calvinists in Reformed history from the late sixteenth century through today. Simply described, Christ died for the sins of the elect alone in a nonquantitative, equivalentist manner. This view of limited atonement was espoused by John Owen, and many others past and present such as B. B. Warfield, R. C. Sproul, and John MacArthur. Modern-day Baptists who hold this view include D. A. Carson, Al Mohler, and Michael Haykin.

The third category of those who can be labeled as particular redemptionists are Calvinists who affirm an unlimited atonement such that Christ died for the sins of all people. This view was held by all the first generation of the Reformed, including Calvin. Amyraut fits in this category as well. These are moderate Calvinists. This third view is yet another variety *within* the self-described particular redemption camp, as Dagg observed. Andrew Fuller should be placed in this category of particular redemptionists, as I will demonstrate below. Modern-day Southern Baptists (who may not use this label for themselves, but still hold the same moderate concepts) would include

---

35.   John L. Dagg, *Manual of Theology* (Harrisonburg, VA: Gano, 1990), 326.

Danny Akin, president of Southeastern Baptist Theological Seminary; David Dockery, former president of Union University, Trinity Evangelical Theological Seminary, and now Distinguished Professor of Theology at Southwestern Baptist Theological Seminary; and Russell Moore, president of the Ethics and Religious Liberty Commission of the Southern Baptist Convention.

ANDREW FULLER

Beyond question, the single most influential particular Baptist in late eighteenth- and early nineteenth-century England was Andrew Fuller. Fuller's impact on Baptists in America is well documented.[36] The early Fuller was committed to limited atonement. His early writings, especially the first edition of his now famous *The Gospel Worthy of All Acceptation* (1785), demonstrate this clearly. But in time, Fuller came to abandon his belief in limited atonement.[37]

There are several strands of evidence pointing to Fuller's shift on the extent of the atonement: (1) the influence of the English hypothetical universalists, (2) the influence of Jonathan Edwards, (3) the influence of the New Divinity men, (4) a comparison of the first and second editions of his famous *The Gospel Worthy of All Acceptation*, (5) his Letter III to John Ryland, (6) the testimony of contemporary and subsequent theologians and historians, and (7) the testimony of Fuller's biographer, Morris. We will survey each below.

First, however, there is one key factor that played a central role in Fuller's shift on the extent of the atonement—his debates with the leader of the New Connection General Baptists, Dan Taylor. Taylor (1738–1816) was the leading light of the English General Baptists in the late eighteenth and early nineteenth centuries. He and Fuller engaged in a series of debates, chief among them being the extent of the atonement.[38]

As a result of these debates, Fuller was persuaded that particular redemption in the sense of limited substitution for sins did not comport with Scripture. Taylor had argued the case for unlimited atonement and that universal invitations for sinners to believe the gospel could only be properly grounded in a universal provision in Christ's death. Taylor continued to point out that if limited atonement were true, then there is no provision at all for the non-elect in the death of Christ.

---

36. Anthony L. Chute, Nathan A. Finn, Michael A. G. Haykin eds., *The Baptist Story: From English Sect to Global Movement* (Nashville: B&H, 2015), 101.

37. See David L. Allen, "Andrew Fuller: Particular Redemptionist Who Held to Universal Atonement," in *Understanding Andrew Fuller: Life, Thought, and Legacies*, vol. 1, eds. N. A. Finn, J. Robinson Sr., and S. Shaddix (Peterborough, Ontario: H&E Academic, 2021), 103–28. See also my volume *The Extent of the Atonement: A History and Critique* (Nashville: B&H Academic, 2016), 478–97.

38. For narratives on Fuller's engagement with Taylor, consult John Webster Morris, *Memoirs of the Life and Writings of the Rev. Andrew Fuller* (Boston: Lincoln and Edmonds, 1830), 275–96; and Adam Taylor, *Memoirs of the Rev. Dan Taylor* (London: Baynes & Son, 1820), 172–82.

Fuller felt the brunt of this argument and could not answer it. He later confessed in 1803: "I tried to answer my opponent . . . but I could not. I found not merely his reasonings, but the Scriptures themselves, standing in my way."[39] As a Calvinist, Fuller's concept of redemption was still "particular" in the sense that the particularity was now located not in the *extent* of the atonement, but in the *design* and *application* of the atonement. Fuller believed the elect were determined to salvation in the elective purpose of God in eternity past. This is, of course, what Amyraut also believed.[40]

Fuller's debates with Dan Taylor also concerned the grounds necessary for the free offer of the gospel. Taylor had argued that only an unlimited atonement could ground the free offer of the gospel.[41] If Christ only substituted himself for the elect alone, then the salvation of the nonelect would be "naturally impossible," as Fuller said.[42] For Fuller, a universal atonement safeguarded the grounds for the universal offer of the gospel.[43]

This is Fuller's point of agreement with Dan Taylor, and he stated it clearly in Letter XII in his *Reality and Efficacy of Divine Grace*.[44] Fuller admitted he had been mistaken about the terms "ransom" and "propitiation" being applied only to those who were among the elect. Now these terms were "applicable to all mankind in general," an admission which clearly shows Fuller had abandoned limited substitution/atonement, not merely his earlier quantitative commercial views. No one affirming the kind of particular redemption that has a limited substitution component would ever say Christ's death serves as a "propitiation" and "ransom" for the sins of all people.[45]

Peter Morden pointed out how Fuller, in his reply to Dan Taylor, "Stated his revised position on the atonement clearly and openly."[46] Morden's conclusion is striking and important: Fuller's view of the extent of the atonement "could now properly be called 'general.'"[47]

---

39. Andrew Fuller, "Six Letters to Dr. Ryland Respecting the Controversy with the Rev. A. Booth," in *The Complete Works of Andrew Fuller*, 3 vols., ed. J. Belcher (Harrisonburg, VA: Sprinkle, 1988), 2:709–10.

40. Quick, *Synodicon*, 2:354.

41. See Taylor, *Observations on the Rev. Andrew Fuller's Late Pamphlet entitled The Gospel Worthy of All Acceptation* (London: Paternoster-Row, 1786); *Observations on the Rev. Andrew Fuller's Reply to Philanthropos*, 2nd ed. (London: T. Bloom, 1788); *The Friendly Conclusion Occasioned by the Letters of Agnostos to the Rev. Andrew Fuller Respecting the Extent of Our Saviour's Death* (London: W. Button, 1790).

42. Fuller, "Six Letters to Dr. Ryland—Letter III: Substitution," in *Works*, 2:709.

43. Fuller, "On Particular Redemption," in *Works*, 2:374.

44. Fuller, "Reality and Efficacy of Divine Grace: Letter XII," in *Works*, 2:550.

45. See Fuller, "Reply to Philanthropos," in *Works*, 2:496 and 550, respectively. See also Fuller, *Works*, 2:555, where Fuller agreed with Taylor on John 3:16, Matt. 22:1–11, and John 6:32 with respect to the extent of the atonement covering the sins of all people.

46. Peter Morden, *Offering Christ to the World: Andrew Fuller (1754–1815) and the Revival of Eighteenth-Century Particular Baptist Life*, in Studies in Baptist History and Thought, vol. 8 (Milton Keynes, UK: Paternoster, 2003), 70. For Fuller's reply, see "Reply to Philanthropos," in *Works*, 2:488–89.

47. Morden, *Offering Christ*, 70.

Fuller both clarified and modified his theology of salvation between the years 1785 and 1801, years in which this theology was a crucial motor for change in the life of the Particular Baptist denomination. The most important change was his shift from a limited to a general view of the atonement during his dispute with the Evangelical Arminian Dan Taylor.[48]

Fuller was a particular redemptionist who came to hold unlimited atonement. Amyraut was also a particular redemptionist who held to unlimited atonement, but labeled his position as universal redemption, following the terminology of the first-generation Reformers.

In addition to his debates with Dan Taylor, there were other influences on Fuller which may have played a role in his shift from limited atonement to unlimited atonement, or served for him as confirmation of his shift. First, by his own admission, Fuller was influenced by early English hypothetical universalists. Fuller spoke of the English Reformers who "fully avowed the doctrine of predestination, and at the same time spoke of Christ's dying for all mankind." Fuller not only affirmed this historically, but stated his own agreement with it as well. He then listed Cranmer, Latimer, Hooper, Ussher, and Davenant, all of whom were examples.[49]

Second, the influence of Jonathan Edwards, himself a proponent of unlimited atonement, should not be discounted.[50] Edwards held to universal atonement.[51]

Third, the New Divinity movement in America exerted great influence on Fuller. What pulled Fuller out of his hyper-Calvinism was the influence of Edwardsianism and the New Divinity. The New Divinity interpreted "sufficient" with respect to the atonement to mean more than just "hypothetically" sufficient. They understood and used the term to mean an actual sufficiency in that Christ actually substituted himself for the sins of all people. This can be discerned in the writings of Joseph Bellamy and other New Divinity proponents.[52]

Fuller's mature position on the extent of the atonement is all but identical to that of the New Divinity. Fuller had come to the place where he understood

---

48. Morden, *Offering Christ*, 75–76.
49. Fuller, "Reality and Efficacy of Divine Grace," in *Works*, 2:545. All of these early Reformers and Reformed theologians labeled their view as "universal redemption," but their conceptual categories on the extent of Christ's death were the same as the later moderate particular redemptionists.
50. See Chris Chun, *The Legacy of Jonathan Edwards in the Theology of Andrew Fuller*, in Studies in the History of Christian Traditions (Leiden: Brill, 2012), 142–82. Chun referred to Jonathan Edwards as Fuller's "theological mentor" (182). Peter Morden, *Offering Christ to the World*, 4, spoke of Edwards's writings as "particularly important in shaping Fuller."
51. Michael David McMullen, "'The Wisdom of God in the Work of Redemption': Soteriological Aspects of the Theology of Jonathan Edwards, 1703–1758" (PhD diss., University of Aberdeen, 1992). McMullen demonstrates beyond doubt that Edwards held to unlimited atonement. Many works that address Edwards's view on the extent of the atonement fail to reckon with the McMullen dissertation. For example, see Chun, *The Legacy of Jonathan Edwards*, 173–76.
52. Chun, *The Legacy of Jonathan Edwards*, 142–82.

the atonement of Christ to be "sufficient" for the sins of all people because Christ actually substituted himself for the sins of all people, even while continuing to maintain Christ's effectual purpose to apply the saving benefits of His death to the elect alone. Again, Fuller and Amyraut are conceptually at one on this point, though differing terminologically.

Fourth, strong evidence for Fuller's shift can be seen in a comparison of the first and second editions of his famous *Gospel Worthy of All Accepta-tion*. In the first edition, written in 1781 but published in 1785, it is evident that he was committed to particular redemption in the Owenic sense of that term.[53] Proof for Fuller's shift can be found in a comparison of the section where he discussed particular redemption.[54] The section in the first edition is almost completely rewritten in the second edition.[55] All references to particular redemption in the sense that Christ suffered only for the sins of the elect are excised by Fuller. Fuller believed that no inconsistency ensued from God's "special design" in the death of Christ in its application to the elect and the fact that all people everywhere were under obligation to believe the gospel. Only if limited atonement is maintained is there an inconsistency.[56] Unlike the first edition of *Gospel Worthy*, there is no statement in quotation or by Fuller in this section of the second edition advocating limited atonement.

Fifth, Fuller's Letter III to John Ryland on the subject of substitution (1803) demonstrates his belief in unlimited atonement.[57] Here is Fuller's affirmation of particular redemption in the sense of God's ultimate *intent* in the atonement: to save the elect and them only. This statement alone indicates that in Fuller's mind there is a distinction between for whom atonement was made and for whom it was designed to save (as in Amyraut). But this does not implicate Fuller as a proponent of limited substitution. He said nothing about a limited extent, merely a limited intent and application.

Paragraph six continues this topic:

In like manner concerning the death of Christ. If I speak of it irrespective of the purpose of the Father and the Son, as to its objects who should be saved by it, merely referring to what it is in itself sufficient for, and declared in the gospel to be adapted to. . . . It was for sinners as sinners; but if I have respect to the purpose of the Father in giving his Son to die,

---

53. See Andrew Fuller, *The Gospel of Christ Worthy of All Acceptation* (Northhampton: T. Dicey, 1785), 132–39.

54. Morden, *Offering Christ*, 73–74, illustrated some of the substantive changes. Morden's work is very important in showing Fuller's shift on the extent of the atonement.

55. See Fuller, *Gospel of Christ Worthy of All Acceptation*, 132–39; and "Gospel Worthy," in *Fuller's Works*, 2:373–75.

56. See Morden, *Offering Christ*, 68–76.

57. Fuller, *Six Letters to Dr. Ryland*, Letter III, "Substitution," in *Works*, 2:705.

and to the design of Christ in laying down his life, I should answer, It was for the elect only.[58]

Throughout this letter, Fuller distinguished the *intent*, the *extent*, and the *application* of the atonement,[59] as did Amyraut. Again, the later Fuller was a hypothetical universalist.

Sixth, many historians and theologians, Baptist and otherwise, have concluded the later Fuller held to unlimited atonement.[60] Baptist historian W. Wiley Richards stated, "Limited atonement . . . was to be the most prominent position held until the middle of the nineteenth-century. Through the influence of Andrew Fuller and others, limited atonement was supplanted by general atonement."[61]

Seventh, Fuller's first biographer, J. W. Morris, himself asserted, not once but three times, that Fuller had conceded the universality of the death of Christ for the sins of all people in his debates with Dan Taylor.[62]

Like Amyraut, Fuller was a particular redemptionist (with "redemption" referring to the effectual application to the elect alone) who held to unlimited atonement. Like Amyraut, Fuller made a clear distinction between the atonement's intent and extent. With respect to the extent of the atonement, Fuller's view was Amyraldian and was often so-called. Fuller was a hypothetical universalist in the mold of Amyraut, though with some elements of disconti-

---

58. Fuller, *Six Letters*, Letter III, "Substitution," 2:707; emphasis original.

59. Failure to recognize this distinction in Fuller's writings is perhaps the key reason many today fail to recognize Fuller's shift on the extent of the atonement. See, for example, Tom J. Nettles, "Andrew Fuller (1754–1815)," in *The British Particular Baptists 1638–1910*, vol. 2, ed. Michael A. G. Haykin (Springfield, MO: Particular Baptist Press, 2000), 97–141; Michael A. G. Haykin, "Particular Redemption in the Writings of Andrew Fuller (1854–1815)," in *The Gospel in the World: International Baptist Studies*, in Studies in Baptist History and Thought, ed. David Bebbington, vol. 1 (Carlisle, UK: Paternoster, 2002), 129–64; and *Understanding Andrew Fuller: Life, Thought, and Legacies*, vol. 1, ed. Nathan Finn, Jeff Robinson Sr., and Shane Shaddix (Peterborough, Ontario: H&E Academic, 2021), 61–75; 77–102.

60. See *Sermons, Essays, and Extracts by Various Authors Selected with Special Respect to the Great Doctrine of Atonement* (New York: George Forman, 1811); James R. Willson, *A Historical Sketch of Opinions on the Atonement, Interspersed with Biographical Notices of the Leading Doctors, and Outlines of the Sections of the Church, From the Incarnation of Christ to the Present Time; with Translations from Francis Turretin, on The Atonement* (Philadelphia: Edward Earle, 1817), 116; David Benedict, *Fifty Years Among the Baptists* (New York: Sheldon, 1860), 141; Tom Nettles, *By His Grace and for His Glory: A Historical, Theological and Practical Study of the Doctrines of Grace in Baptist Life*, 2nd ed. (Cape Coral, FL: Founders, 2006), 153; Henry C. Vedder, *A Short History of the Baptists* (Philadelphia: American Baptist Publication Society, 1907), 249; Philip E. Thompson, "Baptists and 'Calvinism': Discerning the Shape of the Question," *Baptist History and Heritage* 39, no. 2 (2004): 67–68; A. Chadwick Mauldin, *Fullerism as Opposed to Calvinism: A Historical and Theological Comparison of the Missiology of Andrew Fuller and John Calvin* (Eugene, OR: Wipf & Stock 2010).

61. W. Wiley Richards, *Winds of Doctrine: The Origin and Development of Southern Baptist Theology* (New York: University Press of America, 1991), 193.

62. Morris, *Memoirs of Fuller*, 204, 206, 207.

nuity with him in some areas, such as in certain terminological preferences, his federal construct, and so forth.

HYPOTHETICAL UNIVERSALISM, AMYRALDIANISM, AND THE SOUTHERN BAPTIST CONVENTION: 1845 TO THE PRESENT

The late eighteenth and nineteenth centuries marked a period of the decline of Calvinism among Baptists, both in England and in America. The softening of strict Calvinism among British Baptists in the late eighteenth century began with the move away from the hyper-Calvinism of John Gill and John Brine. As the most important Particular Baptist in the late eighteenth and early nineteenth centuries, Andrew Fuller's influence played a crucial role in this shift, which is seismic in its consequences for Baptist history and theology in England and in America. His views on the free offer of the gospel coupled with unlimited atonement were foundational.[63]

In America, most colonial Baptists who self-identified as Calvinists had adopted the "New Light Calvinism" of Jonathan Edwards and, subsequently, the modified Calvinism of Andrew Fuller. "Virtually all major eighteenth-century colonial Baptists were modified Calvinists," according to Michael Williams, who also stated, "Some of the colonial Baptists who emerged by 1790 could even be typified as 'Calminians' due to their unique blend of a softened form of Calvinism."[64]

The Baptist historian David Benedict explained that, by the late eighteenth and early nineteenth centuries, a more moderate Calvinism, which he called "the Fuller system," had already softened the older Calvinism, teaching that Christ died for all, and all are called to salvation.[65]

Long before the founding of the Southern Baptist Convention in AD 1845, Baptists in the north and the south differed among themselves on the specific question of the extent of the atonement. According to Hackney, until the mid-eighteenth century, General Baptists were more numerous than Particular Baptists in New England and the Southern colonies.[66]

Peter Lumpkins has chronicled the shift from strict Calvinism among Baptists Associations in the nineteenth-century American South. Many local associations drafted articles of confession that made no mention of unconditional election, limited atonement, or irresistible grace.[67] Seventy years prior

63. William H. Brackney, *Historical Dictionary of the Baptists* (Lanham, MD: Scarecrow, 2009), 572.

64. Michael E. Williams, "The Influence of Calvinism on Colonial Baptists," *Baptist History and Heritage* 39 (2004): 37–38.

65. David Benedict, *Fifty Years among the Baptists*, 141–43.

66. William H. Brackney, ed., *Baptist Life and Thought: A Sourcebook*, rev. ed. (Valley Forge, PA: Judson, 1998), 97.

67. E. Peter Frank Lumpkins, "The Decline of Confessional Calvinism among Baptist Associations in the Southern States during the Nineteenth Century" (PhD diss., University of Pretoria, 2018). As Lumpkins has demonstrated, only 23 percent of the 424 Baptist Associations he surveyed had a confession of faith that could be described as strongly Calvinistic in their articulation of three key

to the founding of the Southern Baptist Convention, a significant number of Virginia Separate Baptist ministers were not in accord with high Calvinism on the issue of particular election or particular redemption. They were "Arminian" on these points.[68]

When the Southern Baptist Convention was founded in 1845, only thirteen percent of Southern Baptist associations were represented. Two factors likely played into this small attendance: the hasty way in which the convention was convened, and the fact that most Southern Baptists were agrarian and lacked means to attend. The most heavily represented state, Virginia, saw only eighteen percent of her associations represented, and approximately seventy-one percent of its delegates hailed from a single association.[69]

Evidence of the shift away from strict Calvinism, including adherence to limited atonement, can be seen in a comparison of the Philadelphia Confession of Faith (1742) with the New Hampshire Confession of Faith (1833). The latter exhibits a clear moderation of the stricter Calvinism of the Philadelphia Confession. Mark Noll spoke of its softening "the Calvinistic doctrines of unconditional election and limited atonement."[70] James Leo Garrett, the distinguished professor of systematic theology at Southwestern Baptist Theological Seminary, said of it, "Although called 'moderately Calvinistic,' it could as well be denominated 'moderately Arminian.'"[71]

It seems clear that some, though not all, of the founding fathers of the SBC were Calvinists who affirmed limited atonement.[72] The historical record indicates that most Baptists in the south at the time of the founding of the SBC adhered to a theology somewhere between Calvinism and Arminianism.[73]

The theological focal point of the moderation of high Calvinism in America prior to the founding of the Southern Baptist Convention was a shift from limited atonement to unlimited atonement. Though several factors played a role in this shift, one cannot discount the influence of Andrew Fuller. The Southern Baptist historian Albert H. Newman said that "his [Andrew Full-

doctrines: unconditional election, limited atonement, and irresistible grace. Lumpkins, "The Decline of Confessional Calvinism," 440–45.

68. George W. Paschal, *History of North Carolina Baptists*, 2 vols. (Raleigh: The General Board North Carolina Baptist State Convention, 1955), 2:5, 432.

69. Lumpkins, "The Decline of Confessional Calvinism," 178–282.

70. Mark A. Noll, *A History of Christianity in the United States and Canada* (Grand Rapids: Eerdmans, 1992), 178–79.

71. James Leo Garrett, *Baptist Theology: A Four-Century Study* (Macon, GA: Mercer University Press, 2019), 151.

72. Allen, *Extent of the Atonement*, 553–70.

73. Steve Lemke, "History or Revisionist History? How Calvinistic Were the Overwhelming Majority of Baptists and Their Confessions in the South until the Twentieth Century?," *Southwestern Journal of Theology* 57 (2015): 227–54. See also Paul A. Basden, "Theologies of Predestination in the Southern Baptist Tradition: A Critical Evaluation" (PhD diss., Southwestern Baptist Theological Seminary, 1986), 95–96.

er's] influence on American Baptists" was "incalculable." Steve Weaver characterized Fuller's influence on the Southern Baptist Convention:

> His legacy was carried forward on both sides of the Atlantic. . . . Fuller's *The Gospel Worthy of All Acceptation* formed the theological foundation for the modern missionary movement. Perhaps his most lasting legacy is the Southern Baptist Convention, the largest body of Baptists in the world today, which was founded by "Fullerites" and continues his missionary vision with over 5,000 international missionaries supported through the Cooperative Program.[74]

What came to be called "Fullerism," a modified form of Calvinism that affirmed an unlimited atonement, was one of the major influences on nineteenth-century Baptists in America, including Southern Baptists at their founding in 1845.

CONCLUSION

All Baptists who affirm unlimited atonement, whether Calvinists or not, can be roughly described as hypothetical universalists with respect to the actual death of Christ for the sins of all people. When Calvinists today call themselves "Amyraldian," they are usually simply meaning to convey the notion that they are Calvinists who affirm unlimited atonement as did Amyraut. "Amyraldian" becomes something of shorthand for "four-point Calvinist." All these Calvinists really have in common with Amyraut is the view that Christ suffered for the sins of all people, while they may not hold to any of the other distinctives of the Amyraldian school of thought historically considered.

At the Southern Baptist Convention annual meeting in 2009, Danny Akin, president of Southeastern Baptist Theological Seminary and a moderate Calvinist, spoke at the Founders Breakfast. He said: "Most of you would know me—I am basically an Amyraldian. I am a four-pointer who does understand and appreciate why many of you affirm particular redemption." In that same year, Russell Moore described himself as one "who believes in personal election and universal atonement."[75] These comments are illustrative of where most Baptists who identify as moderate Calvinists, past and present, stand with reference to Amyraut and Amyraldianism. They identify with Amyraut because of his rejection of limited atonement and acceptance of unlimited atonement.

---

74.   Steve Weaver, "Ten Baptists Everyone Should Know: Andrew Fuller," https://credomag.com/2019/11/ten-baptists-everyone-should-know-andrew-fuller-2. Emphasis added.

75.   Russell Moore, "Learning from Nineteenth-Century Baptists," in *Southern Baptist Identity: An Evangelical Denomination Faces the Future*, ed. D. S. Dockery (Wheaton, IL: Crossway, 2009), 112.

218   David L. Allen

Though it appears Amyraut did not have *direct* influence on Baptists, hypothetical universalism, of which Amyraldianism is a branch, has indeed directly influenced Calvinistic Baptist theology, including the Southern Baptist Convention. This influence was predominately mediated through the impact of Andrew Fuller and his theology.[76] Fuller's influence here is truly incalculable.

When it comes to the extent of the atonement, General Baptists in the early seventeenth century were more influenced by the Anabaptists and Mennonites, all of whom affirmed an unlimited atonement. From the seventeenth century to today, all non-Calvinist Baptists follow in the steps of their General Baptist forefathers.

All Baptists who affirm unlimited atonement—in fact, all who affirm unlimited atonement, regardless of denomination and regardless of how they define election—are hypothetical universalists *with respect to the belief that Christ died for the sins of all people* ("universalism" in "hypothetical universalism"), and thus all are rendered saveable, and would in fact be saved, if they were to believe ("hypothetical" in "hypothetical universalism"). In this broad sense of hypothetical universalism, within all Christendom, only high and hyper-Calvinists are excluded.

---

76. Phil Roberts, "Andrew Fuller," in *Baptist Theologians*, eds. T. George and D. Dockery (Nashville: Broadman, 1990), 132.

CHAPTER TWELVE

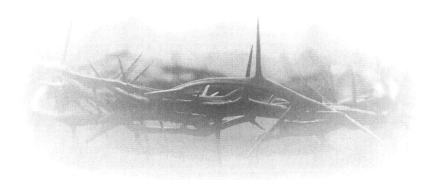

THE SIGNIFICANCE OF THE ATONEMENT FOR THE WORLD

The Cross of Christ, the Church, and the Common Good

Michael Jensen

THE CROSS AND THE PROBLEM OF THE COMMON GOOD

The cross of Jesus Christ is not always seen as a symbol of that which benefits society as whole—namely, "the common good."[1] In 2002, a sixty-six-meter-high cross, called "the Millennium Cross," was erected high on the Vodno mountain above the North Macedonian capital of Skopje, in the heart of the Balkans. Opulently lit at night, the Cross appears to float in mid-air. It has become the unmistakable symbol of the city. The Cross was funded by the government of North Macedonia (then called by the unfortunate and unmusical name "The Former Yugoslav Republic of Macedonia"), the Macedonian Orthodox Church, and by private donations. Although appeals were made to the history of Christian missions to Macedonia, no one was under

---

1. Professor Michael Sandel of Harvard University said in a 2020 interview: "The common good is about how we live together in community. It's about the ethical ideals we strive for together, the benefits and burdens we share, the sacrifices we make for one another. It's about the lessons we learn from one another about how to live a good and decent life," in Thomas Freidman, "Finding the 'Common Good' in a Pandemic," *The New York Times*, March 24, 2020, https://www.nytimes.com/2020/03/24/opinion/covid-ethics-politics.html.

any illusions as to what it was intended to say—least of all the 32 percent of Muslim citizens of the city beneath it. As Anastas Vangeli writes, the Millennium Cross "had implicit role of a territorial mark of the nationalist IMRO-DPMNU [the ruling party], or, as it popularly known it was meant, 'to serve as a reminder to whom the city belongs.' It has become since an important national/political symbol for the ethnic Macedonian nationalists regardless of their party affiliation."[2]

The North Macedonians were certainly not the first to hold up the cross as a symbol of ethnic identity and as a talisman of power. This has been a theme, played with many variations, since the Battle of the Milvian Bridge in AD 312.

There is a deep disconnect (it hardly needs saying) between this use of the cross as a symbol of victorious power and the actual Christian doctrine of the atonement. In the last 1,700 years, the cross has been too often a sign of exclusive triumph rather than a shorthand for an inclusive declaration of grace (as it is in, say, Eph. 2:11–22). Its description of a victory in defeat has been shorn of its irony; its revelation of mercy in judgment has been recast as simply "judgment"; its narrative of the reconciliation of enemies, to God and to one another, has been obscured. This is particular redemption in an ethnic or national sense.

The prevalence and persistence of this disconnect is revealing. What Scripture teaches about the significance for humankind of the death of Jesus has too often been an awkward starting point for a theological account of the common good. This is for two particular reasons. First, it is an awkward starting point because navigating the scriptural tension between the particularity of the atonement and its universal scope is not easily done. As the other chapters in this book have shown, this of course was the concern of Moses Amyraut. The tendency is to ease the dilemma between Jesus's death for *us* (1 Thess. 5:10), and his death for *the whole world* (1 John 2:2), by siding with one aspect over against the other. If the former, then Jesus's death is a sign around which an *us* gathers as opposed to a *them*. If the latter, then the cross loses its moral and unitive force and becomes merely the generator of universal ethical principles—an evocation, say, of "forgiveness," quite apart from the historical actuality of Christ's reconciling work on the cross.

Second, the cross is a sign of Christ's rejection by the world he came to save, and his judgment upon it. It is a signal that there is something deeply at odds between the God of Israel and Israel, the creator God and humankind. The death of the Messiah is the "abominating sacrilege" (Mark 13:14)—the ultimate blasphemy of rebellious humanity against the divine being. The collusion of mob, religion, empire, and former friends against Jesus is deliberately highlighted in the gospel narratives. Psalm 2, which depicts the gathering of

---

2.   Anastas Vangeli, "Religion, Nationalism and Counter-secularization: The Case of the Macedonian Orthodox Church," *Identity Studies in the Caucasus and the Black Sea Region* 2 (2010): 91.

the nations against the Lord and his anointed one, seems to be fulfilled at Calvary. And the wrath of the Lord against those who oppose him is surely also marked by this moment in time. In John's gospel, Jesus claims that he has not come to condemn the world, but to save it. Yet his rejection by the world is a sign of the world's condemnation by God, in and of itself (see John 3:16–21).

What then is the significance of Christ's work on the cross for that which is not, and for those who are not, the church? In what sense can we speak of a "common good" that is achieved by or taught by the cross? In what ways might the atonement connect with the imperative to "seek the welfare of the city" (Jer. 29:7)? The imperative for answering such a question is surely illustrated by the example with which I opened. In addition to that, however, a number of contemporary commentators have called for a revival of the concept of the common good because of the increasingly divided and individualistic moral landscape of contemporary culture.[3]

This chapter attempts to explain how, when held together, both particular *and* universal aspects of the doctrine of the atonement ought to, and indeed do, provide a resource for clear theological thinking about the church's relationship to the world—a species of what might be called its "social ethics." Especially this is so in terms of the inclusive constitution of the community of the cross and the evangelical—and cruciform—practice of loving one's neighbor, even when these are one's enemies. Christians are called upon to live cruciform lives for the sake of the world. Established by the cross of Jesus Christ, the church is not an "us" *opposed* to them, but an "us" who exists *for* the sake of "them."

In Augustine of Hippo and the Dutch Calvinist theologian Herman Bavinck we shall find two exemplars of our problem. For Augustine, an account of the common good is given without reference to the atonement. For Bavinck, an account of the atonement is given with a somewhat thin account of the common good. From there we shall explore three key New Testament passages on the cross: 1 Corinthians 1:18–33, Colossians 1:15–23, and 1 Peter 2:11–3:24, before drawing the threads together.

AUGUSTINE, *THE CITY OF GOD* 19, AND THE COMMON GOOD

A theological approach to the question of the common good has a venerable history, but the cross of Christ features very little in it. For example, in his great work *The City of God*, Augustine outlines the waxing of the heavenly city against the waning of the earthly one. Yet, even as they await the coming transformation of all things, Christians are not to wish for or to pursue the destruction of society. In Book 19 of *The City of God*, Augustine addresses the question of whether human flourishing is social—especially given the

---

3. See, for example, Michael J. Sandel, *The Tyranny of Merit: What's Become of the Common Good* (Harmondsworth: Penguin, 2020); and Jonathan Sacks, *Morality: Restoring the Common Good in Divided Times* (London: Hodder & Stoughton, 2020).

prevalence of misery and evildoing within human society. Society offers little
security to individuals. As he writes: "Even when a city is at peace and free
from sedition and civil war, it is never free from the danger of . . . disturbance
or, more often, bloodshed."[4]

Seeking the common good is, under the fallen condition of human nature,
often a miserable and even tragic necessity. The magistrate must judge, even
when he cannot know the full truth. Just wars must of occasion be waged—
but this is not a happy business by any means.

For Augustine, the desire of the earthly city for an earthly peace and the
desire of the heavenly city for the enjoyment of eternal peace coincide. The
denizens of the heavenly city should pursue earthly peace because this bodily
peace will produce a desire for peace of the soul.[5] For love of neighbor, the
Christian will "take care to ensure that his neighbor also loves God"; and this
will mean that he will "be at peace with all men as far as in him lies." He will, if
truly loving God, his neighbor, and himself, pursue a "well-ordered concord."
This concord has two parts: that the Christian should harm no one, and that
he should do good to all. In particular, he serves the common good by ordering his own household well, ruling out of a dutiful concern for those they
command.

Augustine does not advocate flight from the things of the world, but their
proper use in light of the coming heavenly kingdom. The Christian household
"makes use of earthly and temporal things like pilgrims: they are not capti-
vated by them, nor are they deflected by them from their progress towards
God."[6]

The earthly individual and household and the heavenly pursue the same
peace and order, but for different ends. An earthly peace is established, and
the cooperation of human wills are secured, in order that the things of this
life may be obtained—since they are the ultimate goal of the earthly city.
The heavenly city also makes use of this peace and must promote it, for now.
It must seek "the things necessary of the support of this mortal life," since
it shares this mortal condition with the earthly city. The benefits of social
order—food, education, justice, and so on—are necessary for both cities.

There is one difference: the heavenly city cannot consent to the religious
laws of the earthly. It cannot cooperate with its worship and must dissent
from the earthly city at this point. And this has, inevitably, led to persecution.
The earthly city and the heavenly have often been at odds. But this should not
be because the heavenly city pursued a path of conflict. Rather, the heavenly
city calls people of every nation to join her in her pilgrimage without thereby
destroying "the customs, laws, and institutions by which earthly peace is

---

4. Augustine, *The City of God against the Pagans*, ed. and trans. R. W. Dyson (Cambridge: Cambridge
   University Press, 1998), 19.5, 926.
5. Augustine, *The City of God*, 19.14, 940.
6. Augustine, *The City of God*, 19.17, 945.

achieved of maintained." On the contrary, so long as they do not impede true worship, they are to be preserved. Thus,

> Even the Heavenly City makes use of earthly peace during her pilgrim-age, and desires and maintains the co-operation of men's wills in attaining those things which belong to the mortal nature of man. . . . Indeed, she directs that earthly peace towards heavenly peace. This peace the Heav-enly City possesses in faith while on its pilgrimage, and by this faith it lives righteously, directing towards the attainment of that peace every good act which it performs either for God, or—since the city's life is inevitable a social one—for neighbour.[7]

But what of the cross? For Augustine, the cross does not feature directly in his rationale for the common good. His theological rationale for seek-ing the common good lies in an eschatological direction. The church is on a pilgrimage and must tend to the needs of the body as well as the soul—for now. It cannot neglect the agonistic processes of rule, war, and justice, even as it recognizes that they are imperfectible. It needs to share in them so that it can more readily call others to join its pilgrimage, which is an expression of love. But Augustine also, without perhaps giving it much exposition, simply sees the earthly city as the sphere for the righteous living and doing good to which the church is called. In this account, the cross and atonement are only implicitly present.

HERMAN BAVINCK ON "THE UNIVERSAL SIGNIFICANCE OF PARTICULAR ATONEMENT"

In more recent times, the concept of the common good has been strongly associated with Roman Catholic social teaching of the mid-twentieth century. With its emphasis on natural law, the doctrine of the atonement features little in this body of work.

Is there anything more explicit on the Protestant side? One might assume that, given the central place that the atonement plays in Reformation and post-Reformation dogmatics, that it might appear more as a resource for social ethics. In the thought of Moses Amyraut, God's grace was certainly extended to all humankind not simply via general providence but also through the intent to save. Objective grace is offered universally, because of God's kind-ness to all his creatures. Not all are saved because not all are given the gift of faith. But to what extent is this thought adapted to a vision for the common good (an expression that Amyraut would not have himself used, of course)?

It is not well known that Amyraut was one of the great theological ethi-cists of his age. His *La morale chrestienne* was published as four volumes (in

---

7.   Augustine, *The City of God*, 19.17, 945.

six parts) and totals more than 4,600 pages.[8] Over this vast opus, Amyraut traces the foundations of moral thought and behavior. We must consider the "school of nature," but we must also take into account the distorting effects of the fall. The Old Testament Law has a particular focus for humanity under the impact of Adam's sin. However, the Christian revelation in the gospel of Jesus Christ engenders the full account of morality. There's nothing in particular that distinguishes Amyraut's theology from that of his Reformed contemporaries at this point. He argued strongly that despite the effects of sin we are justified in deploying reason in understanding theological and moral truths.

That Amyraut does not significantly differ here from his contemporaries is significant, since one might have assumed that his view of the atonement would have knock-on effects in his theological system, including ethics. However, one looks in vain in his corpus for an application of the atonement to what we might call "social ethics."

The Dutch Calvinist theologian Herman Bavinck includes in his *Reformed Dogmatics* a section titled "The Universal Significance of Particular Atonement."[9] Bavinck begins this chapter by coming at the problem of the cross and the common good from the question of the significance of the atonement for all: "Although vicarious atonement as the acquisition of salvation in its totality cannot . . . be expanded to include all persons individually, this is not to say that it has no significance for those who are lost."[10]

What is this significance? In particular, Christ's work has value for all since it is on account of Christ's work that all the human race was spared—and continue to be spared the foreclosing of judgment. Christ illumines the world—not that all respond or are open to seeing by his light, but that his light nevertheless shines. For Bavinck then, unbelievers benefit from the work of the Christ, even if not salvifically. How? Because the final judgment on the world is postponed.

This seems like pretty thin gruel, especially when compared with the grand terms in which Bavinck paints the universal scope of the atonement in other respects. At least, we may say, Bavinck has attempted to draw a line from the cross to some idea of the "common good," but it remains sadly undeveloped. Or at least his emphasis on the particular aspects of the atonement completely overshadow any sense in which attention to the common good may be prompted by a doctrine of the atonement.

That is not all that Bavinck has to say about social ethics. In a well-regarded essay published in 1909, Bavinck expounds Calvin's doctrine of

---

8.   Richard A. Muller, "Beyond Hypothetical Universalism: Moïse Amyraut (1596–1664) on Faith, Reason, and Ethics," in Martin I. Klauber, ed., *The Theology of the French Reformed Churches: From Henri IV to the Revocation of the Edict of Nantes* (Grand Rapids: Reformation Heritage, 2014), 214.

9.   Herman Bavinck, *Reformed Dogmatics*, vol. 3, *Sin and Salvation in Christ* (Grand Rapids: Baker Academic, 2006), 470–75.

10.   Bavinck, *Reformed Dogmatics*, 3:471.

common grace with a perceptive enthusiasm.[11] Even reprobation does not mean a complete withholding of the divine grace. On the contrary, the condition of humanity after the fall is not what it could have been, were God to have not shown to us a measure of his grace. It is still the case that "heaven and earth with their innumerable wonders are a magnificent display of the divine wisdom."[12] The gifts of human reason, art, and civil society are signs of grace that all may enjoy, and which the Christian should not despise. On the contrary, these blessings are to be honored and received with thanksgiving.

The doctrine of common grace, taught by the Calvinian tradition, prompts a concern for the common good since it teaches Christians to recognize the activity and presence of God in all human flourishing. The goodness of God in the world confirms what we learn about him in the gospel. Creation and redemption are works of the same God, "whose property is always to have mercy" (as the 1662 *Book of Common Prayer* puts it).

But is the doctrine of the atonement, which is the central hinge of redemption, related to the doctrine of common grace? In his appreciative reading of Calvin's teaching on common grace, Bavinck does not highlight the atonement. Certainly, the Christian who has been brought to the foot of the cross has learned there complete humility and subsequently been restored to all things in God—which "teaches us to love our neighbour, to value the gifts bestowed upon him and to employ our own gifts for his benefit."[13] However, for Calvin and for Bavinck, this is more to do with the sovereign will of God in election. The gospel reveals God's sovereign will, which gives to Christians the assurance of his power, and is confirmed by "the operation of that same will in the world at large." Common grace teaches us that every aspect of human life and every moment of human living is to be consecrated to the Lord.

Our brief examinations of both Augustine and Bavinck demonstrate that accounts of the common good and the doctrine of the atonement are not often, or at least not explicitly, related to one another in the tradition. It must be admitted, however, that the New Testament itself does not provide many passages where the connection is drawn, either. But that is beside the point: if the goal is to give a properly theological account of the common good, then the voice of the doctrine of the atonement ought not to be muted. The task of the systematic theologian is not simply repetition of the scriptural witness, but the drawing out of connections between the various claims of Scripture perhaps only implicit in its pages. In what follows, then, I offer three exegetical soundings in the search for a more overt and generative correlation. What vision of social ethics does the theology of the cross outlined in the New Testament prompt?

---

11. Herman Bavinck, "Calvin and Common Grace," in *Princeton Theological Review* 7, no. 3 (1909): 437–65.

12. Bavinck, "Calvin and Common Grace," 454.

13. Bavinck, "Calvin and Common Grace," 462.

THE CROSS, THE CHURCH, AND THE WORLD IN PAUL AND PETER

1 Corinthians 1:1–2:5: The Cross as an Exposé of Human Power and Wisdom

The theme of Paul's first letter to the Corinthians is the unity-in-diversity of the church, which is the body of Christ. The factions of the church, outlined in 1:10–17, are a contradiction to the very being of the church. They represent the infiltration into the church's life of worldly—and not cruciform—patterns of being. In 1 Corinthians 1:1–2:5, Paul pits his theology of the cross against the wisdom of the Greeks and the Jewish thirst for signs of power: "For Jews demand signs and Greeks desire wisdom, but we proclaim Christ crucified, a stumbling block to Jews and foolishness to Gentiles, but to those who are the called, both Jews and Greeks, Christ the power of God and the wisdom of God" (1 Cor. 1:22–24 NRSV).

The cross stands as a rebuke to the overweening pride of human cultures, but is then simultaneously the principle by which both Jews and Greeks may enter God's kingdom together. The weakness of "the called" corresponds to the weakness of the cross itself, which turns out to have a hidden power and a hidden wisdom: the things of the world are reduced to nothing in the face of this divine "foolishness" and "weakness."

Although there is nothing quite like a worked-out theology of atonement in this passage—nor arguably even in the letter itself—the institution of the church itself is presented as a living example of the power and wisdom of the cross, in its very weakness. Christ Jesus "became for us wisdom from God, and righteousness and sanctification and redemption" (1:30)—which occurred on the cross. In one simple sentence, Paul blends together his core metaphors for atonement: God has revealed his surpassing wisdom, he has made just his own judgments and declared his people righteous, he has made holy the unholy, and he has purchased and liberated his people for himself from their slavery to the world—all on the cross of Jesus Christ. His righteous obedience makes possible the redemption of the foolish and the weak—and, as it will turn out, the criminal and the sexually immoral (see 1 Cor. 6). They were "brought with a price": namely, the crucified body of the Lord.

The cross of Christ thus stands as an exposé. It scandalously reveals the impotence of human power and the foolishness of human wisdom. By dying to reconcile the weak in their weakness—and not the strong because of their strength—Christ strips bare human pretentions to power. The atonement of the weak and the foolish shames the powerful and the wise "by human standards" (κατὰ σάρκα), revealing as it does those human standards to be a sham in any case (1:26–7).

In what sense might Paul's exposition of the cross in this passage relate to a vision of the common good? The cross is God's ironic display of power: a defeat that is a victory, a foolishness that is a profundity. But because it is, when seen with the eyes of the Spirit of Christ (1 Cor. 2:15–16), exactly where God's wisdom and authority are instantiated and displayed in the world, it stands as a judgment against the alternatives. A cross-shaped social ethics must sound a note of warning against the world that defies the Lord and his anointed. It has been exposed; it cannot stand.

In seeking the common good, then, the servants of the cross must not fail to say "No" to overweening human pride, especially when it is expressed in human wisdom and human power. The testimony of the cross does not destroy human aspirations to seek earthly goods, whether these be advances in medicine, more just government, or technological inventions—all which may reduce human suffering significantly. But the theology of the cross exposes them if and when they become idolatrous alternatives to divine power and wisdom. The witness of the church to the power of God in the cross, in its proclamation and its practices of living with one another and in the world, brings an appropriate modesty to human power. This is indeed a great service to the common good, even as it may cause the witnesses to the cross to suffer the same rejection that the cross itself represents.

Colossians 1:15–25: The Cross as an Act of Universal Peace-Making

The Colossian hymn is of interest to our question about the common good because of the cosmic scope of the atonement it depicts. Christ, in whom the fullness of God dwells, dies on the cross not simply to rescue his people from their sins and from the fallen world, but to reconcile *all things* to God. The Son is the true *imago dei* (1:15), the fulfillment of God's design for humanity, who precedes all things and in whom all things cohere. The hymn ranges between that particular humanity over which Christ rules, the church, and the reconciliation in his body of all things, whether in heaven or on earth. There is nothing outside the purview of the peacemaking work of his blood shed on the cross. He is "the firstborn from among the dead," so that in all things his supremacy might be unquestioned. Not only is all humankind summed up in the incarnate Son as the true image of the invisible divine being, but the shedding of his blood on the cross is the centerpiece of God's mission to reconcile all things to himself. That peacemaking act is not simply directed toward the church but is the means by which God accomplishes the reconciliation of all things.

Nevertheless, his people, the church, feature centrally, since he is their head (v. 18): "he is the head of the body, the church; he is the beginning and the firstborn from among the dead, so that in everything he might have the supremacy."

What is the connection between the two parts of this verse? How is his supremacy connected to the church? Jesus's resurrection from the dead establishes his supremacy because his resurrection life animates his body—the church. His victory constitutes a new people, since he is the firstborn from among the dead—many must surely follow.

This extraordinary, cosmic act of reconciliation involves the Colossians themselves, as Paul explains in verses 21 to 23. They were once in a state of alienation and outright enmity from God. This was a condition that had come about because of their evil behavior. It was, in other words, a matter of deliberate rejection of the divine moral will. The process of atonement thus involved both the justification ("free from accusation") and the sanctification ("present you holy in his sight") of the Gentile Colossian believers, which they take hold of by faith (1:22–23), having heard the gospel that Paul serves. And this gospel, which the Colossians have believed—the gospel of the reconciliation of all things in the blood of Christ—is preached "to every creature under heaven" (ἐν πάσῃ κτίσει τῇ ὑπὸ τὸν οὐρανόν). It is, that is to say, an announcement not simply to the individual human beings whose sin is atoned for, but to the entire created order. This seems to be a similar thought to that which Paul expresses in Romans 8, where the creation's temporary subjection to futility is linked to the redemption of human beings.

This is not a doctrine of universal salvation. Reconciliation and peace, presumably, involve the repudiation of that which is evil. It is, however, a doctrine of cosmic redemption in the blood of Christ. The whole of the creation is the object of his work in dying for sin and rising to new life. All of creation has suffered the effects of human sin; now, in the blood of Christ, since sin has been atoned for, the creation has been reconciled to the Creator just as it was made in him, through him, and for him. Jesus Christ completes the mission of humanity as God's true image and becomes for the created order the presence of the fullness of God. He becomes firstborn twice: once over all creation, and again as the "firstborn from among the dead."

Paul does not here, or elsewhere in Colossians, make any direct connection between his theology the cross and "the common good." He only mentions "outsiders" in 4:5–6, when he enjoins Christians to "be wise in the way you act towards outsiders." However, the cosmic scope of his work on the cross surely invites us to consider the implications of the atonement for social ethics. The reconciliation of all things—and the declaration of peace—is a reality established by the blood shed upon the cross. What might we infer here? The gospel is the declaration that God's peace has been established by means of the cross. It is an invitation for every creature under heaven, including every human being. The peace of God is a reality in which the whole creation now stands, by the power of the cross. The powers and authorities have been disarmed by the cross (2:15)—not just as an exposé, but as a triumph. Thus the community of believers—renewed in God's image (3:10)— are called to practice this cross-shaped peacemaking with one another, since all earthly distinctions have been eclipsed in Christ (3:11—see also Gal. 3:28; Eph. 2:11–22). Their perfect unity, stemming from love, is to be an expression of the peace of Christ ruling in their hearts (3:14–15). They know peace with God and so they practice reconciliation with one another, forgiving as the Lord forgave them (3:13–14).

Those who know the peace of Christ also know that God's purpose in the atonement was the reconciliation of all things. They see in Christ a refocusing, with great clarity, of the image in which all human beings have been made.

They discern in Jesus's death God's loving intent to reconcile to himself even his enemies—which is what they once themselves were. They now become the agents of that love and peace—not just by their proclamation of the gospel of peace but their imitation of God's cruciform love for the world.

1 Peter 2:11–3:22: The Cross as a Model of Suffering for Doing Good

Peter's letter is explicitly addressed to Christians in the mode of exiles (1 Pet. 1:1–2).[14] He begins by assuring his readers of their "new birth into a living hope" (1:3) in the resurrection of Jesus Christ from the dead. This sure hope brings a security in the midst of the trials that are sorely testing them.

In the middle sections of the letter, however, (2:11–3:22), Peter reaches for the cross of Christ as the mode of hopeful living in the present. Perhaps more explicitly than any other New Testament author, he attaches his theology of the atonement to the way Christians should live in foreign, if not hostile, territory. They are not to withdraw from pagan society—even if that were possible—but are to live in an exemplary way among them (2:12). In fact, their lives are to be recognized by the pagans as good—at least in the final analysis. For here Peter makes an important distinction: it is not that the Christians are to do good on the terms set for them by the pagan world. Indeed, not so. They may well, in the present time, be falsely accused of any number of crimes—incest, treachery, and cannibalism were just three such crimes leveled against Christians in the first and second centuries, as is well known. Peter rather strikes an eschatological note here: on the day that God visits, the pagan world will finally recognize the good that Christians have done.

Is this then an exhortation to live, not according to some commonly agreed vision of the good, but according to a good particularly revealed to Christians and frequently concealed from pagan eyes? By no means. Peter makes appeal to Christians to silence people by doing good (2:15), to show honor to the emperor (2:17), and to respectfully submit to human authority because God has sent them to maintain justice (2:13–14). These are common goods that any person could recognize and from which all should benefit. That Christians, in serving God primarily, also seek to respect (pagan) human authority may frequently not be recognized as such by pagans—but implicitly this is because of their perversity, fear, and corruption, not because these things are not commonly recognized goods.

And that perversity was not abstract for Peter's readers. In addressing slaves who were subject to cruel and unjust masters, he refers them to the example of Christ on the cross, who bore in his body our sins. He was an innocent suffering for the guilty. In saying Christ bore *our* sins in his body on the cross (2:23), Peter shows that he considers the cross to have involved believers in a spiritual exchange—the righteous for the unrighteous. That is not what the slaves are to do with their masters—suffer "for their sins." Nevertheless, there is

---

14.   I remain unconvinced by interpreters who claim that 1 Peter is written to Jewish Christians.

a sense in which this is true. The slaves, by bearing literally in their bodies the unjust cruelty of the master without retaliation, do indeed engaging in an act of sin-bearing—one which may indeed win over their masters—as submissive wives may likewise win over their husbands (3:1).

Not just those in particular roles but in general, Christians should be persistent in doing good—in particular in not returning evil for evil, but in responding with a blessing (3:8–9). This is a pattern of response learned directly and uniquely from the cross of Christ. In 3:18 and the following verses, Peter makes this explicit. The great exchange of righteous for unrighteous embodied in the cross brings the believers to God. They are likewise to accept the suffering directed at them by the unrighteous—a righteous act, which may bring their persecutors to God. The suffering of believers does not make atonement in quite the same way as the blood of Christ does, but by following the model of Christ's death, Christians may become the agents of reconciliation—shaming their persecutors into possible repentance.

For Peter, the atonement in an impetus for Christians to bear the sins of the world—in the sense of accepting suffering for doing good, and not retaliating. This was how Christ achieved his victory, after all. What is good is, interestingly, not a matter for negotiation, or decided by consensus. It may well be that the Christian is viewed as detrimental to the common good by the pagan, and thus made to suffer. Nevertheless, the Christian answers with gentleness and respect, especially for those in authority. If that means suffering as a witness to the rule of Christ, then so it must be. To pursue the glory of God as an ultimate end means, penultimately, to pursue the common good.

THE CROSS AND THE ATONEMENT, FOR THE COMMON GOOD

Ordinarily, Christian accounts of the common good have been built from a foundation of the theology of common grace. Human beings are made all alike in the image of God. The world is preserved by God from his ultimate judgment, and in the meantime the rain falls on the righteous and the unrighteous alike. The call of the law is to love one's neighbor, for no other reason than because God commands it. The cross fits awkwardly into this picture, if at all. It is the badge of the church for whose sins Christ atoned—a point of separation and judgment rather than of inclusion and embrace. As we have seen, this is not at all the full story. My expository soundings have shown that there are a number of points at which the atonement generates an even richer account of the common good then is customarily given and provides a particular impetus for a Christian concern for and action to secure the same.

First, *the atonement establishes a community of people eager to seek the common good.* The cross forms the church. By reconciling a people to himself, God establishes the means by which his rule can be expressed upon the face of the earth for the good of the whole creation. As John Stott wrote in his classic study *The Cross of Christ*:

The community of Christ is the community of the cross. Having been brought into being by the cross, it continues to live by and under the cross. Our perspective and our behaviour are now governed by the cross. All our relationships have been radically transformed by it. The cross is not just a badge to identify us, and the banner under which we march; it is also the compass which gives us our bearings in a disorientated world.[15]

The people gathered together under the sign of the cross are called to take up their own crosses. They have been constituted by an extraordinary act of divine enemy-love.

Second, *the atonement reinforces the original grounds (we are created equal) for a biblical account of the common good.* As we have seen from our reading of Colossians 1:15 and following, the original marking out of humankind as the *imago dei* finds its consummation in the savior who sheds his blood. The commission of human beings for dominion is completed in his reconciliation of all things by his blood shed on the cross. Whether we accept a particular or universal view of the atonement, few would deny that the love of God, vividly expressed in the mission of the Son to die for the world, is inclusive of all those made in his image—whether those are saved or not (2 Pet. 3:9). The gospel of grace is to be preached to all nations—which surely means all people, not simply those who will accept it (Matt. 28:16–20). The cross creates a new humanity by uniting in Christ human beings regardless of the old distinctions of ethnicity, social status, and gender (Eph. 2:11–22; Gal. 3:28). By doing so, it strengthens the primordial biblical contention that the first humanity, "in Adam," has been created with a profound equal dignity and for a common purpose.

Third, *the atonement shows us how to the order the common good in terms of two great themes: sin and grace.* Theologically speaking, these are propositions that a purely "natural" account of the common good may not readily discover. The death of Jesus Christ marks out Christian faith as realistic about human nature. It provides an antidote to utopianism of all kinds. The atonement was necessary because of universal and irremediable human rebellion. The cross is a sign of God's judgment, as we saw from our reading of 1 Corinthians, on the hubris of humankind. It is both a demonstration of the worst that human beings can do in their idolatry and corruption, and the Word of God against them. Any account of the common good must reckon with insidious human evil. The cross is a divine intrusion into a world that has gone badly awry: a revelation that all is not well, and that God has said a definite "No" to humankind at just this point.

In this way, for the sake of the common good the church—the community of the cross—must join in saying "No" to the world which continues to defy its Creator. The cross teaches us the humble and suffering mode by which

---

15. John Stott, *The Cross of Christ* (Leicester: IVP, 1986), 256.

the church must stand against the world. It is called not to reply to defiance with defiance, but to bear witness to the Christ of the cross, and to expect rejection. This is an agonistic note to strike, for the church will not always find agreement as to what actually defines the common good. It may well be a bitterly contested notion. The church may have to "lay down its life," as it were, for the sake of a common good that the world refuses to accept as such.

But grace and mercy are also revealed in the cross. The atonement discloses God's determination to redeem and to reconcile his creation to himself. His character is as merciful as it is just. In the cross, he both metes out his divine justice, satisfying the requirements of his own law, and justifies the guilty. In the midst of a fallen and hostile world, Christ's command to love our enemies is revealed as God's own posture to the inimical world. What ought the followers of the crucified Christ do but seek to be exemplars of this cruciform grace, not returning evil for evil but rather replying to it with good (see 1 Pet. 3:9; Rom. 12:21)?

What might this mean in practice? Having seen that the cross compels them and teaches them, how might Christians pursue the common good? One recent public debate in Australia might serve as an example. Religious groups have been campaigning for several years for legislation that would protect religious freedom in Australia. The case against pursuing such legislation, sometimes made from within the churches themselves, has been that it represents a form of tribalism. It is seen as self-protective. For their part, secular voices have argued that the churches are pursuing freedoms that permit them to (in their view) harm other groups, such as LGBTQI+ minorities.

The problem is made more complex by the way in which contemporary liberal society invites social groupings and communities to advocate for their own legal and literal space, to be mediated from above by bureaucratic means. In arguing for religious freedom, are not churches merely doing what other communities have done to protect their own interests? Isn't this how the game of social arrangement is now to be played? If churches do not show vigilance here, will their ability to preach and to live the gospel not be curtailed—which will certainly be to the detriment of the common good?

However, if the church operates as the community of the atonement, it will be uncomfortable about advocating simply for its own rights, protections, and privileges without reference to its neighbors, some of whom may well be its enemies. It exists "for the sake of" the world, and not for its own sake. It may be that churches should be ready, as a witness to the cross of Christ, to lay down some of their rights in the interests of others. At the very least you would expect Christian advocates for religious freedom to take on a non-defensive tone when making their case—recognizing that religious freedom is not simply to be won for their own freedom, but a freedom to be enjoyed by all citizens, and which includes the freedom *not* to believe. The cross teaches us, surely, that what it is to "win" is not what the world means by victory. The church needs to make its case that preserving its own freedoms to operate in space governed by a secular-liberal paradigm benefits not just its own interests. That case may well not succeed, since (as the cross reminds us) an agreed view as to what the common good is may not be found. In that case, the church must be prepared to "lose"—since that is what its Savior did.

CONCLUSION

What I have attempted to show in this chapter is that the theology of the atonement ought not be as awkward a companion for a biblical account of the common good as it often has been in the Christian tradition. It is not too strong to say that the use of the cross as a tribal and cultural symbol is a blasphemous repudiation of its very meaning. Christ's blood reconciles human beings to each other in reconciling them to God. In establishing a new humanity, the atonement does not obliterate but severely relativizes the tribes that divided the old. The motive for a Christian pursuit of the common good—our common humanity—is redoubled in the cross. But we are also shown in the cross the real meaning of "the good," parsed out in terms of sin and grace. It gives us, to repeat the words of John Stott, our bearings in a disoriented world.

CHAPTER THIRTEEN

"HE PREPAREST A TABLE IN THE PRESENCE OF HIS ENEMIES"

A Sermon on John 13:1-30 for Maundy Thursday

Amy Peeler

Have you ever shared a meal with your enemies?

I would imagine most of us try not to have too many enemies, and this is a good practice for Christian discipleship, not to mention mental health. But sometimes it happens even when we wish it wasn't true; a series of events spins out of control, or deeply held convictions set us on opposite sides than others.

It was the latter kind of situation that I found myself in a few years ago. I'm part of an organization called the Center for Pastor Theologians that brings together people involved in both the academy and the church for mutual encouragement and learning. They very intentionally draw from a wide spectrum of denominations within Christianity, denominations that hold very different convictions on important topics. But over the course of the several days together, over prayer, Bible study, and meals we got to know one another not as entities—"the Episcopalian," "the academic," "the Southern Baptist," "the pastor"—but as people, people with names and stories, hurts and victories, a sense of humor. During the final meal, which stretched past two hours, the conversation quite naturally turned to some of our differences. And something amazing happened. No, we didn't change each other's minds, but we heard one another, learned from one another, came to appreciate one another, saw Jesus in one another. As I came home from that event, I found myself thinking about Psalm 23. It seemed to me that the Lord had prepared a table before me in the presence of my "enemies," who were now, though we did not all agree, truly my friends.

On Maundy Thursday, we remember and reenact and enter into Jesus's meal with his disciples, but it is also fitting to say that this is Jesus's meal with his enemies. And his story doesn't end quite as rosy as mine, for they did not all end up as friends. Clearly Judas qualifies as an enemy here, but also, painfully, Peter and the other disciples who so quickly ran away. Jesus knew all of that, but he still ate with them, served them by washing their feet, and loved them, all of them. This day and this text invite us to consider what it meant for Jesus to demonstrate his love for all by preparing a table in the presence of his enemies.

As Jesus's life as an itinerate preacher nears its end, John's gospel recounts Mary's anointing of Jesus, Jesus's entry into the Holy City to shouts of "Hosanna!", and then Jesus's teaching about what is to come: his death and his glorification. Some believe in him, and others are not willing, for they, John says, "loved human glory more than the glory that comes from God" (12:43). That glory, Jesus will show in this account, is awfully uncomfortable.

And now, on Maundy Thursday, at the beginning of John 13 the evangelist says that the hour has come. Jesus knows it is time for him to depart from the world, and up until that last minute, the very end, he loves his own. Such a statement seems quite limited, indicating love only for the elect. This seems a poor place to argue for an unbounded atonement. But a wrinkle in the lovely account calls that limited conclusion into question.

Would that love even include Judas? John does mention Judas right after the statement about Jesus's love. In fact, Judas appears in this story early and often.

In verse 2, the evangelists notes that by the time the supper happened, the devil had already put it into the heart of Judas to betray Jesus. The tempting idea had already been planted and found fertile ground in the mind of Judas.

In verse 10, when Jesus is conversing with Peter about washing, Jesus says, "Not all of you are clean." John makes it clear to his readers in the next verse that Jesus knew who was going to betray him.

In verse 18, Jesus tells them they are blessed if they follow Jesus's example of service, but this blessing will not apply to all of them. He says, "I know whom I have chosen." Readers might think Jesus is saying he choose the eleven, with the exception of Judas, but this is not the case at all. In 6:70, using the same word for choosing, Jesus says, "Did I not choose you, the twelve? Yet one of you is a devil." John then clarifies: He was speaking of Judas son of Simon Iscariot, for he, though one of the twelve (and hence one of the chosen) was going to betray him.

Jesus chose Judas, and yet he became, to the point of bringing about his death, Jesus's enemy. Jesus's love for his own at first might seem very limited, for it suggest that he loves only those whom he has chosen. Yet, because of the *types* of people they are, including even his enemy Judas, although these twelve disciples be small in number, his love of them shows that his love knows no limits.

Jesus goes on to say that his choice even of Judas happened in order that the Scripture might be fulfilled: "The one who eats bread with me, he lifts up his heel upon me." This statement comes from Psalm 41 (NRSV) which evokes the image of someone putting their foot on the neck of another, a degrading and dangerous situation. In the psalm, even when faced with this level of betrayal, David is trusting in the Lord's protection from his enemies.

Hear it in full:

Ps. 41:8   They think that a deadly thing has fastened on me,
              that I will not rise again from where I lie.

Ps. 41:9   Even my bosom friend in whom I trusted,
              who ate of my bread, has lifted the heel against me.

Ps. 41:10 But you, O Lord, be gracious to me,
              and raise me up, that I may repay them.

Jesus's words evoke another echo from Israel's Scriptures as well. Having mentioned the devil and a heel, readers may very well remember the curse to the enemy of God, the serpent in Genesis 3. There God says to the serpent who has deceived the woman,

Gen. 3:15 I will put enmity between you and the woman,
              and between your offspring and hers;
              he will strike your head,
              and you will strike his heel.

The promise is that the snake will try to bite at the feet of humanity, but humanity will crush the snake's head. At very least this statement is something like Aesop's fables, an etiology for why snakes are dangerous yet conquerable. But, of course, Christian readers saw much more. A particular descendent of a particular woman may be wounded in the heel by the serpent, but that Son will ultimately crush the serpent.

But I get ahead of myself. That is the rest of the weekend following Maundy Thursday. We aren't quite there yet.

In this instance, in this last meal he shares with his disciples, the positions are switched. The one who has been influenced by the serpent, who has heard and responded willingly to the parsel-tongued plan for betrayal, stands above the descendent of a woman and drives his heel into the Son's neck. The serpent that should be crushed is about to do the crushing.

Jesus doesn't take this stoically. John says that Jesus's spirit is troubled, and he testifies, proclaimed as a stark and crushing truth: "One of you will betray me!" Is he angry, heartbroken? His specific demeanor is not completely clear, but without a doubt, he is deeply disturbed.

His cry upsets the disciples too.
"Who could it be?" They ask.
Peter gestures to John, the beloved disciple, "Is it him?"

Jesus puts an end to his effort of putting down another close friend of Jesus. "It is whomever I give the bread to." And he hands it to Judas. At this point, the text says, Satan enters into him (13:27). Temptation has taken root and will now bear its fruit of evil action.

Jesus allows Judas to act. "What you are going to do, do quickly." Jesus is not surprised; he allows that which is so painful for him, betrayal unto death. Judas takes the bread that has been handed to him by Jesus, and he goes out.

"Now," Jesus says, "the son of man is glorified and God is glorified in him." Divine glory appears most brilliantly in this moment of betrayal unto death.

After this Jesus states that it is time for him to go, and gives a commandment: love one another as I have loved all of you (13:34). This statement in this moment invites a pressing question: How did he love them? For in a reflection about the universal scope of the atonement, one might counter that Jesus's love for all types of people does not necessarily translate into Jesus's atonement for all people. John is very careful to show, however, that his love is not at the level of feeling, but of action—salvific action.

We know at some level the answer to this question of "how he loved" because we hear it and even experience it each year in the service of Maundy Thursday: he washed their feet. He filled the water basin, and wrapped a towel around himself. The descriptions are drawn out, and the pace of the reading slows, so that you get a sense of the expanded time as the disciples wonder at what he is doing. And he kneels with each of these he's known so well. Did he remember all the unique exchanges with each person, their individual quirks, the memories they had shared over the years of ministry?

Notice that he loves them in this way and serves them *before Judas has left*. He did this for them all, and that included Judas. It would have been tender, powerful to wash the feet of a friend, but what was it to wash the feet of an enemy? The feet that would soon carry Judas to his deed of betrayal, Jesus prepared them. The heel that was even then bearing into his neck, Jesus washed it. Instead of striking at the heel of his enemy, Jesus cleansed it.

How else does he love these disciples? He feeds them. In the midst of this meal that will be his last, he takes a piece of bread, dips it, and gives it to Judas.

At this point the ambiguity of the New Testament text leaves a space for the development of different theological traditions. Did Jesus share not just a meal, but his last meal, the Eucharistic meal with Judas?

Calvin says no: *"Augustine* was wrong in thinking that this sop was an emblem of the body of Christ, since it was not during the Lord's Supper that it was given to Judas."[1] Jesus giving bread to Judas was a further act of kindness, but not the emblem of the Lord's salvific body.

I surmise that the theological *via media* of Moses Amyraut would have held the question in its appropriate exegetical tension. Without question Jesus tangibly expressed his love for his disciples, even Judas, by washing his feet and sharing a meal with him. The work of Amyraut actually helps to uncover the agreement between the theologians that one might imagine were at odds with another. Calvin, Amyraut, and Arminius all affirmed the universal scope of God's love and the universal sufficiency of Christ's death. With affirmations in the Scriptures such as John 13, how could this ever be denied?

Disagreement comes in the mysteries of God's will, which John 13 itself holds in tension, with its interweaving of Jesus's acts of love alongside affirmations of Judas's status as an unclean betrayer. Amyraut, following Calvin, would have affirmed the sufficiency of Christ's death for all but the effectiveness of Christ's death for only the elect. The bread is offered even to Judas, but he does not accept the saving relationship of the hand that gives it. Calvin and Amyraut on one side, and Arminius on the other, would offer a different reason why—either Judas's choice to reject (Arminius) or God's choice not to elect him (Calvin and Amyraut).

The good news for believers, and this is always very good news, is that we are not Jesus and can never know the mind of God. Jesus's words to all who are his disciples could not be clearer: "Just as I have loved you, so also you should love one another" (John 13:34). If he loved even Judas by washing his feet and sharing a meal with him, we are called to do the very same for all people, for we never know before the end who might end up being a disciple and who might end up being a betrayer. On this side of the eschaton, we are only called to love. As God "stretches out his hand to all alike,"[2] so too should we.

You might need to reflect on an enemy God wants you to dine with, to serve, to love. That's impossible unless the Spirit of God is at work.

That might be what you need to consider, but I do not think believers can be about the good work of dining with our enemies until we realize we are one. Romans says it explicitly: while we were God's enemies, we were reconciled to him through the death of his Son (5:10).

Our sins make us the enemy of God. We did not betray Jesus two thousand years ago, but we hold the potential to do so. Hopefully the season of Lent and the global unsettledness of recent years has afforded you the opportunity to

1.   John Calvin, *Commentaries on the Gospel according to John,* vol. 2, trans. Rev. William Pringle (Grand Rapids: Baker, 1979), 71.

2.   John Calvin, *Commentaries on the Second Epistle of Peter,* trans. Rev. John Owen (Grand Rapids: Baker, 1979), 419.

face your own sinfulness, to acknowledge your failures. To see your status as sinful, as corrupt, as fallen, as God's enemy.

In Psalm 23, the psalmist praises God for preparing a table before him in the presence of his enemies. Most commentators note that the picture is that God sets a lavish table for the Psalmist and serves him even while the enemies are kept at bay, standing outside watching but unable to hurt him. That is a good picture of protection, but the Christian gospel does something different. God doesn't just prepare a meal before our enemies. God prepares a meal for us and our enemies and invites us to dine together. This is possible because God has prepared a table for us *as his enemies*. God has prepared a table for us. God washes our feet, serves us, gives us *the bread and the wine*.

The good news is that because of Jesus's love for all, we do not remain enemies of God—because of what we celebrate this weekend, we can be reconciled. But tonight, sit in the uncomfortably overwhelming glory of your enmity with God and, in the full knowledge of it, Christ's service to you. If Jesus loved even Judas, he loved us all with his life.